THE
ACT
APPROACH

Timothy Gordon, MSW
Jessica Borushok, PhD

Foreword by **Kevin Polk**, PhD

Praise for *The ACT Approach*

"*The ACT Approach* is a marvelous must have desk resource for any practicing therapist. Tim and Jessica present the ACT model in easy to understand terms, masterfully blend in various ACT concepts and associated techniques, and show the evolution of the model over the last two decades. They even supply highly useful client handouts that the therapist can use to support learning and offer very entertaining and useful experiential self-guided exercises for the therapist who is new to ACT. Through the use of clinical transcripts, which have unique sidebar commentaries, Jessica and Tim demonstrate how to use ACT principles with a wide range of common clinical problems. This book is a wonderful primer for any therapist who wants to learn ACT. It is clearly written, entertaining, informative, and very clinically focused. The book shows very clearly the authors' complete mastery of ACT concepts and clinical strategies. Highly recommended!"

-Kirk Strosahl, PhD,
Co-founder of Acceptance and Commitment Therapy

"Timothy Gordon and Jessica Borushok have written a superb therapeutic guide for conducting ACT. In clear prose, with engaging illustrative examples, they explain ACT and show how practitioners can use ACT to help their clients live meaningful lives consistent with their values. I strongly recommend it."

-Andrew Christensen, PhD,
Distinguished Research Professor at the University of California, Los Angeles
Co-developer and author of *Integrative Behavioral Couple Therapy (IBCT)*

"Learning ACT is often confusing. This great book takes an interested clinician by the hand and leads them through a challenging learning path. Written by working clinicians for working clinicians, the book is engaging and clear. Particularly useful are the places where the authors discuss how they apply ACT principles to their own lives and the clinical transcripts. It seems the clinicians learn best by "seeing" the work. And the transcripts give a very clear sense of how to do ACT in a natural, non "techique-y" manner. Transitioning to ACT doesn't mean letting go of the clinical practices that work, but adding precision, scope and depth to the processes. I highly recommend this book."

-Joanne Steinwachs, LCSW,
Peer Reviewed ACT Trainer

"As both a basic scientist and ACT researcher, I like that the authors have brought sufficient focus to these topics in the early parts of the book. However, having reviewed plenty of ACT books I must say that this one has a slightly different feel to it. Specifically, it is a hands-on and process focused account of ACT that I believe will be of huge and practical benefit to the people on the front lines of human suffering."

-Nic Hooper, PhD,
Co-author of *The Research Journey of Acceptance and Commitment Therapy*

"ACT is one of the most popular treatments nowadays; despite its popularity, its dissemination is compromised by the lack of clear, hands on, and clinically relevant materials for mental health providers from different theoretical orientations, backgrounds, who work at different settings. *The ACT approach* conveys the theory and the practice of ACT in a way that it's clear and easy to understand, covering different ACT lenses and without losing the sophistication of delivering ACT in a therapy room. This books is clearly written by clinicians who spend hours and hours working with a broad range of clients and therefore it's full of real-life examples, clinical recommendations, and reflective comments for ACT learners. I really wish this book was written many years ago when I first learned ACT."

-Patricia Zurita Ona, PsyD,
Author of *Parenting a Troubled Teen*

"This book is a treasure for any therapist interested in learning about ACT, or any trained ACT therapists looking to apply their skills to children, groups or marginalized and oppressed populations. The authors scaffold concepts throughout the book; the simple concepts in earlier chapters are, by the end, rich and complex. This makes the text invaluable to novices and experts. The images are simple and useful. The annotated transcripts are a wonderful way of demystify what ACT looks like in practice, and demonstrating how master clinicians use ACT. This text would be a wonderful resource to graduate students and professionals alike. "

-Jonathan B. Singer, PhD, LCSW,
Associate Professor of Social Work, Loyola University-Chicago
Founder and Host of the Social Work Podcast

"*The ACT Approach* has cleverly integrated all the newest advances in the field of ACT into the text in an accessible and immediately useable format. The book is written in an accessible style teaching the reader ACT concepts while bringing them along in a compassionate and gentle style. The examples are easy to identify with and the exercises well timed. A great way to be introduced to the ACT model. An excellent contribution from innovative authors in the ACT field."

-Louise McHugh, PhD,
Co-author of *The Self and Perspective Taking*

"A clear and accessible guide to understanding and using ACT in daily practice. The process discussions added to the therapy transcripts are very helpful in guiding the reader in applying the principles of ACT in their own sessions. Whether you are an ACT therapist or a therapist looking to incorporate ACT into your own work, the activities and worksheets are tools that you and clients alike will find helpful."

-Niki Gomez-Perales, MSW, RSW,
Author of *Attachment Focused Trauma Treatment for Children
and Adolescents and Attachment Focused Toolbox*

"This very accessible book is both a great way to get in to ACT and a nice friend to hold your hand as you explore it in more depth. I particularly like the clinical vignettes with cheat-sheets attached that makes it clear what is going on in session and helps the reader do the same in their own practice."

-Andreas Larsson, PhD,
Co-author of *The Research Journey of
Acceptance and Commitment Therapy (ACT)*

Copyright © 2017 by Timothy Gordon and Jessica Borushok

Published by
PESI Publishing & Media
PESI, Inc
3839 White Ave
Eau Claire, WI 54703

Cover: Amy Rubenzer
Editing: Bookmasters
Layout: Amy Rubenzer & Bookmasters

ISBN: 9781683730811

Printed in the United States of America.

PESI
Publishing
& Media
www.PESI.com

Dedication

To all children lost, may you be found.

— T.G.

For my clients: Your strength and heart inspires me daily.

— J.B.

About the Authors

Timothy Gordon, MSW, is a social worker in Canada and internationally recognized peer-reviewed ACT trainer. He specializes in treating attachment and trauma related disorders. Tim is also a yoga teacher who integrates movement and yoga practices into his work. Tim's research has included yoga as a mental health intervention, ACT for chronic pain, and ACT with neonatal intensive care units. Tim is passionate about empowering people in various settings to use ACT, he has worked with Canada's Parliament and is involved in bringing ACT to sub-Saharan African countries with his colleagues at Commit and Act.
Visit Tim's website: www.TheZenSocialWorker.ca

Jessica Borushok, is a clinical psychologist and founder of Busy Mind Reboot. She has consulted on a multi-site, grant-funded program to help parents of children in neonatal intensive care units and has co-facilitated a classroom-based prevention program for fourth graders designed to teach problem solving and coping skills in an effort to reduce risk associated with environmental stressors. In addition to clinical work and research, Dr. Borushok provides ACT trainings. Visit Jessica's website: www. busymindreboot.com

Table of Contents

Foreword

Dear Reader:

Tim and Jessica told me to 'just be yourself' and write your experience of ACT. This was cruel. They told me to do that right after I read the latest neuroscience that shows that it's impossible for anyone to 'be' the self because the self changes each moment. Me as the 'being me' is the one doing the writing, but as I write I keep slipping back into the imagined and static 'noun me' instead of the 'evolving verb me.' Fortunately, I managed to forget this nonsense long enough to get back to being myself again so I could write the following.

My early experience with ACT was that it was quite complicated. Then I realized ACT was "learning by doing," and it did not need to be complicated. One day while standing in front of a whiteboard I got lucky and came up with a learning-by-doing diagram that a lot of people have found useful for doing ACT instead of talking about ACT. Then a Buddhist monk came along and named the diagram The Matrix because he figured that Keanu Reeves sex appeal would help it out. He told me that Buddhists are often right about such things. No way I was going to argue with a Buddhist monk. They have that Karma thing going.

The Matrix has been utilized by ACT practitioners, and probably many others, to increase a person's psychological flexibility. Because of the success of the ACT Matrix (it really was named by a Buddhist teacher), some really cool people have come into my life, and Jessica and Tim are two of those gifted people. In this book Jessica and Tim have used the ACT Matrix to enhance their already clear and concise explanation of all things ACT.

What I love most about *The ACT Approach*, is how accessible the authors have made ACT for all practitioners. Whereas other ACT manuals and therapy guides read very academic, and confusing with all its jargon, this book makes it easy for therapists to implement acceptance and commitment therapy into treatment. It provides a theory and science basis for the work while incorporating all the fun, cutting-edge clinical applications and practices to put you at the top of your game.

If you're like me, and appreciate a "learning by doing" way of understanding ACT, this is the resource you need. Trust me when I say you are about to have a great read.

That my diagram has helped inspire these fine authors humbles me.

Kevin Polk, PhD
Co-author, *The Essential Guide to the ACT Matrix* and *The ACT Matrix*

Introduction

Acceptance and Commitment Therapy, abbreviated as ACT, said aloud as the word *act*, is a cutting-edge, modern approach to direct practice. Whether practice settings are individual or group psychotherapy, counseling, coaching, community or organizational interventions, ACT has widespread applicability. ACT is about assisting people to recognize when fighting, avoiding, attempting to escape or suppress painful experiences does not work and when accepting that pain is a more workable way to move forward with their lives, to bring them closer to the life they most wish to commit to and live.

In this book, you will discover a model, not just a set of techniques or ACT skills—don't worry we will give you those too. You are likely reading this book after already having your own clinical experiences in other orientations (attachment-focused, cognitive therapy, CBT, DBT, EMDR, Gestalt, narrative, psychodynamic, solution-focused, to name a few). Our hope isn't to indoctrinate you, converting you to being solely ACT therapists; we find value in the experiences and knowledge you already have. Instead we wish to inspire you to bring this approach to the clinical wisdom that is already working for you. We will continue to address this concept throughout this book with an overarching question: How can ACT be useful to you in what you're already doing?

To fully understand what we mean by ACT as an approach, you will need to have a little background. ACT is based on a philosophy of science called functional contextualism: *function* meaning what works, and *context* meaning in a certain situation. **Our main goal is to help you view your clients through the lens of what works in a certain situation and learn to work with your clients when their behaviors are not functioning to move them toward the life they want in a given context.** It would be incredibly short-sighted and unaccepting of us to tell you that all the things that work in your clinical toolbox need to be discarded in order for you to practice ACT. Instead, this book brings you in full contact with ACT, both conceptually and experientially, offering a challenge: Bring ACT to the work you're already doing and see how you can target the function of your clients' behavior. What can you do to change the way their painful experiences work in their lives rather than trying to alter the form or frequency of their most difficult thoughts, feelings, sensations, and memories?

This distinction is an important one, and we wish to underscore it here: Practicing ACT doesn't simply mean learning some new tools to teach acceptance and mindfulness. Functional contextualism is a scientific philosophical perspective of the world and the things with which humans struggle. You can learn this perspective and use it to understand why your clients do what they do and why they suffer, and work to create interventions that target their struggles and inspire real-world behavioral change that impacts their long-term quality of life. You can use this same scientific perspective to increase your effectiveness as a therapist and reduce burnout (Brinkborg, Michanek, Hesser, & Berglund, 2011).

The bottom line is this: Regardless of your practice setting or clinical orientation, we believe ACT has something for you. And if you're reading this book seeking to immerse yourself in ACT and learn how to do all ACT all the time, understand that in reading this book we will arm you with everything you need to start. This book is meant to be a jumping-off point into developing your practice, and we hope that after reading it you have the foundation necessary to take the next step into intensive workshops and clinical consultation or supervision.

Before we move on, the first chapter of this book has a daunting title: "Basic Science and Theory." We hope that we have created a sufficient argument for you to not shy away from the chapter and instead read it. Understanding the basic science, the foundational underpinnings of ACT, can bring ACT to life in your practice. **We want to give you the tools so that no matter what shows up in the therapy room, you know how to approach it in an ACT-consistent way.** More explicitly, we are only interested in giving you what can be most useful to you in your work—an approach that functions in your practice context.

We are clinicians. Our full-time job is seeing clients individually and running groups. Although both of us are in independent practice now, we have also worked extensively in other settings: Jessica in primary care–mental health integration, behavioral medicine, consultation–liaison, skilled nursing home and rehabilitation, adult developmental disability program, and hospital settings, and Tim in Parliament, policy reform, single-session walk-in clinic, community counseling nonprofit organization, forensic assessments, and former director of a mood disorders support program. We work on research projects, develop programs, give workshops and write, but our day job is doing the work you will be reading about in this book: doing ACT. And that means this book is presented with a focus on how to use ACT in your moment-to-moment work with the people you serve.

How to Use This Book

We've written this book to be a detailed account of doing ACT clinically. At times you may find ACT confusing as it lacks a circumscribed or strictly laid out method or set of techniques to follow. Unlike other evidence-based therapies, ACT does not prescribe a stepped system from one session to the next telling you to use one technique before another and so forth. Instead, ACT is process based, encouraging flexibility in delivery and allowing for treatments that are tailored to the person sitting across from you in the therapy room, but are approached from a theoretically sound and evidence-based perspective. **Our aim in this book is to provide you with both the foundation and theory as well as the exercises and techniques so that no matter what setting, what client, what problem you encounter you are able to meet the challenge and the need of the moment; you are able to respond to whatever shows up and adjust accordingly.**

This book contains many valuable and unique opportunities to learn and practice. We provided handouts that we have carefully chosen based on our own experience as therapists and expertise with the model. Most are meant for you to use with your clients, while some are meant to assist you in learning ACT through ACT-consistent case conceptualizations of client problems and treatment planning, as well as other handouts and activities for you, meant to benefit you personally as a therapist beginning or advancing your ACT practice.

To help highlight the subtle process-based work of ACT we have included therapist-client dialogues that while not verbatim transcripts from our sessions, are very close to it with real qualities and circumstances representing the many clients we've encountered in our work. **Most of the transcripts include something that we think is special and unusual in a clinical guide: a sidebar transcribing the process-based approach of the therapist's interactions with the client.** Similar to the Shakespeare plays you might have read in school with side-by-side descriptions and translations that provided more substance to the dialogue, the sidebars in this book provide an in-depth analysis of what the therapist is saying and doing along with suggestions about how the therapist might be conceptualizing a client issue and how you might do the same while engaging in similar or different behaviors in your own practice. This is included to advance your understanding of how ACT might look in the moment-to-moment practice of psychotherapy rather than exclusively spelling out large interventions with experiential exercises that only last a number of minutes and could potentially leave you wondering what to do next. And yes, we have also included our favorite and most useful metaphors and exercises in this book to aid your practice.

For those who appreciate visual representations, you will also find diagrams and other depictions of information that we hope will assist you in understanding how ACT works and will serve as heuristics for remembering and using ACT as an approach to the work you're already doing.

To demonstrate the broad application of ACT, this book covers a variety of presenting clinical problems:

- **Substance Use Disorder**
- **Anxiety and Panic**
- **Obsessive-compulsive Disorder**
- **Post-traumatic Stress Disorder**
- **Borderline Personality Disorder**
- **Depression**
- **Chronic Pain**
- **We have also presented ACT for use with couples, children, adolescents, parents, and groups.**

ACT was derived from the ground up, focusing first on basic science and building upon the theoretical orientation an integrated approach to working with clients. Thus, we have laid out the book in a similar manner, beginning first with the basic science to provide a strong foundational understanding, then moving through the six core processes, providing multiple perspectives through which to view psychological flexibility–ACT's model of health–and approach various clinical populations, and concluding with insight into how we can not only practice and do ACT, but also live ACT through acknowledging what we as therapists bring into the therapy room with us and understanding how we can become more aware of not only our clients' patterns of responding to pain, but also our own.

Happy reading!

Chapter 1

Science and Theory

Historically, Acceptance and Commitment Therapy (ACT) is known as a bottom-up approach, a therapy built on basic science with each of its processes validated and controlled in mediational analysis before being rolled out as a treatment package (Villatte, Villatte, & Hayes, 2015). ACT's long history dates back to conceptualization in the late 1970s and an early version in 1982 referred to at the time as "comprehensive distancing." Between 1985 and 1999, it went through a development period in which relational frame theory (RFT), the theory that underpins ACT, was presented (Zettle, 2011). Since 1999, ACT is in a new period and is no longer a bottom-up approach; instead, it is a reticulated model of science in which research informs practice and practice informs research.

Understanding the basic science may seem like a purely academic pursuit, but knowing the basic science creates a foundational understanding of the ACT approach so that when things go wrong—when a client does not respond to a technique or skill the way a client did in a book, or when you start feeling stuck and have that "I don't know what I'm doing" moment—you can let the *approach* guide you by providing a safe space to experiment, grow, and get creative with the model. The interventions we give as examples in this book provide only a sample of how one could do ACT. There is no one way to do ACT, nor does any one set of techniques or method work for all clinical situations. Instead, understanding how the processes make the interventions work is far more helpful for tracking the function of clients' behaviors and creating interventions on the spot that facilitate change in a powerful and long-lasting way that beneficially impacts their quality of life.

LEARNING, LANGUAGE, AND COGNITION

Many people are shocked when they hear ACT is a modern approach to applied behavior analysis. Typically, we associate behaviorism with laboratory experiments involving pigeons pecking buttons not as conversations about acceptance, personal values, self-compassion, and practices designed to help us commit to a meaningful life or develop mindfulness. Thankfully, behaviorism has come a long way from the pigeon-pecking days (though weren't those experiments cool?). As a science, it has evolved to understand our most private experiences (thoughts, feelings, memories, sensations) as behaviors and the ways in which they shape who we are today.

An early part of this evolution is Skinner's breakout *Verbal Behavior* (1957), which was a theoretical book about applying the scientific program behaviorists had been using with animals to humans as well as to human language and cognition. Language means our words, the things we say, but Skinner also uses it to refer to cognition, the things we think and feel. Cognition includes all of our private experiences including memories and sensations and thinking about thinking, which may be referred to as metacognition. Metacognition is also included as a private experience that is game for a scientific behavioral analysis. Essentially, whether observable aspects such as walking and talking or those known only to the person experiencing them (e.g., thinking and feeling), they are all things people do. For example, right now you may be having the thought, "How is this relevant to ACT?" Modern-day behaviorists would consider that a private behavior is just that: a behavior, even though only you can observe it (and we promise it's relevant).

Language and cognition are considered private behaviors, a classification of behavior that only the individual can observe. ACT has a special focus on private behaviors, and we would argue that contextual behavioral science, the program supporting ACT, has the most robust scientific understanding of the role of acceptance in our private experiences thanks to the experimental research on relational frame theory that undergirds ACT. Contextual behavioral science offers widespread applicability to the clinical work you do in your practice.

RELATIONAL FRAME THEORY (RFT)

In order to understand ACT and its theory, relational frame theory (RFT), we need to situate RFT historically in its evolution from behavioral approaches. Early behaviorists Pavlov and Watson developed respondent learning (or conditioning) and identified that we learn through associations. Think of Pavlov's early experiments pairing the sound of a bell with food to create an explicit relationship between bell and food such that dogs in this experiment soon salivated at the sound of the bell without food being presented. Skinner's work, operant learning (or conditioning), demonstrates that our behavior is shaped by our environment. We learn based on the consequences (what happens as a result of) our actions (Skinner, 1971). As a quick note, learning by consequences might be confusing to you if, like us, culturally the word *consequence* was typically associated with punishment. In behavioral science, consequence means *anything* that happens as a result of a behavior; and *anything* could be as complex as an infant crying and then winning the attention of a parent who changes the infant's diaper or as simple as an early-morning commuter feeling a little more energized after a morning cup of coffee.

The newest behavioral approach on which RFT is built, relational learning (or conditioning, sometimes called "derived relational responding"), gives evidence that humans, unlike the dogs in Pavlov's experiments, can make connections that are not easily perceived or apparent. These connections are, in fact, private. Steven Hayes and many other colleagues, including Barnes-Holmes, Brownstein, and Zettle, pioneered RFT's focus on how language, thoughts, and all other private experiences (cognitive content) are something that someone does, and therefore are behaviors (Dymond & Roche, 2013; Hayes, Barnes-Holmes, & Roche, 2001). Relational learning shows how humans relate events in combination with one another. For example, when children are learning the names of animals, if you (A) say "cow" and then (B) point at a picture of the cow, they may learn that when you (B) point at a picture of the cow to (A) say "cow." This basic training is reinforced by your smiling or touching the child and saying, "Yes! Good job." If you later (A) say "cow" and (C) write the letters C-O-W, they would derive that (C) the letters C-O-W are the same as the (B) picture of the cow without the two ever being shown together. It sounds relatively simple to our adult human minds because all things we interact with have many symbolic meanings, but for other animal species, these tasks are incredibly difficult if not outright impossible.

More so, these relationships between events are not solely based on its stimulus properties (form or topography, how something is perceived publicly). Take for example a diamond and a boulder. Both are considered rocks: one is shiny and one is large. If we look at the physical properties of each it may seem weird that anyone would pick the diamond over the boulder, because the boulder is larger and can be used to smash things or hold something in place while a diamond may have little utility in the heavy-lifting and smashing department. However, if you ask anyone who speaks English and is familiar with both a diamond and a boulder which they would choose, most if not all would select the diamond because it is worth a lot more. We have applied an arbitrary meaning to the diamond; the meaning or value of the diamond is not based on any objective, observable, topographical elements, but rather on the symbol it represents.

Being able to create symbolic representations of objects, including our private experiences, allows us to hand someone a piece of green, crumpled, stained paper and receive a latte or slice of pizza in return. If aliens landed on Earth and observed such a transaction, they might think the person who accepted the paper was not very bright. If, however, they were similar to humans and could learn an arbitrary relationship between the paper and the idea of currency, and they calculated how much we paid for a single latte, they would realize that we likely have a slight caffeine addiction.

Relational framing helps us understand how humans bring thoughts, memories, sensations, and feelings that we are not directly presented with into our present-moment experiencing. This process is arbitrary, meaning it is socially constructed. Humans constantly derive arbitrarily applicable relationships between things, even things you've never before considered. Take for example, in what ways is the United States of America larger than Canada? Based on stimulus properties alone, we know this is not true: Canada is a larger country than the United States in physical size, but one could say the United States is larger based on population. The 300 million U.S. citizens clearly outnumber the 36 million Canadians. One could also say the United States is larger because of its more varied regions—it has 50 states and one federal district whereas Canada has ten provinces and three territories. This is simply one example of our ability to derive arbitrarily derived applicable relationships between things, in this case countries. Let's look at some more examples.

As you read the words on this page you may not be presented with a large, ice-cold glass of water right in front of you, however you can begin to relate to it as we describe it. The large glass filled with water is so cold the clear glass has become clouded with condensation. What are you noticing right now? You may be having the thought, "I could go for a glass of water right now," or an image may be forming in your mind of ice-cold water in a glass that you have in your kitchen cabinet. Without the physical object in front of you, your mind can come up with many private experiences related to the representation of that physical object as described. This skill is unique to humans and has been helpful in learning from others' experiences and making decisions based on past precedent or predictions for the future.

Imagine living in a world where you actually had to interact with bad-tempered bosses to learn what mood they were in rather than asking your coworker who already met with them earlier that day; we are guessing you would have a lot more unpleasant experiences. However, the ability to construct these relational frames in our minds can come at a cost: We can respond the same way to private experiences as we do to the external event or object. Take for example a person who responds to the thought of a terrible interview as if it were an actual interview gone wrong. That person may be less likely to work on a resume, apply for a challenging job, or work toward advancing a career all in an effort to avoid an imagined outcome. This ability alone can cost people a lot, limiting possibilities, creating rigid rules, avoiding potentially painful but meaningful situations all because of these relational responses that cannot be shut off or pruned. This distinction is important because other orientations often support changing or eliminating certain private experiences deemed "negative" or unhelpful.

The science of relational frame theory proves that once these relational frames are constructed, they cannot be eliminated or deleted. Relational frames are additive not subtractive, which means that when working with our clients, the focus is on expanding their behavioral repertoire or broadening their relational frames rather than trying to remove or change any private experiences. **The science shows that removing private experiences cannot be done.** Instead of focusing on whether thoughts are "good" or "bad," we turn back to the functional contextual philosophy of science and look at the function of a behavior (including private behaviors) in a given context—or more simply, how a behavior works.

FUNCTION OVER FORM

In our introduction, we told you that ACT is based on a philosophy of science called functional contextualism. When it comes to identifying client problems and how to target them in clinical settings, this science is extremely helpful. Focusing on how the behavior works (functions) in a given situation (context), rather than simply saying a form of a behavior is wrong, bad, or maladaptive, enables a richer understanding of client problems with more accuracy in how to assist clients in growing and shaping different behaviors. This functional contextual view of clients and their behavior is also helpful because even behaviors that do not topographically seem to make sense have a function—the behavior will serve some purpose—and this analysis in our experience allows for clients to be pulled out of the "something's wrong with you" conversation into a more useful conversation about how a behavior they are doing is not effective in helping them live the kind of life they want or would choose to live, this problematic behavior is in fact creating more difficulties for them. For example, clients with substance use disorders often face criticism from themselves (shame, guilt, etc.), their families, and their providers (especially questions about why they would continue to use or abuse a substance). However, if we look at it from a functional standpoint, we come to see that a substance, let's say alcohol, is an effective way to avoid painful private events, such as thoughts, memories, feelings, and sensations in the short-term.

Those who struggle with alcohol abuse or misuse will often mention the "numbing" effect alcohol has and frequently report struggling with abstaining from alcohol without replacing it as a coping strategy with another avoidance coping strategy that is once again perceived as harmful. From the ACT perspective, we validate attempts to numb and describe how alcohol has been successful at doing so; however, we illuminate the long-term unworkability of this pattern and instead motivate coping strategies that promote contact with the unpleasant private events and move them in the direction of long-term benefits: connecting with who and what matter most to them. And depending on the client, this move can come in many forms. For a client using alcohol to avoid thinking about past traumatic memories, using ACT to address symptoms of posttraumatic stress disorder is demonstrably effective, whereas a client with chronic pain may use alcohol to numb sensations, and so working to address chronic pain may be the way forward. **In either case, looking at the function of the behavior rather than the form or topography—what the behavior looks like—can be an extremely meaningful intervention for both you and your client.**

This issue of the function of behavior begs an important philosophical discussion for clinicians that is best not left to the pages of obscure philosophy textbooks: Our criteria for knowing the "truth" in our clinical practice is strictly practical. In other words, we focus only on what works in a given situation. Our analysis and assessments target how client behaviors work in a certain situation to achieve a specified goal, outcome, or valued direction. That last part is important: we don't mark behavior as good, bad, true, or false. We seek a truth that answers how effective a behavior is in achieving the desired outcome.

Diagnostic systems that favor the form of behavior, its topography, or what a behavior looks like rather than how a behavior functions (e.g., syndromes defined by the *Diagnostic and Statistical Manual of Mental Disorders* [DSM]) can help us talk about patterns of client behavior as an organizing title, but the helpfulness of that classification (depression, anxiety, posttraumatic stress, and the like) typically ends there. A DSM diagnosis does not include a functional analysis, how a behavior works (see Chapter 4 for a robust application to clinical problems). The function of behavior—whether it is workable in a given context—is the focus of our analysis in ACT. **This focus also means that ACT is a transdiagnostic approach because we are not looking only at symptomatology, but rather function. More important, it is a functional contextual approach, which means you can apply ACT to any presenting problem.** It is a bold statement, we know. At the time this book was written, more than 100 randomized controlled trials included applications of ACT to various clinical populations (A-Tjak, Davis, Morina, Powers, Smits, & Emmelkamp, 2015):

- Aggressive behavior
- Agoraphobia
- Alcohol use disorder
- Anxiety
- Behavioral problems in children with cerebral palsy
- Borderline personality disorder
- Chronic pain
- Depression in adults and adolescents

- Eating pathology
- Generalized anxiety disorder
- Medical problems
- Obesity
- Obsessive-compulsive disorder
- Panic disorder
- Posttraumatic stress disorder
- Psychosis
- Social phobia
- Substance abuse
- Stress
- Treatment-resistant populations with various diagnoses
- Trichotillomania

ACT has also been applied to nonclinical populations for other problems:

- Classroom collaboration and conflict
- Eating and weight concerns
- Emotional burnout
- Enhancing psychological health of students abroad
- Health behavior with cancer patients
- Mathematics anxiety
- Parenting
- Procrastination
- Psychological well-being
- Public speaking anxiety
- Smoking
- Test anxiety
- Tinnitus distress
- Workplace stress

This list is not exhaustive—ACT has been applied to many more populations and problems. If you are curious about ACT's empirical basis and wish to better understand the many interesting research projects supporting ACT, we recommend exploring the book, *The Research Journey of Acceptance and Commitment Therapy* (Hooper & Larsson, 2015), which covers all research conducted in English over the past 30 years.

RADICAL BEHAVIORISM BASICS

We realize that, in picking up this book with an aim to learn about ACT, you may have got more than you bargained for: a philosophy of science, relational frame theory, functional analysis, and all of this behavioral jargon! All when you simply wanted to learn how to add acceptance and mindfulness to your work. Bear with us, we're going to introduce you to a few of the behavior analysis concepts that we will use throughout this book. We use the scientific terminology and jargon because we hope this scientific perspective empowers you in your practice to adapt and use ACT in the different practice settings or clinical populations you may work with. We also hope it provides a basis to communicate through a common language with others who share or are interested in this perspective.

Reinforcement

Behaviors, the things people do, are more likely to recur as a result of a desired or reinforcing consequence that follows the behavior. Said more scientifically, behaviors are operant responses. In ACT, we spend a lot of time analyzing and generally attempting to understand patterns of reinforcement. This analysis helps answer the questions concerning why people do what they do, what is reinforcing to a certain person, and how that specific reinforcer maintains a behavior for them. We emphasize understanding what is reinforcing to a certain person because again what provides reinforcement to one person may not do the same for another, it depends on the context.

We want to make a specific note about types of reinforcement in session. Therapists from our functional contextualist view of the world have the ability to reinforce client behavior in session by paying attention, empathizing, making eye contact, and asking clarifying questions. Throughout this book we will challenge you to become somewhat directive or intentional in using ACT and to pay careful attention to what client behaviors you reinforce in session. Even without your direct awareness you are reinforcing behaviors. Through the intentional practice of discriminating between behaviors to reinforce and behaviors to not reinforce, you create another tool in helping to shape client behavior. In this way, you set the culture in session to one of vulnerability and moving toward a meaningful life rather than staying stuck in stories or holding fast to an eliminative agenda.

In ACT, we have interventions that focus on a person's unique reinforcers, we just call them values or more simply use the names of the people they most care about, the qualities that they most wish to live, and describe what they care about the most. As you expand your awareness in therapy, notice when clients begin to talk about their values or actions that are a step toward their values. In those moments make a special effort to reinforce: smile, ask a follow-up question, make eye contact, nod your head, appear engaged, or comment on what you are noticing and thank them for sharing it with you. Over time you will begin to notice a shift in language used in therapy that aligns with your shared mission to help them struggle less and live more.

Stimulus

A stimulus is anything that happens in the environment that triggers a behavior. This first term is particularly important because the process of evaluating the function of a behavior starts with how a stimulus works in a certain situation for someone, as in what they do when something shows up. Let's take something innocuous as an example, a phone ringing. When a phone rings, sending a loud ringtone, it might be a *stimulus* for one person to pick up the phone and say hello. In a different context or situation, let's say a movie theatre, a phone ringing might be a stimulus event for someone to quickly search their pockets or bag for their phone to turn it off. In one last situation, an anxious parent waiting up for their adolescent to return home after midnight may be holding their phone in their hand willing it to ring, and when the phone finally does ring it's a stimulus for them to pick it up and immediately say, "Are you okay?" or "Where are you?" In these three examples the same stimulus, a phone ringing, functions in different ways based on the context or situation.

This concept is important in our functional contextual view of the world because we cannot begin to understand how our clients are interacting with and reacting to their environment without understanding how a stimulus functions for that person in a specific context. For example, the feeling of sadness may function differently for one person than the next. A passing feeling of sadness may serve as a stimulus event for one person to pause and reflect on a recent loss in their life and what that person meant to them, while it may elicit a crippling reaction from another resulting in a day spent at home, in bed, hiding from their experiences.

Aversive Stimulus

Simply said an aversive stimulus is any experience public or private that someone may work to avoid, escape, or control (Catania, 1998). Think of *aversive* as something that is unpleasant, an experience that one would dislike. Remember, we are referring to a stimulus (see earlier definition), so what one person may find aversive may function differently for someone else. For example, the sight of a large black dog reminds us, the authors, of our childhood dogs. You would see us smiling and reminiscing about playing with Bart and Bear as children, whereas, for a colleague of ours, a large black dog is scary and something he would cross the street to avoid. Same form, same stimulus, but different functions.

Appetitive Stimulus

Appetitive stimulus is the opposite of aversive. It is any experience that someone may work to gain or receive. Think of appetitive as something that is pleasurable or enjoyable. Expanding on the previous example, seeing a large black dog is an appetitive stimulus for us, the authors, and triggers memories from childhood that are pleasurable to us.

Discrimination of Stimuli

In ACT we seek to help clients learn how to tell the difference between the outcomes of different contexts. People can become insensitive to context, the situations they find themselves in, including mental contexts such as thinking, feeling, sensing, and remembering.

A failure to discriminate between different situations and their outcomes can create problems where an experience generalizes to another in an unhelpful way. Such situations may arise when people respond to private events as if they are actually happening or when people make decisions on how to act next based on rigid rules they have created that are not sensitive to the actual situation. Said technically, problematic stimulus generalization happens when contexts fail to produce discriminative operant responding. Because of humans' unique ability to respond arbitrarily, that is, they can react to a stimulus not based on its formal properties but rather socially constructed ones (see relational frame theory earlier in this chapter for more), they may experience difficulties in this discrimination task.

Take for example a person with a trauma history who is standing in line at a coffee shop when someone else stands too close in line. For this person who has suffered a trauma the awareness of their body in relation to the other person triggers some implicit trauma reaction in which they are unable to discriminate between trauma memory and standing in line at a coffee shop, in a safe environment, far away from their attacker and not currently presented with their trauma. The outcome here could be dire for this person, experiencing many painful private experiences, but what's more is there could be no foreseeable end to the suffering; perhaps this person decides the coffee shop is no longer a safe place to go due to their unwillingness to experience another traumatic reaction.

As we mentioned at the beginning of this section, helping clients to discriminate between outcomes in different contexts creates space between stimulus and response in which the client can begin to notice contextual factors, which allows a moment to pause and choose how to respond. With the example just mentioned, the ability to notice the difference in context between the trauma memory and the current coffee shop, such as the smells, the details of the building, the purpose of going to the coffee shop, the sounds of the other customers, allows the person to discriminate between their memory and where they are in this moment and choose to behave in accordance with their values based on the situation they are actually in (the coffee shop) even in the presence of unpleasant internal stuff.

Stimulus Control

When something happens in a person's environment, when presented with a stimulus event, we know that discrimination is important because it changes what the person might do in the presence of that stimulus. How a person behaves in response to a stimulus is based on the reinforcement (consequence) that follows that behavior. When a learned history exists between stimulus and response, the stimulus is labeled a discriminative stimulus, meaning when this specific stimulus occurs in this specific context this specific response happens. For example, hearing "time for dinner" (discriminative stimulus) when you are visiting your mom's house (context) may elicit feelings of excitement, getting up and going to the dining room table, and salivating (response) because you have learned that your mom is a really good cook and often makes your favorite meals when you are visiting. On the other hand, if you hear "time for dinner" (discriminative stimulus) when you are home (context) you may put a smile on your face, and say "you shouldn't have," and have the thought "seriously you really shouldn't have" (response) because you have learned that your spouse, who decided to surprise you with dinner, tends to burn food. Similarly, a child in a grocery store with one parent may start crying, fall to the ground, and yell when that parent says, "no, you can't have a candy bar" because the child has learned that throwing a fit leads to them getting a candy bar whereas when at the grocery store with the other parent who says, "no, you can't have a candy bar," the child stays quiet because no matter how loud the child got, that parent did not relent.

Here is the heart of Skinner's operant conditioning mentioned earlier in this chapter: **Learning happens through consequences.** Clients' repertoires of behavior, the many things they could do like laugh, sing, dance, create, and talk, typically narrow when under the control of an aversive stimulus event; they can do relatively little when presented with a painful experience except in instances where the outcome of their behavior is about escaping, eliminating, controlling, or avoiding the aversive stimulus. When a behavior is under the control of an aversive stimulus, people tend to be insensitive to the long-term outcomes of attempting to escape, eliminate, control, or avoid their experience because they are focused on immediate short-term relief. This mind-set is helpful when a person is crossing a street and a car is zooming down the road not paying attention because we want that person to react and jump out of the way rather than stand around and think about what is the right thing to do in this situation. Clients get into trouble and find aversive control problematic or unhelpful when, for example, they curse at or hit their partner during an argument to avoid an unpleasant interaction without pausing to consider the long-term consequences of that behavior. Notice how aversive control is neither "good" nor "bad" but rather functions in different ways based on the context.

In this book we will encourage you as therapists to treat the contexts of therapy, your presence in the therapeutic relationship, your time together with clients, and the space in which you practice as the opportunity to apply stimulus control in favor of promoting psychological flexibility. This opportunity means paying attention to the instances of unhelpful aversive stimulus events that a client may be experiencing in session or are reporting as happening outside of sessions as well as other situations such as when a client's behavior is guided by consequences, the outcome of the client's responses. Stimulus control in those instances is constantly in flux, and your ability to bring a client's attention to what may be happening is an incredible strength. This focusing attention and encouraging noticing what is happening will increase your ability to practice stimulus control in your sessions and offer your clients insight into their own stimulus control problems inside the therapy room and outside in the real world.

PUTTING ACT IN CONTEXT

We are often asked in workshops and supervision how ACT applies to physical, real-world problems such as homelessness, poverty, abusive spouses, or a tangible aversive experience (e.g., the fear of having an allergic reaction when environmental cues trigger anaphylactic shock), the list goes on; functional contextualism works just the same. *Function* describes how a behavior works in a given situation. *Context* needs to be broken down further: there are physical, real-world contexts such as your office, a geographical location like the city a client lives in, or one's genetic makeup—these are all examples of independent variables. They are a context. There are other kinds of contexts too: social contexts or private contexts—one's thoughts, memories, sensations, and feelings. Experiences that happen in a private context can influence behavior both publicly, in the observable realm, what you see someone do, as well as in private, what someone thinks, feels, senses, and remembers.

Functional contextualism seeks to analyze how a behavior works in a given situation: when a child has a history of allergic reactions to peanuts and has been traumatized by a near-death experience of anaphylactic shock, it is workable for that child to fear and avoid places or people that could trigger an allergic reaction. For example, avoiding a child on the playground known to disregard the peanut-free policy at school functions in that context to keep the child with the allergy safe from someone who brings peanuts to school. However, this functional behavior can become problematic or unhelpful if that peanut-bearing child on the playground happens to have blond hair, and the child begins to avoid all blond children, even those in completely different contexts such as daycare or a local park, due to the derived relationship between blond hair and fear of peanut contamination. In that example, the fear towards a peanut allergy and the derived relationship between blond hair and peanut contamination are enough to make this young person insensitive to the context (child at school who does not listen to peanut-free policy versus all other children) and avoid thereby costing them the ability to play with other children and make friends. We have shown you how this ability can go awry, but it is important to remember that this ability to create relationships between seemingly disparate events, people, objects, and things serves a purpose, it is a part of human evolution.

EVOLUTION SCIENCE

The basic science you have been reading about in this chapter emerged from evolutionary approaches. Behavior scientist B. F. Skinner greatly influenced the contextual behavioral science movement and was interested in how biology and physiology linked learning principles of behavior to evolution (Skinner, 1984). Radical behavioral approaches are a great example of that linkage. For example, Skinner described selection by consequences such that behaviors that reoccur are a product of being reinforced. And what of the behaviors that do not get reinforced operantly? They become extinct—the behaviors don't persist because they haven't been reinforced.

Contextual behavioral science is a form of modern evolutionary science (Hayes, Barnes-Holmes, & Roche, 2001). All behaviors that exist, even ones we label problematic such as the substance use example mentioned earlier, persist because something in the context of that behavior reinforced it. A person with persistent anxiety in the face of enclosed places, for example, will be reinforced with a decrease in anxiety every time they avoid an enclosed space, which creates an immediate sense of relief and an increase in anxiety the next time the person faces an enclosed space. The only way to extinguish or make extinct the private behavior of anxiety in the context of enclosed spaces is to remove the reinforcer, which oftentimes is an avoidance behavior.

Functional contextualism is a good fit with modern evolution science, because the contextual view of the world focuses on behaviors in a certain situation. Context includes everything that influences a behavior from its current situation to historical factors such as development and learning history, social and cultural variables, and even biological factors. Epigenetics, a modern evolutionary science, has considerably advanced the understanding of deoxyribonucleic acid (DNA)—the chemistry inside all living organisms that is codified and associated with the transmission of genetic information. Epigenetics demonstrate that contextual factors and different experiences in the environment alter genetic expression in considerable ways with long-lasting impact (Jablonka & Lamb, 2014). This point is important for our clinical practices and is not merely relevant to the world of experimental research. We can use evolution science and, specifically, epigenetics to understand that the world our clients live in and their reactions to that world based on their learning history affects them not only by shaping their behavior but also by shaping their biology. This shaping happens as the result of doing what works in a given context.

The fascinating part is that evolution does not end there. It can also include social learning and cultural practices as they too are based on reinforcement contingencies. Researchers such as David Sloan Wilson, author of *The Neighborhood Project*, are learning how to shift environments and reinforcers in those environments to alter behaviors through providing a new context and function, **and why we, as clinicians, withhold judgment from our clients as we understand that given their context, their world, and their history they have come to this moment with you by doing the best they can: doing what works** (Wilson, 2011).

Another scientific approach that influences the context in which our clients exist and is confluent with modern evolutionary thinking is attachment science. The scientific program of analyzing how infants and their primary caregivers interact in a behavioral system is relevant to the conceptualization and treatment of young people, including creating parent training programs. These early attachment experiences have long-term implications for intimate relationships and explain how classes of attachment behaviors can be used to enrich our functional perspective of the world, assisting us in answering the questions of why people do what they do. We will explore this concept in greater depth in Chapter 8 when we dive into ACT with children and adolescents. **For now, it's time to turn our attention from the basic science and foundation of our work to the core of ACT: the six processes of psychological flexibility.**

Chapter 2

ACT's Six Core Processes

A number of things make ACT unique among therapies and approaches. One of ACT's differences stands out: **It is based on a scientific program that does not simply theorize what helps; rather, each component of ACT is analyzed and presented separately to explicitly detail how it helps people live a richer, more vital life.** ACT is composed of six such components that we refer to as the six core processes. Each of the processes is individual but not mutually exclusive. This means that each one of the processes works with the others. When combined, the six core processes form a circular model that represents psychological flexibility.

The six core processes of ACT can be viewed separately and defined individually. In this chapter, we look at each process in detail, which will be helpful to you in learning ACT as you will see how each process makes ACT work. Furthermore, each process is individually mediated to be a valid mechanism of change. That means if you successfully focus on any one of these processes in your clinical work, you should see an improvement in psychological flexibility. This last term, *psychological flexibility,* represents the whole ACT model of health. All six processes seek to increase psychological flexibility or coming in full contact with painful experiences and with uniquely chosen values, while consciously choosing the actions to engage in a meaningful life. Notice from this description that psychological flexibility does not prescribe one's attempts to escape or avoid painful experiences but instead invites experiencing them. To work with our pain where painful experiences do not exclusively govern our behavior. That is what ACT's six processes are about. **The six processes include acceptance, defusion, present moment, self-as-context, values, and commitment.**

ACCEPTANCE

Acceptance is practicing openness to private events (thoughts, feelings, sensations, memories). We often focus on our clients' most difficult private events (e.g., anxiety, sadness, physical pain, etc.) as targets for therapy. In ACT, individuals are encouraged to be accepting of their experience, rather than avoiding private events such as anxiety, sadness, or physical pain. Because the term *acceptance* can have different meanings to others, it is important to note that **in ACT, acceptance means a willingness to come into contact with a person's whole experience**, including the unpleasant internal stuff that shows up. Acceptance is *not* liking or wanting these experiences, is *not* begrudgingly or angrily saying they exist, and is *not* giving up and not doing anything; rather we encourage a willingness to notice those difficult private events, to allow them to be there as part of your experience.

Now, because unpleasant private events can be painful, we do not encourage this contact with private experiences without a function. The function of acceptance is to further the goal of working toward a meaningful life. Often when we experience unpleasant internal events we tend to work hard to escape or avoid those private events and anything that may evoke those experiences. The problem with this is that the things that cause us pain often point us in the direction of what is important to us. We would not have the thoughts, "everyone will hate this book, we have nothing original to say," if doing a good job, helping others, and furthering professional development were not important to us. If we exert all our effort trying to distract, ignore, or avoid unpleasant internal experiences, we are not moving toward who or what matter most to us. We will talk more in this book about how a control or eliminative agenda is not a functional or workable solution and actually can lead to greater distress over time. Note that acceptance is not an end in itself; it is one part of the larger whole, increasing psychological flexibility.

ACCEPTANCE IN PRACTICE

Take a moment to pause and notice the thoughts and feelings that show up while reading this book. Maybe you have sounds or other people in your environment distracting you from reading; maybe you are feeling rushed or frustrated and thinking, "I don't have time for this." Maybe your mind keeps wandering off to all of the things you have to do today or trying to make connections between what you are reading and the therapy session you had last week. As you notice these private events, rather than trying to avoid or escape or ignore them, instead try to allow yourself to experience and notice them.

Begin to practice opening up to these experiences and develop a willingness to sit with frustration or difficult thoughts as you turn your attention back to the book. Would you be willing to have these thoughts and feelings if it meant staying committed to learning or professional growth?

DEFUSION

Defusion is a made-up word that places focus on a cognitive component encouraging awareness of private experiences (thoughts, feelings, sensations, memories), the response to them, and the consequence (what happens as a result) of that response. Defusing creates space to pause and notice the effectiveness of a response to a private experience and an awareness that we have the flexibility to choose how we respond to private experiences rather than being reactive or automatically trying to eliminate or avoid them with poor results. For example, imagine that every time you are presented with the opportunity to go to a party and meet new people you have the thought, "I'm going to make a fool of myself and everyone will laugh at me," the feeling of anxiety, the sensation of your heart pounding and palms sweating, and the memory of saying or doing something embarrassing at a party. Now imagine that you were so caught up in those sensations, as if you wrapped that feeling of anxiety around you like a blanket and you began to believe that those thoughts were the only option, were inevitable. If you believed those thoughts were the truth, would you go to the party? The answer, we're guessing, is no. **If we buy into our thoughts and private experiences to the point where we believe they are literally true, it is likely we will react automatically and attempt to avoid or escape a situation.**

Now, imagine that same scenario, but instead of being caught up in those private events, like standing in the inside of a tornado, we are on the outside seeing the swirling cone and feeling the wind whipping by, but also able to see the whole scene in front of us. Defusion is similar—still experiencing our private events, but having the ability to pause, take a step back, and notice that, for example, the thought, "I'm going to make a fool of myself and everyone will laugh at me," is just that: a thought. Creating space allows us to recognize that escaping that anxiety and not attending the party might provide relief in the short-term, but it is only increasing our anxiety of interacting with others and working against our goal of having meaningful relationships in the long-term. When we take a step back to see the whole picture, we are able to see that an alternative is to acknowledge that going to the party means that we will likely feel an increase in anxiety and be bombarded with many similar thoughts, but we will also be taking steps to work closer to the life we want to live. **Defusion creates choice.**

DEFUSION IN PRACTICE

Pause and notice any thoughts that you're having about reading this book right now. Maybe you are having the thought "this doesn't make any sense to me, maybe I just can't learn this" or "there are so many technical terms that I don't understand, maybe ACT isn't for me" or "I don't remember struggling so much when I was learning [different therapy], maybe I'm not as sharp as I used to be."

Notice any urges following that thought to close the book and stay within your comfort zone or any conversations your mind is having trying to rationalize why it would be a good idea to stick with what you already know. Notice also how those behaviors are not working toward your goal of learning ACT. Notice what your options are when those thoughts pop up and choose what is more helpful for you—to continue reading?

PRESENT MOMENT

ACT orients people to the ***present moment,*** encouraging their awareness of their experience here and now. Inside us exists a rich and complex private world, and although it can be helpful to get caught up in that world, ACT encourages awareness of private experiences (thoughts, feelings, sensations, memories) and an acknowledgment of how in this moment these private experiences influence you. One of us, Jessica, is a daydreamer. She has spent many hours caught up in the imaginary world in her mind. She is creative and enjoys coming up with stories, characters and faraway places, and taking the time every once in a while to spend an evening caught up in those worlds helps feed her creativity. It serves a function. But sometimes getting caught up in her mind and not paying attention to the world around her can become problematic: crossing a busy street, sitting across from a client in therapy, writing an ACT book. Most activities that are meaningful for life require some degree of present-moment awareness, but staying in the present moment when there is no immediate threat or crisis can be difficult because our minds can come up with endless "pay attention to me!" "look out!" "danger ahead!" situations.

Take a client with generalized anxiety disorder who spends all of their time planning their life to avoid danger, catastrophes, or simply messing up. While on the surface it may not seem like it, planning requires taking ourselves out of the present so that we can think about a future potential experience. Although planning is an excellent skill to have, when we look at the function of the behavior, rather than the observable movement of the behavior, we can begin to notice situations in which a lack of present-moment awareness can work against us. This client may benefit from sitting down to write out a five-year plan for saving up for a down payment on a house, or a plan for how to complete the degree or certificate needed to begin their dream job. However, when they are spending all of their time planning, it can be helpful to pause and notice the cost. Clients may actively avoid being in the present moment for fear of unpleasant internal experiences popping up or to ignore unpleasant situations in their environment.

Working with clients to clarify what is important to them and whether spending time in their minds focused on the past or future "what if" alternative realities is helping them move closer to what is important. Also, creating a greater awareness of their experience here and now may help them identify problematic patterns of behaviors or responses to internal stimuli that they were otherwise blind to. **We cannot work to modify our behavior if we are not aware of how behaviors are problematic or unworkable.** Building a practice of present-moment awareness into every session can be a good way to model the importance of noticing. We like to begin every session after the initial session with a brief present-moment activity. In Chapter 6 we offer a few examples of what these exercises may look like.

PRESENT MOMENT IN PRACTICE

Take a moment to notice your experience here and now. Notice the feel of the book in your hands, the texture of the pages or the coolness of the device it is displayed on. Pause to notice where you are right now as you read this sentence. Is the environment quiet or noisy? Are you cold or warm or just right? Notice the places where your body meets the chair or couch where you are sitting, or the places where your feet touch the ground if you are standing. See if you notice anything in your environment or inside your mind that surprises you, that you didn't realize was there.

SELF-AS-CONTEXT

Self-as-context is a way of experiencing oneself. It invites people to see themselves as separate from their private experiences (the opposite would be seeing oneself as their content or self-as-content). This is a unique way of viewing our experience. It is in this way that self-as-context allows a person to see themselves as a stable entity and the experienced content (private and public behaviors, contextual stimuli, etc.) as changing. From this perspective, a person is seen as the observer of their own experience, rather than saying they are their experience. From this perspective in any given context it is the experiences that change, not the self who is observing. The observing self is constant and is the same self that existed in the past and the same self who will exist in the future. The part that changes is what the self is observing in any given moment. This concept can be a difficult one for clients, and for clinicians, to grasp, but it need not be complicated or involve any spiritual view of the self. It is simply the idea that our selves are the observer of our experiences and not the content we notice and interact with; the self interacts with experiences both private and observable, but is separate from them.

SELF-AS-CONTEXT IN PRACTICE

Pause and notice you, the person behind your eyes, observing the words on the page and noticing the thoughts your mind generates. Notice that this you, this observer self, is the same you that first purchased this book and the same you that sits across from your clients. Regardless of the roles you don or the time that passes, the you looking out of your eyes noticing is the same you that has always been there.

VALUES

Values are the who and what that personally matter to an individual and are uniquely chosen principles or standards. For example, being a loving partner may matter to one person who also states that their partner is important to them. Another person may state that athleticism is important to them, that taking care of their body and increasing their skill level are what they value. In both examples, the value of who or what is important has been clarified. Values go beyond goals, not simply professing love to your partner or performing well at an athletic event; you can't check a value off a list and call it done. Values are a sort of beacon that guides how we live our lives based on what creates a meaningful life to us. In that sense, there are no right or wrong values, only who and what is important to us now with the understanding that as we grow and change, so too may our values. In the therapy room, it is important to be aware of both what the client's values are as well as what your values as a therapist are. Values will be the guiding force of therapy, helping to outline what success looks like for this client. We can evaluate the function of clients' behaviors in terms of whether the behaviors work to take them closer to or further from their values.

COMMITMENT

Commitment is about doing the observable behaviors or engaging in activities in the service of one's values (the who and what that are important). Examples of committed actions will look topographically different for all people: taking time out of the day to have a nap or go to bed early may be a committed action for one person, pursuant to values such as sleep management, sleep hygiene, or taking care of oneself, whereas for another person, sleeping may be functionally about avoiding unpleasant private experiences: "I'm feeling down and hate this feeling. I'm going to go to bed and just sleep the day away." As with private experiences, observable behaviors are neither good nor bad, but rather are dependent on their function: does the behavior move me closer to whom and what matters most to me (committed action)? **If values are true north, then commitment can be viewed as the mile markers along the way.** They are observable behaviors that can be checked off as complete.

There is often the misconception that engaging in committed actions leads to happiness. However, depending on where the client is in their own journey, sometimes engaging in behaviors consistent with their values can cause an increase in unpleasant internal experiences. Take for example a client who values having a family and being a loving father, but is in a marriage with a woman he is not close to and who refuses to have children. A committed action for this client may be getting divorced and dating again or even adopting on his own. Even though these behaviors certainly function to take him closer to his values and the life he wants to live, they are in no way easy or even pleasant. Again, the focus is on the function of behavior rather than the removal or elimination of unpleasant internal experiences.

ACT IS A CIRCULAR MODEL

The following illustration depicts the six core processes as a circular model in which the processes are connected. Although we began the list of six core processes with acceptance, and acceptance is also the first word in the acronym of ACT, we wish to be explicit that the circular model means you can begin with or target any process at any time in any order in your work; you do not have to begin with acceptance or touch on only one process at a time. You are free to weave different processes into a single session or begin with any process you please while being consistent with the model. Whichever process you focus on depends largely on what your client presents with and what would be most beneficial for that client in that moment.

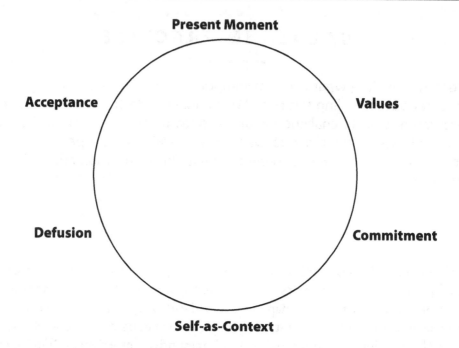

Bringing the Six Core Processes Together

To give you a sense of how these six core processes interact with one another and how they can all be used effectively in a single session with a client, we are including this transcript of a typical interaction between a therapist and client using the six core processes with explanatory notes. Please note that this is not the only way to do ACT, this is simply an example. The way you introduce the six processes into your practice may sound different and that is okay. In our experience teaching and supervising others in ACT, having your own flexible approach to ACT works best.

Therapist: I know this is an incredibly painful topic, but let me make sure I'm getting this right, what makes this sadness so hard for you isn't just the self-doubt that shows up when you're at work and criticizing yourself but the absence of something?	This is an early attempt to assess why this hurt is showing up in this client's life. What does the client value that causes this pain?
Client: Yeah, I want a relationship. My little sister is getting married. It's like she has everything figured out; she's got a great career, she's successful, she's great at her job, has an awesome guy, her fiancé loves her so much and I'm just at home, alone, with no one.	The therapist attempts to role model slowing down with this action of taking a breath and being in the present moment.
Therapist: [Pauses and takes a breath.] That sounds hard to compare yourself to her like that.	The therapist attempts to expose the function of this behavior, demonstrating how fusion works practically to this client: when certain feelings and thoughts show up that are painful for you, you begin to criticize yourself—a behavior the client has reported as problematic.
Client: It is, I hate it. I love her but it's hard for me to see her doing so well.	
Therapist: And that's what you do when this hurt shows up is reach for an answer, like criticize yourself.	

Client: Well that's what I usually do, yes.

Therapist: Bear with me, can you tell me what this hurt is exactly, like what thoughts and feelings occur to you in those painful moments?

The therapist again purposefully slows down, drawing more attention to the here-and-now, asking this client to not shy away from the experience but more closely identify it. This could also be seen as preparation for defusion work, bringing the client's potentially out-of-awareness experience into awareness.

Client: That I'm not as smart or good looking as my sister and this is why I'm single, lonely, and not successful at my job.

Therapist: Pause right there with me if you will. Could we both just take a breath and feel that right now?

This is an example of the present moment process enacted.

Client: [Tearfully] Yes.

Therapist: [Slowly] And what is it like to be here in this moment?

The therapist again draws on present-moment process combined with an early priming for self-as-context work—experiencing the moment, observing it. Notice how the therapist is gently inviting the client to come into contact with the experience.

Client: Sad. Hard. I just want to shut down.

Therapist: I know. Try not to turn away from that hurt. It's natural to want to shut it down but stay with me for a moment and let's not fight this.

This is an example of acceptance in action where the therapist invites the client to not engage in experiential avoidance.

Client: [Pauses] Okay.

Therapist: And what does your mind tell you about this now?

The therapist uses the present moment to enact defusion, separating the content of the mind, what it may be telling this client, from what the client may do next.

Client: That this is a bad idea.

Therapist: Yes, and what do you typically do with this hurt?

Again, the therapist uses defusion to draw on what might happen in this instance if the content of the mind was taken literally or acted upon.

Client: Just sleep or stay in my room, eat, watch TV.

Therapist: And right now, what does this hurt tell you to do?

> Based on the client's ease of self-reporting, the therapist enacts another intervention with present-moment process work focusing on the interpersonal relationship between the client and therapist in the here-and-now.

Client: I just want to feel better so I would change the subject.

Therapist: Even here, right now with me, your mind wants you to turn and run away?

> The therapist again brings the focus to the client's behavior and experience in the room with the therapist.

Client: Yes. I hate it, it's embarrassing.

Therapist: What's important about that? Why does this hurt matter?

> The therapist asks a values-driven question, clarifying what is it about this painful experience that uniquely matters to this client.

Client: I'm alone. I want a relationship and not just a romantic one. I don't even feel connected to my family, and I live with them.

Therapist: It's like a flip side of a coin: you value relationships, a romantic relationship but also a relationship with your family and that's beautiful, but the flip side of the coin is when that comes into conflict and that sounds like it brings a lot of pain. And yet, they're flip sides of the same coin, they're indivisible, it's almost as if you don't get one without the other. You can't have relationships matter to you without feeling alone when there's an absence of them.

> The therapist describes what the client values and parallels values with pain using the metaphor of a coin. The therapist then also outlines the perils of experiential avoidance by explaining that walking away from this hurt is akin to walking away from values.

Client: [Making eye contact] You're so right.

Therapist: So what if that is what our work could be about, not focusing on us getting better at eliminating your self-doubt, criticisms, the comparisons you make between yourself and your sister. Instead we focus on the life you most want for yourself, looking at ways to bring yourself closer to the relationships you want with your family, and explore ways you can pursue the romantic relationship you want.

> The therapist promotes a noneliminative agenda, encouraging acceptance and commitment over avoidance and fusion.

Client: I'd like that, it makes sense to me and feels concrete.

Therapist: Could I take this one step further?

> Giving options, creating the context of choice in the therapeutic environment, is important and respectful from our perspective.

Client: Yes, please.

Therapist: Let's both of us take a step back for a moment. What is it like to see your self-doubt, criticisms, and the comparisons you make? To bring them alive here, to not shy away from them, and for us to just talk about them and go on being here, working together?

> This is a present-moment activity leading into defusion and perhaps also promoting self-as-context in this client.

Client: I don't know, I've never thought about it this way. It's different and helpful.

Therapist: [Smiles] I'm really happy to hear you say that because we just did something unconventional, we broke a social convention. I asked you to do something hard and you courageously did it, you brought your most painful thoughts and feelings here. Then I asked you not to turn away and you didn't. You stayed in this moment with me and we were able to loosen the shackles of what your pain was telling you and now we're here, connecting despite your mind telling you to shut it down.

> The therapist reinforces the client's accepting and present-moment committed behaviors in the session with the goal of increasing the occurrence of these behaviors in future sessions and outside of the sessions as well.

This interaction may not have looked like any particular exercise, but it is ACT and did touch on all of the six core processes. In this book we want to teach you how to approach all interactions with your clients through this perspective and have the foundational understanding of ACT so that no matter what shows up in the room you can flexibly respond in an ACT-consistent way whether you touch on one, two, or all six of the core processes. We have similar therapist-client scripts throughout this book with explanatory notes to help broaden your own relational frame when it comes to doing ACT.

ACT Informed Consent

Practicing ACT means you are creating an entirely different kind of therapeutic contract. Introducing ACT to your clinical practice is not merely about using a set of ACT methods or techniques, like introducing mindfulness and sprinkling in metaphors that involve acceptance and connection with values. ACT offers a unique approach to the informed consent that breaks the commonsense eliminative agenda that clients largely visit therapists for: to reduce or fix painful private experiences and feel better. Instead, the ACT informed consent encourages engagement with painful private experiences because research shows we cannot escape that pain and that attempts to rid ourselves of painful private experiences get in the way of living a rich and meaningful life that improves quality of life in the long-term.

The ACT therapeutic contract as demonstrated in the previous therapist-client dialogue acknowledges the short-term relief of attempts to control, avoid, and escape painful private experiences yet parallels how those attempts can serve to limit one's life and may have a reinforcing effect on those painful experiences. This realization can be incredibly validating to clients suffering with chronic or persistent problems from medical health issues such as diabetes, chronic pain, or even severe mental health issues like a diagnoses of schizophrenia or borderline personality disorder. Clients suffering with these chronic or severe problems can become frustrated by their own lack of control over private experiences and feel demoralized by former therapies that may have also failed in curing or fixing their painful private experiences. This statement is not meant as a critique of other therapies or previous attempts to eliminate painful experiences; rather, it is meant to bring a modern behavior analytic understanding, informed by evidence of how therapists can create validating therapeutic contracts free from the pitfall of a promise to eliminate or control a human experience that research demonstrates is out of our control.

We have included a sample of what we have written in our own informed consent. How it appears below is verbatim in the introduction to treatment letter that all of our clients receive at the beginning of individual and group treatments. Note that this excerpt is brief; we have left out the limits to confidentiality, billing information, and other administrative details because that information will look different based on your region and legislation/laws.

INFORMED CONSENT EXCERPT

———

Our work is very important to me and it may focus on helping you struggle less with the thoughts, emotions, sensations, and memories you don't want so as to help you better move toward what's important to you in life. Sometimes our own personal histories can make things more difficult for us. In this work together, we will always be focusing on your hopes, goals, or possible outcomes important for you in life. Through our work, I hope that you will gradually learn a new way to relate with the things you've long struggled against.

Bringing this language into your informed consent ensures that clients are aware not only of confidentiality and other legal considerations, but also of what to expect from you and your time together. Creating an ACT-based informed consent can help to facilitate the initial conversation in that it outlines directly in the therapy agreement what therapy with you will focus on, allowing them the opportunity to ask questions and collaborate in their care and set the stage for increasing connection with what matters rather than reducing or eliminating unwanted symptoms. **An ACT-based informed consent highlights three main points.**

1. Your work together will help them struggle less with the thoughts, emotions, and memories that they don't want to experience so as to help them better move toward what's important to them in life. This point provides an excellent opportunity to discuss their prior efforts and the central idea that you will not be removing or reducing their symptoms because truthfully you can't (and now you know you have science on your side to back you up).

2. Valued living is the focus rather than symptom reduction, which means you will always focus on their hopes, goals, or possible outcomes that are important to them in life. Clients, particularly those who may come from a different background from you—whether that be race, gender, religion, culture, disability, or anything they judge to be different from you—may have concerns that you will project your own values or goals on them, prescribing how they ought to live their lives. Highlighting that the focus will be on what they want for themselves, who and what are important in their lives, can help to alleviate some of these concerns. A direct conversation about this can also be a powerful therapeutic relationship builder as can acknowledging to yourself that at times your desires for their life and their desires for their life may differ and bring you back to your governing goal to help them live the life that they want. In our experience that can take a lot of pressure off of therapists to "fix."

3. Sharing your own hope that they will gradually learn new ways to relate with the things they've long struggled against and learn to move forward in their lives means that even though you cannot get rid of their painful experiences, you can show them a new way to connect with that pain, perhaps how to create space for their pain, validating it and moving forward with the life they want to live, doing the actions that bring them closer to an increased quality of living.

Subscribing to an ACT therapeutic contract with relevant informed consent also energizes the work of therapy in our experience. By creating this new type of therapeutic contract, you expose the cultural forces of "feeling good" as a rigged game. The point of therapy becomes not how do we get better at escaping pain and feeling good but instead how do we build a meaningful life and get good at feeling. It also means that nothing a client says is inherently wrong or problematic. Their most painful experiences can be validated with empathy and when appropriate, the therapist can skillfully ask where energy could be redirected in order to grow toward values and a richness of living.

The Hexagon Model

We would be remiss if we did not show you the most common way to present the six processes as a hexagon model, it is often colloquially referred to as the *hexaflex* (Hayes, Strosahl, & Wilson, 2011). Now, you may look at the next diagram with puzzlement and wonder to yourself, "ACT is a circular model and that hexagon is not a circle?" And you would be completely correct. **We use a hexagon to depict the model and the six processes because a hexagon has six points and each process can be overlaid with each point on the hexagon and connected to all of the other points.** We can then use the hexagon to depict how each process is separate, on its own point, but each connects with one another to make up a larger whole: psychological flexibility. The term *hexaflex* is meant to be a play on words: combining hexagon with psychological flexibility. We have adapted the hexagon model of psychological flexibility and presented it here demonstrating how the whole model is psychological flexibility and how the model is made up of six smaller, independent parts that are interconnected.

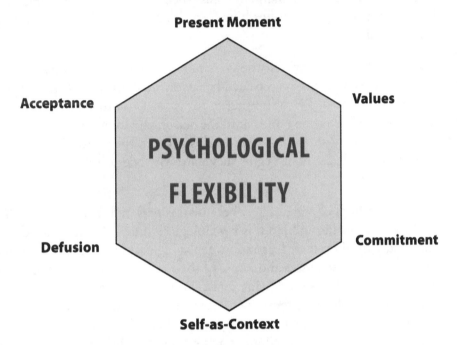

Using the hexagon to depict a greater whole in the ACT model, psychological flexibility, is important. In Chapters 5, 6, and 7, we demonstrate process-based interventions with specific presenting problems, but the goal is not to simply target acceptance alone or defusion exclusively. Instead, we focus on growing a measure of psychological health: psychological flexibility.

PSYCHOLOGICAL FLEXIBILITY

By now you should have a sense that ACT is based on a philosophy of science called functional contextualism that looks at what works in a given situation. ACT's theory, relational frame theory, is based on functional contextualism and looks at a person's private behavior. Here is where we get the *psychological* portion of psychological flexibility. If we did not apply ACT to thoughts, feelings, memories, and sensations, we would simply have a model of behavioral flexibility. ACT's six processes combine to target behavior but not just publicly observable behavior such as walking, talking, hugging, kissing, fighting, and arguing. ACT's six processes also target private behavior that includes thinking, feeling, remembering, and sensing.

In ACT, we seek to increase *flexibility* **both publicly and privately through broadening behavioral repertoires.** Adding flexibility to a repertoire of behavior, either public or private, is especially pertinent when someone is suffering or coming in direct contact with something painful, because people often narrow their lives in unproductive ways when faced with painful events. For example, a person with agoraphobia may create rigid rules around what is considered safe, reacting to feelings of fear when exposed to anything outside of these rules. Over time that person may be limited by rules or thoughts or feelings never leaving their house or even a specific room in their house. They have trapped themselves with their own mind.

Now, this isn't to say psychological inflexibility or the narrowing of behavioral repertoires is "bad." Again it is dependent on the function of the behavior. For example, typically people need to add flexibility not in their happiest most joyous moments but in their darkest and most painful moments. It can be helpful at times to be completely focused or immersed in what you are doing, say, when you are at home watching a movie or streaming an interesting show. You want your behavior to be pretty inflexible there, affixed to the screen, immersed in the story and the characters when a major moment occurs that makes you jump from your seat—these are all examples of psychological inflexibility. Or imagine a basketball player taking a foul shot. The player tends to have restricted, almost ritualistic behaviors in that situation; the rhythm and consistency is what helps the player perfect the shot and maintain focus when thousands of opposing fans are screaming at them. The bottom line is that psychological inflexibility can also be good! **When in doubt, always stop and ask WTF: What the function?**

Let's look at how we break psychological flexibility down to understand it more closely. Picture a person arguing with someone they care about. Maybe this is a repeated behavior: a conversation begins that they do not want to have and the person feels frustrated. By continuing to focus solely on their frustration, memories pop up replaying old arguments, and the frustration builds until the person says something hurtful, ends the argument, and later creates feelings of regret. *What the function?* In this context, the person has both private and public restricted behavioral repertoires: when a fight begins they narrowly focus on the frustration, and act in a way to escape an unpleasant conversation.

These behaviors later lead to feelings of regret, likely because this person does not want to hurt someone they love; therein lays his values: to be loving and kind. Is psychological inflexibility functional in this context? No. Rather than becoming rigidly fixed on their frustration, replaying past arguments, the person could learn to become more open to all of their experiences and aware of their restricted pattern of responding. They could notice the urge to react and instead focus on slowing down, noticing the other person's face, listening to what the other person is saying, acknowledging their own frustration, and connecting with why it is important they have a productive conversation with this person they care about. Then, in the face of frustration they can choose a more workable behavior, perhaps a different action, one that brings them closer to the loving and kind relationship they want to have with this person. With those actions they are broadening their behavioral repertoire and becoming more psychologically flexible because in that moment of frustration they now have two options for how to behave: argue or slow down.

Most clients do not come to our offices because what they are doing is working for them or because they are too psychologically flexible. Generally, they come because their lives are not what they want them to be and they feel stuck or trapped by their minds or private behaviors. Working to increase psychological flexibility may sound abstract at times, but it has real world implications and promotes tangible behavioral outcomes. We have a helpful way of tying all the processes together in a single sentence that highlights what we are working toward: **"In this moment, I'm holding my pain so that I can choose to do the things I care about."** We feel that sums up the whole model succinctly and exposes what psychological flexibility is about: being present with our experience, even pain, and choosing to make a life that is about living what we value.

Chapter 3

Life Map:

ACT Made Easy for Individual and Group Therapy

In our experience, the easiest way to learn the ACT approach and model of psychological flexibility is through a diagram called the ACT Matrix, or simply "the Matrix." The Matrix was created by Kevin Polk, Jerold Hambright, and Mark Webster; it offers a quick and easy, hands-on way to do all six processes of ACT in a single diagram with clients (Polk, 2014). It's also a useful tool for showing your clients what our work is about in ACT—creating a noneliminative agenda where we as the helping professionals do not rid our clients of painful experiences but instead aim to foster and model acceptance with the goal of decreasing their reactive behaviors that are problematic in their lives and instead simply notice those painful private experiences and then choose what they want to do next, based on their values.

A quick note before we move on with the Matrix: we never call it "the Matrix" with our clients. We have created our own adaptation we call a Life Map that works with our style and our clients. We have deviated from the current dominant method of presenting the Matrix and will encourage you to also do what works for you in your practice based on your experience with this diagram. We call it a Life Map because it represents everything that clients experience both in the observable world and within their private experience mapping where they have been going and where they wish to go with their behavior.

LIFE MAP

Setting up the Life Map diagram is simple: we draw a horizontal line with arrowheads at each end, and a circle in the middle, and that's it for the artistic portion if you choose. Although in making a Life Map feel free to get fancy, the rest of completing the Life Map is about writing. We'd also like to encourage you, the reader, to create your own Life Map, following the steps so you know what it looks like in your own life. That way you can even tell your clients that you use this in your life too! That it isn't some skill only for people in therapy, but rather is a tool that can help everyone orient to where they are and where they want to go.

A quick note: going forward, we're going to use the same language that we use with clients, referencing "you" rather than the client.

The bottom right quadrant lists who and what matter most to you, the values that you most wish to move toward. The bottom left identifies private experiences: the thoughts, feelings, memories, and sensations that get in the way of moving toward who and what matter. The top left quadrant is about the observable behaviors you use to move away from, avoid, or escape painful private experiences. And the top right identifies observable behaviors you use to move toward who or what matters. We can view the top half as representing the public world (behaviors that are observable publicly), while the bottom half identifies private experiences (thoughts, feelings, sensations, memories, values, etc.). The right side identifies what moves us toward the life we want to live and the left encompasses what we do to move away from painful experiences. Here's what it looks like:

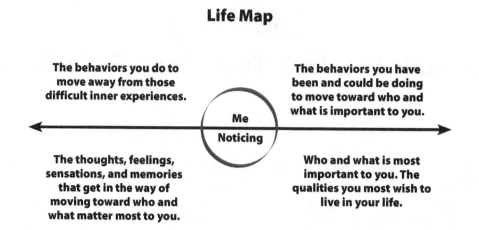

Life Map

The behaviors you do to move away from those difficult inner experiences.

The behaviors you have been and could be doing to move toward who and what is important to you.

Me Noticing

The thoughts, feelings, sensations, and memories that get in the way of moving toward who and what matter most to you.

Who and what is most important to you. The qualities you most wish to live in your life.

The Function of Toward and Away Moves

We use the Life Map to train our clients to look at the work functionally. This functional perspective is fundamental to the work we will be doing with them in ACT and we wish to point out that moving toward does not simply mean "good" behavior just as moving away does not mean "bad" behavior. Both directions are vital to survival. In science, we have a special name for the species that only moves toward the who and what that are most important to it, the species that never attempts to escape painful situations and disregards threats: extinct. They die quickly; these species wander into open, grassy fields to munch grass without a care for predators, making lots of noise and rarely looking around. There is also a scientific term for the species that only moves away from painful experiences, never leaves its comfort zone and remains in the safety of its shelter, not out eating and drinking, engaging with others: extinct. Moving toward who and what is most important functions in certain contexts just as moving away from painful experiences or perceived threats also works in a given situation. Avoiding dark abandoned alleys that give you a cautious, fearful chill accompanied by the thought, "something's not right" is generally a smart move, while avoiding going anywhere outside of your house because you feel afraid or cautious, depending on the context of course, may be less functional.

We will explain these concepts to our clients: that toward moves aren't good just as away moves aren't bad after we show the Life Map because we do not wish to turn the therapeutic context into one in which clients receive more rigid rules about how they ought to behave: toward good, away bad! That could be an irreversible mistake. With this caution understood, the Life Map is an incredibly useful and simple diagram to draw and facilitate with clients. In our experience, clients can instantly begin using the Life Map.

Setting Up the Life Map in Five Easy Questions

We generally ask five questions to construct a Life Map with our clients and do so in the numbered order you'll see attached to the next diagram. We encourage you to experiment with the Life Map, write one for yourself in your personal life. Later in Chapter 9 we will invite you to create a Life Map based on your behavior as a therapist in session.

Five Questions to Set Up the Life Map

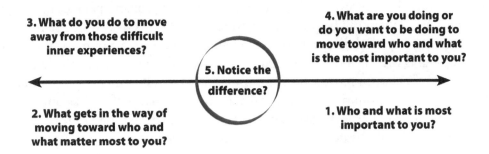

3. What do you do to move away from those difficult inner experiences?

4. What are you doing or do you want to be doing to move toward who and what is the most important to you?

5. Notice the difference?

2. What gets in the way of moving toward who and what matter most to you?

1. Who and what is most important to you?

Question 1: Who and what is most important to you?

This first question is an early focus on values with curiosity about the people and qualities that a client most wishes to have a connection to in their life. In a first session with a client you may be listening to their story and making mental notes as you pick out what you perceive to be their values: who and what matter most to them. Perhaps a client enters your office and in an intake they begin speaking to you about their history of substance abuse, telling you about the relationships they have lost because of their behavior. You may wish to slow them down and politely ask, "Who is it in those relationships you've lost that really matter to you?"

Question 2: What gets in the way of moving toward who and what matter most to you?

We often pose this second question by saying, "Inevitably, painful thoughts, feelings, sensations, and memories get in the way of us moving toward the life we want. What gets in the way of moving toward who and what matter most to you?" In our experience, this is an easy question for clients to answer. However, in some situations, we will additionally prompt, "What feelings get in your way of moving toward?"

Question 3: What do you do to move away from those painful inner experiences?

We regularly have to clarify this question by adding, "If I was there with you, what would I see you do?" We clarify with additional questions because the upper quadrants of the Life Map focus on behavior that happens in the publicly observable world. If a client offers an answer such as, "I shut down" or "I withdraw," we would applaud them because they are both good answers. You may wish to know more and expose the specific behaviors by asking, "What would I see you do when you shut down?" Additionally, "You withdraw, I think I get that but what exactly does it look like when you withdraw? What would I see you doing if I were there watching you?"

Question 4: What are you doing or do you want to be doing to move toward who and what is most important to you?

When asking this question, we often point to the left side of the Life Map saying, "If you weren't so busy moving away from the painful experiences that show up in your life, what would you be doing or doing more of to move you toward who and what is most important to you?" We often get clear answers in response, but from time to time we will get answers like "be happy" and we once again attempt to get publicly observable behaviors by asking, "Again, if I was there with you, what would I see you doing?"

Question 5: Notice the difference?

We point to the right side of the Life Map and ask, "What does it feel like to move toward who and what is most important to you?" Do not expect all positive comments. For many people, moving toward who and what is most important to them can be profoundly difficult, and that's okay. In these moments we explain to our clients, "This is why our work is about accepting painful experiences and not waiting until we feel better to move toward who and what is most important to us." Secondly, we point to the left side of the Life Map and ask, "What does it feel like to move away from your painful private experiences?" Often we get the answer "awful" or "exhausting," but from time to time someone will say "natural" and again, this is an okay answer. Remember, moving away is not always a bad thing and clients who have a long history of attempting to escape and control their most painful private experiences may not be ready to give up those move away strategies yet as their attempts are at times reinforcing.

Clients Noticing at the Center

We draw a circle at the center of the Life Map and we write our client's name (or write "me") with the verb *noticing*. The client's name goes at the center because the Life Map is about them, it's a map of their life, their behavior, the things they do and say, the things they think and feel, and at the center of all of that is them. And the verb, *noticing*—we write this because the awareness of experience is essential to ACT. The purpose of the Life Map diagram is to get people to pay attention to their experience, notice it on purpose, and choose what they will do next. This is essential because the truth criterion for ACT is pragmatic—focused on function, on what works, which brings us back to our philosophy of science, functional contextualism: how something works in a given situation. It's only the person who is noticing their experience who can tell whether their behavior is a move toward who and what matters most or is a move away from something they don't want to feel. Here's an example:

> This morning I woke up, put on my running shoes, and took my dog for a run. My health is important to me. Is my morning run with the dog a move toward or a move away? You might assume a move toward because you might assume running is a part of my healthy living. You're not wrong, running is a part of what I do to move toward my health. However, what if I told you that the night before I ordered a medium stuffed crust pizza and embarrassingly ate the whole thing myself and feel really crappy about my body and having the thought, "I'm fat and disgusting," so I'm going on a run in reaction to that? You'd likely change your theory about my taking the dog for a run being a move toward and assume it's moving away from feeling gross. Realistically, it's only me who can tell.

The example of going for a run is not severe and we know it, but it's a good example. Going for a morning run with the dog may be an away move that is not problematic, which is okay! The example does however illuminate the functional contextualist definition of truth: We don't assume to know what a client's behavior is about; we subscribe to a practical definition of the truth, what works in a given situation. Even if that person in the example was actually "fat" based on our cultural medical definition of "fat," buying into the thought "I'm fat" and acting to avoid that thought is not helping us move toward the life we want to live. We do not care whether the thought is true or factual, we care about the function. For more on this definition of truth see Chapter 1 and read on to Chapter 4 for an in-depth explanation and demonstration of analyzing the function of client behaviors.

A quick note about the utility and absence of noticing: if a client cannot see personal painful private experiences, if those experiences occur out of the client's awareness or unconsciously, then governance of those experiences can lead to rigid, inflexible repertoires of responding. Clients can become insensitive to the values that they would choose for their life to be about. This is how we conceptualize pathology in the ACT model of psychological flexibility—a lack of awareness of rigid behavioral repertoires of responding and connection to values that leads to patterns of avoidance functioning to take people further from the life they want to live. In the following chapter we explore more deeply the adverse of psychological flexibility (psychological inflexibility) and its six processes. We attempt to underscore this point to clients by saying a variation of the following:

> *When you leave here today I want to get you noticing your experiences and how they influence your life so that you're more free to choose what you do next. This doesn't mean I want you be 100 percent mindful all the time, totally blissed out, only acting on your values. If a bus jumps the curb and is racing toward you, I don't want you noticing the chrome on the bus and being curious about this sense of panic that has just showed up. I want you to move away! You likely want to avoid getting hit by that bus. Having you notice your experience is meant to be practical, a helpful way of you being free to choose what your life is about, not your mind. It's not about what you do next, it's about noticing what's influencing your behavior. We're developing the process of noticing so that you have the flexibility to choose what you do.*

This quote is helpful for wrapping up the Life Map and describing what to do next for clients. After all, as helping professionals we want to do something that clients will find useful. We point out that the strategy is not getting better at feeling less of their painful private experiences, which may seem shocking for some, considering they likely have come to you as a therapist for help in doing just that: feeling less of what pains them the most.

We've included a blank Life Map for you to use in your practice (pg.28). One with the guiding questions to help you remember how to write the Life Map and one with nothing on it at all. We'd like to encourage you to be creative and not rigidly come up with rules about how the Life Map ought to be done or how it should be presented. In our experience, being yourself and using the Life Map creatively yield the best results. We don't always begin with the bottom right quadrant when we fill out a Life Map, and you don't need to either.

With the attached blank Life Map, we'd like to challenge you to use it in a session. Fill out all four quadrants with your clients, even if you only write one or two items in each quadrant; that is okay — this diagram works by having your clients look at their lives in this functional contextualist way. For some it becomes instantly obvious how their behavior works in a given situation. For example, drinking a lot of alcohol when we're feeling depressed or alone numbs us and moves us away from our feelings of depression, which at the time is a relief but brings us no closer to the connected life we want to live.

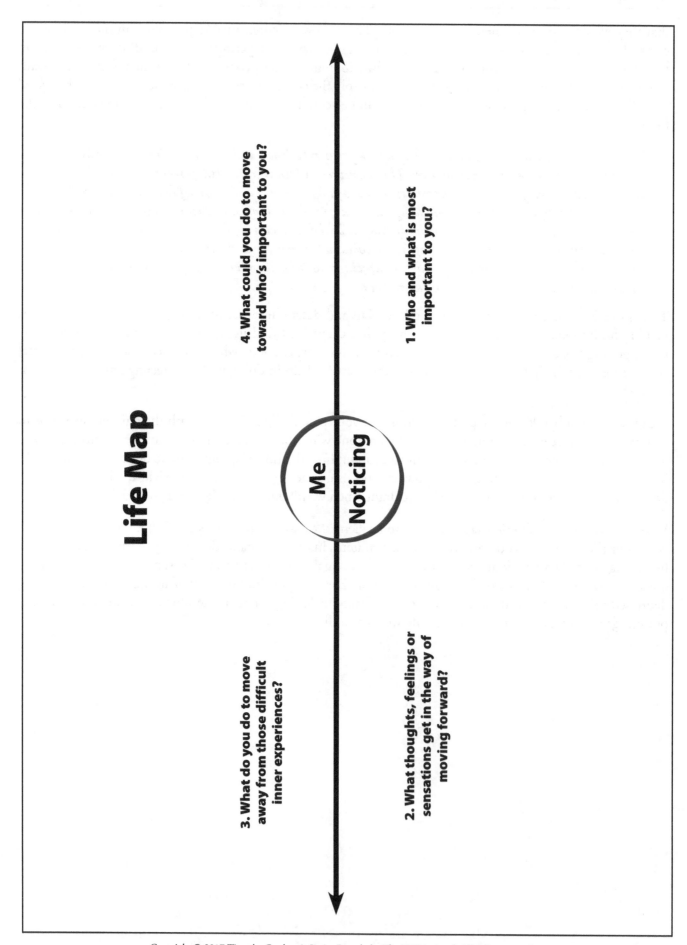

Life Map

Me

Noticing

1. Who and what is most important to you?

2. What thoughts, feelings or sensations get in the way of moving forward?

3. What do you do to move away from those difficult inner experiences?

4. What could you do to move toward who's important to you?

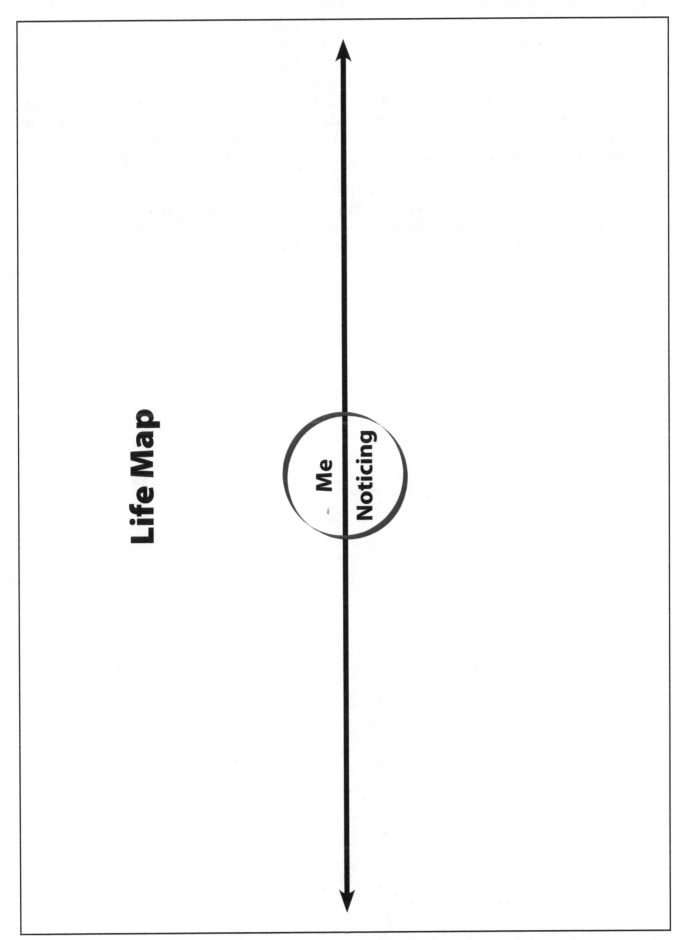

Life Map

Me
Noticing

You may also wish to use images whether you and your clients draw them yourselves, print pictures, cut them out of magazines/newspapers, or use stickers. Be creative. For example, instead of drawing a circle in the middle of the Life Map and writing "me noticing" at times we may put a big star in the center and write "You Are Here" similar to those informational maps at malls that help us orient to where we are in relation to everything else; it's about creating a new perspective and noticing where you are in the experience rather than drawing the perfect line or doing it exactly how we do it. The Life Map is simply about looking at how different behaviors work (function) in different situations (context). As an alternative to using the blank Life Map, you can create your own on a whiteboard or use other materials you may have in your office or practice setting.

We provide a "Mapping Your Life" worksheet, which you may wish to keep handy to give to clients, using it in session and sending it home with them to prompt their use of noticing outside of sessions. We have also had a lot of success giving a blank copy to clients and asking them to make a Life Map for their adolescent, partner, or someone else who is important in their life. We believe that it solidifies their use of the skills by bringing it and explaining it to others.

MAPPING YOUR LIFE

This is a map to your life, it's about paying attention to your experience so that you can choose what you do.

PART 1. GIVE AT LEAST ONE ANSWER IN EACH SECTION

3. What do you do to move away from your painful experience?

4. What could you do to move toward who and what is most important?

Me
Noticing

2. What painful thoughts, feelings, sensations, or memories get in the way of moving foward?

1. Who and what matter most to you? What qualities do you most wish to live in your life?

1. _____

2. _____

3. _____

4. _____

PART 2. NOTICE YOUR EXPERIENCES

What does it feel like to move toward who and what's most important? What does it feel like to move away from painful thoughts, feelings, sensations, and memories? Which side do you spend the majority of your life living on?

_____

_____

_____

_____

LIFE MAPPING IS ABOUT EXPLORING

We especially like using the Life Map with clients because it shows them what therapeutic agreement we are making. With this ACT consistent noneliminative agenda, we may point to the top left quadrant (moving away behaviors) and describe "the behaviors written here are your attempts to eliminate and minimize the painful private experiences you have." Then we point to the bottom left quadrant and list their painful private experiences out loud, saying how these experiences "may be limiting your life and even reinforcing the hold that some of this painful stuff has on you." Before switching our focus to the right side of the Life Map, we say "Our work is about you noticing what is motivating your behavior so that you can have the freedom to choose what you do next." With that, we will encourage clients to explore, tell us what they most wish to be doing if not engaged in a life of attempting to avoid, escape, and control their most painful private experiences.

We find clients enjoy this conversation and often reference the behaviors already listed on the right side of the Life Map, encouraging a broader repertoire of behavior. This last point about more behavior is an important distinction between escaping, avoiding, or controlling painful experiences and exploring new ways to be in the world. It is in this moment where the therapist can explain to clients that they themselves have little success eliminating painful private experiences, both for their clients and for themselves. Instead, the therapist explains having much more success in encouraging exploration of new behaviors in the presence of that pain. It is this exploration that leads to an increased quality of life. This distinction may seem small now, but place it in the evolution of how your conversations will go with clients and the focus isn't on a fixed outcome such as removing painful experiences but instead on increasing flexibility in the presence of painful experiences and broadening their repertoire.

LIFE MAP IN GROUPS

In group settings, the Life Map is especially useful. We stand at a whiteboard, flipchart, or use a wireless device with stylus connected to a projector and draw the horizontal line with arrowheads on each side. We begin by asking a general question to all the members of the group, "Who is most important to you? Just shout it out and we'll try to keep up and write them all down." When someone shouts "my wife" and another person says "Julie," we would actually just write down exactly those responses in the bottom right quadrant. After achieving a sample of who is important, we ask, "And what is important to you or what qualities do you want to live in your life?" We tend to get answers such as "nature" or "parenting." At this point, drawing on the specific qualities can be helpful. For example, you would hear us say in response to parenting, "Parenting! Great. And what kind of parent do you want to be?" Typically someone will say "loving" or "present," and these are exactly the richer details we seek to uncover when we talk about doing values-focused work in ACT.

When in doubt, adjectives are great ways to identify values (loving, honest, kind, outgoing, healthy, creative, spiritual, hard-working, etc.). When we have a number of answers written, we typically poll the room, "By a show of hands, does everyone here see at least one person or thing that matters to you in your life?" We also ask, "If there's anything missing that you feel really needs to go on here, shout it out and we'll add it." There's no magic number of responses. If no one raises a voice of dissent, that is okay and not problematic. We are not seeking a complete picture; we simply want a representation of values by asking these questions because if a person does not connect with something on the board, it is hard to connect with the exercise as a whole.

Moving on to the bottom left quadrant is a natural progression, and we prompt the group by saying, "Inevitably, difficult thoughts, feelings, sensations, and memories show up that get in our way of moving toward who and what matter most to us." We like to make things obvious and will point at the bottom left quadrant. We ask the group, "What thoughts, feelings, sensations, and memories get in the way of you moving toward who and what matter most?" We once again point for emphasis, this time at the bottom right quadrant with the answers just filled in, illustrating the answers we are looking for now are about what gets in the way of moving toward the bottom right quadrant. Answers often include sadness, fear, and other feelings. We prompt someone in those moments, "And what thoughts do you have when fear shows up in your life?" A group participant may respond, "I can't do it" or "There's not enough time!" Or if someone offers a thought such as "I'm not good enough," we may ask, "What feelings show up when that thought occurs to you?" We write thoughts down in quotes to illustrate how thoughts can get in the way. We also include physical sensations—chronic pain or withdrawal symptoms—and other physical dependence sensations or the sensations associated with panic or fear (heavy weight on chest, heart pounding, "feels like someone is grabbing my throat and I can't breathe"). We ask clarifying questions, "Where do you feel that in your body?" and "What thoughts or feelings occur to you when that sensation shows up?" At this point in the group, you will likely already have a sense of who the group members are and why they are here, so if the group is stuck you may repeat things they have said before, "Hey Alex, I remember you saying before during our introductions that you often feel like you can't do anything you want to do with chronic pain. There's a good thought in there that I bet shows up for a lot of people: 'I can't live the life I want with pain.' Would it be all right if I put that in the bottom left? Do other people have thoughts like that?"

It may occur to you that there are wrong answers such as when a participant might say "my brother-in-law is an asshole." We encourage you to be directive and explain what it is that you're looking for again: "We're looking for the thoughts, feelings, sensations, and memories that show up and make it more difficult for us to move toward who and what matter most to us. What do you experience that gets in the way of moving toward the life that's important to you?" Alternatively you might ask, "Yes! And when you're saying 'my brother-in-law is an asshole,' what thoughts or feelings show up there for you?" **The general idea is that all content is grist for the mill in ACT. There is little that we cannot work with in this context, and labeling experiences on the Life Map demonstrates a clear conceptualization of what will be the focus of the group's work.**

We then move on to the top left quadrant and ask the group, "When these painful thoughts and feelings show up [point at the bottom left quadrant], what do you do to move away from them? What are your strategies to minimize, escape, avoid, or control this stuff?" Typical answers involve "drinking," "watching TV," "avoiding people," "sex," "eating," in which case we ask "eating what and how much?" We then ask "what about not eating?" to demonstrate the variability in behaviors and write both down: "overeating, not eating" or some variation on that theme. Sometimes examples show up that therapists assume are adaptive and healthy such as "sleep," "exercise," "go to therapy," or "yoga." None of those answers are wrong, and if they are used to move away from painful private experiences then they truly do belong in the top left quadrant. Remember, the answers here are about the behaviors one does to move away from painful private experiences, we obviously would like to hear about problematic away move behaviors to give us clinically relevant information, but this category of behavior does not need to be populated by exclusively problematic behaviors.

When moving to the top right quadrant we find it an easy transition to ask, "If you weren't so busy doing all this [pointing to the top left quadrant that lists all of the away move behaviors], what are you doing now or could you be doing to move toward who and what are most important to you?" When we ask this question, we point to the bottom right quadrant listing the group's values to emphasize our point. We often get answers such as "spending quality time," "going for walks," "talking to my spouse." Here we ask clarifying questions, "What would you be talking about?" **The idea is to draw group participants' attention to specific behaviors that they are doing or could be doing.** The behavioral model can far too easily take for granted the reinforcing qualities of doing things that move one toward who and what are most important to them. In fact, for most people moving toward can feel difficult or downright unnatural and painful. Every now and then you get a group that will focus on feelings: "I'll be happy," or "I will feel better." In these moments, reflecting back to them a statement that draws out the observable behaviors they are doing can help redirect. For example, we might ask, "If I could see you feeling better, if I were watching a movie about you being happy, what would I see you doing?" You may even notice other group members jumping in and helping each other out. It's a wonderful normalizing activity to realize that others struggle in similar ways. And in one cohesive exercise you have mapped the whole ACT model and connected clients with a different way of viewing their lives.

MAPPING THE WHOLE ACT MODEL

Another way to conceptually view the Life Map is combining it with the hexaflex, depicting ACT's six core processes. Although familiar as you now are with the following diagram, you will note that we needed to flip the values and commitment processes with one another, because they fall on different spots using the Life Map. Remember though that the hexagon is just a way of showing the six processes, so nothing conceptually changes when we swap the values and commitment processes for this demonstration, all processes are still equally represented in the model.

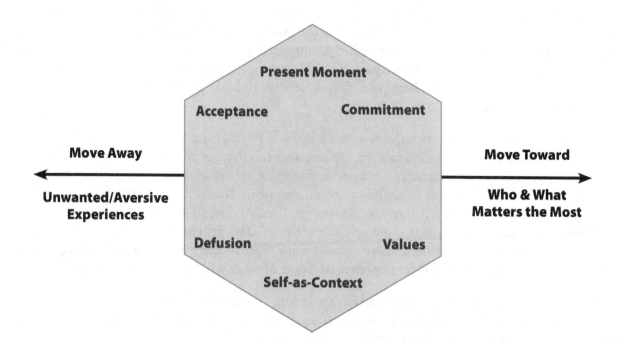

When you overlay the hexagon and Life Map you see: the bottom right quadrant of the Life Map describes who and what matter most; it is what we labeled as values in the hexagon. The painful private experiences that get in the way of moving toward who and what are most important fits into the bottom left quadrant labeled as defusion—these are the thoughts, feelings, sensations, and memories that we wish to defuse from in order to limit their control over our behavior. The top left quadrant lists the behaviors that are attempts to avoid or escape (move away) from painful private experiences, overlaid with the acceptance process where we promote acceptance of painful thoughts, feelings, memories, and sensations rather than an unwillingness to come into contact or make space for them. The top right quadrant is where we expose the behaviors that already do or could move one toward who and what matter most (their values), and once more it is overlaid with the hexagon, this time demonstrating the hexagon's commitment process. Contacting the present moment occurs as one looks at and uses the Life Map, essentially noticing and labeling or tacting to their experience and where it goes, pointing to it, and naming or depicting it on the Life Map, which can only be done in the present moment. Finally, observing the Life Map and seeing the self at the center of the perspective, their experience encompassing both private and public experiences with behaviors that move them toward who and what matter most, and away from what they would avoid or attempt to escape is a self-as-context experience.

Throughout this book we will reference the Life Map as an easy to use way of delivering the entire ACT approach in a single diagram. In Chapter 4, we use the Life Map for case conceptualization and treatment. In Chapter 7, we expose novel applications of the Life Map: using it to create engaging questions that inspire change in client behaviors. In Chapter 8 we use the Life Map with young people to help them tell stories about their lives in a more flexible manner. We find this diagram to be useful in teaching and practicing ACT and hope you will use it in your practice.

Chapter 4

Case Conceptualization
with ACT

The populations we serve as helping professionals tend to make their way to our practices looking for solutions. In this commonsense agenda a new client may think, "I'll visit the therapist so they can help me feel better with the thoughts, feelings, sensations, or memories I'm struggling with just like my medical professional will help me with my high blood pressure, or cold." We addressed creating a noneliminative agenda with clients through an ACT informed consent in Chapter 2. **The bottom line is that this noneliminative agenda focuses on struggling *less* with painful private experiences, instead focusing on growing lives toward meaning, vitality, and an increased quality of life. That increased quality of life is something we seek to grow with psychological flexibility.** In ACT, psychological flexibility is the measure of health that we aim to increase. Inversely, psychological inflexibility is the way that we track pathology. Using the functional contextualist approach, we look for patterns of unworkable behavior, areas where we can work with clients to assist them in modifying their behavior and notice when a behavior is not working to achieve moving them toward their values or increasing their quality of life. Having an understanding of both how psychological flexibility presents in session as well as how psychological inflexibility can look gives us the ability to track not only where our clients are but what core processes we want to target (acceptance, defusion, etc.) with the ultimate goal of increasing workable behaviors and psychological flexibility overall. Essentially, our aim is to change the function of clients' behavior so that they are acting in ways that bring them closer to the life they want to live.

Everyone can develop inflexible, rigid repertoires of responding when faced with aversive experiences—this is the human condition not just mental-health–related problems or a syndrome. When pain shows up, there tends to be little variability in behavior. We respond with a narrow repertoire. Here's an example: Imagine while you are reading this book, someone walks up behind you thinking they're playing a practical joke and blasts a 120 decibel air horn. (If you're not familiar, air horns are small enough to fit in your hand but are about as loud as a thunderclap right in your ear or an obnoxious driver honking at you. Air horns are super loud because they're meant to signal trucks, trains, ships, and emergency vehicles.) If you heard this while relaxing and reading this book at home your ability to respond to your environment became instantly smaller; you'd likely react with a rigid repertoire of behavior. You'd jump or yell, possibly feeling as if your heart just leapt from your chest. Your behavior has likely become *inflexible* and *narrow,* meaning there are very few things you would be engaged in, in that moment.

Before you had been taking in the words on the page, noticing your thoughts and reactions to them, thinking about how these concepts might apply to your practice, sipping tea, or noticing how comfortable you are where you are sitting. Afterward, you might jump from your seat, panic, and have racing thoughts about what could have possibly caused that sound. This reaction is normal, logical, rational, and evolutionarily relevant. Your sympathetic nervous system was developed to activate in times of great stress or danger to keep you safe. Protecting yourself from threats wisely involves narrowed, inflexible repertoires of fighting, fleeing, or freezing so that you may survive. But humans' ability to literally believe our private experiences to be true means that we respond similarly to our private experiences as we do our observable public experiences. **Our minds are unable to distinguish the threats in our minds from the threats in our world.** As a result, reacting to these painful private experiences as if they were tangible threats in our environment means that we tend have narrow and rigid reactions even when there's nothing threatening nearby—we act to avoid, escape, and hide—and we've seen many examples of inflexibility in this book already.

These patterns of excessive avoidance lead us to treat normal experiences as threats; to react to private experiences, such as thoughts or memories or sensations, as threats. Sadness becomes the enemy. Anger becomes dangerous. Anxieties become something to prevent at all costs. Our thoughts become our fate. Memories become the monster under our bed. And our lives can become organized around preventing these experiences from showing up. Eventually, we have one kind of response to everything: avoid and control. Our responses all become like jumping out of our seats in response to the air horn. Consequently, our ability to respond becomes insensitive to other things that are important to us, like our values, our families, our careers, and our vitality. When this happens, we call it *psychological inflexibility*.

ACT's aim is to reduce psychological inflexibility (which we will discuss in detail later in this chapter), or, said another way, increase psychological flexibility. Psychological flexibility as you have learned already means being conscious, present, and willing while engaging in actions guided by our values. That sentence is a mouthful, and the concept itself can be a little bit tricky to wrap our minds around. It's one of the reasons we repeat the definition in slightly different ways throughout this book, to give you more experiences of coming into contact with what psychological flexibility is. We find it helpful to remember that the key to psychological flexibility is workability. In ACT, workability is the yardstick by which we measure any action. In any moment, we might ask, "Given what I'm working toward, how workable is this behavior I'm engaging in right now? Is it taking me closer to that goal? Is it working for me?" From this perspective, no behavior is right or wrong. Behavior is simply workable or unworkable. Thus, avoiding pain and getting wrapped up in our minds might be just fine in the right context. But in other contexts, the same behavior is unworkable and takes us away from building the lives we want to build.

A helpful way to begin conceptualizing the opposite of psychological flexibility is with a hexaflex diagram inspired from Bach and Moran's text, *ACT in Practice* (2008), the hexa-inflex. Just like the hexagon model's hexaflex demonstrating the six core processes, the hexa-inflex shows how the six core processes interact to create one model. In the hexa-inflex though, we see the inverse of these six core processes: psychological inflexibility. This is important because often clients do not present with any of the markers of psychological flexibility, so having an understanding of what the opposite of the processes are can give you, the therapist, a direction for intervention.

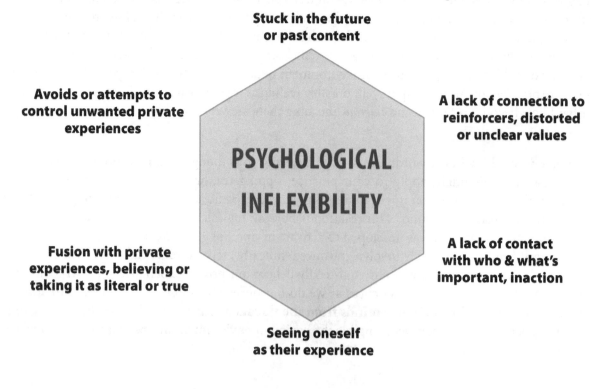

Stuck in the future
or past content

Avoids or attempts to
control unwanted private
experiences

A lack of connection to
reinforcers, distorted
or unclear values

**PSYCHOLOGICAL
INFLEXIBILITY**

Fusion with private
experiences, believing or
taking it as literal or true

A lack of contact
with who & what's
important, inaction

Seeing oneself
as their experience

EXPERIENTIAL AVOIDANCE

The opposite of acceptance occurs when a person actively avoids or attempts to control or escape situations that may elicit unpleasant experiences, what we call experiential avoidance. *Experiential avoidance* can be functional in some contexts: You're driving and notice a truck ahead of you on the road blow a tire. The truck rapidly decreases speed as debris shoots up into the air. You immediately apply the brake, look to your right, and pull onto the shoulder of the road to avoid a collision with the truck and its debris. All of those reactions happen quickly and are all avoidant yet perfectly functional. They work! Next time you're on the road and a truck blows a tire in front of you threatening a collision, we don't want you to just notice the debris, its color and texture, accepting the rhythm of life: we live, we breathe, tires blow, collisions happen. No way. We want you to AVOID! However, when we presented basic science in the first chapter of this book, if the thought occurred to you, "Oh, I'm not a scientist or a researcher, I'll never get this chapter. Reading it will just make me feel stupid," and you put the book down, or maybe you did begin reading the chapter and noticed anger pop up because we started talking about behaviorism and you felt bamboozled like ACT tricked you into reading about operant conditioning and you skipped the chapter; those are examples of experiential avoidance that are potentially less functional and might not help you move toward your values of professional growth, knowledge, or being a well-rounded clinician. **Explicitly, experiential avoidance is a class of behavior focused less on how the behavior works or what the observable experience of the behavior is, but rather how it functions in a given context.**

When we attempt to avoid or to alter, control, or escape a situation that brings about painful private experiences and that behavior is taking us farther from the type of life we want, we are engaging in nonfunctional experiential avoidance. Take, for example, a client recovering from methamphetamine abuse who uses again. After coming down from the episode they may feel sad or ashamed that they had a relapse. When they think about their upcoming appointment with you, they may think to themselves, "My therapist is going to be so disappointed in me. They will be mad and think I don't care about my recovery." In order to escape these feelings and thoughts, this person may not show up to their next appointment and ignore your phone calls. Of course, this behavior only makes the feelings and thoughts grow bigger and larger, and before they know it they are back to using regularly and calling themself a "failure." This pattern of behaving functioned to escape unpleasant thoughts and feelings related to a setback, and although it may work to alleviate or numb his private experiences in the short-term, in the long-term it is in direct opposition to the life they want to live, a life where they are a loving, attentive parent and taking an active role in their recovery in collaboration with people who can help.

When our focus is always on avoiding unpleasant experiences, it is extremely difficult to live a meaningful life, because where there is meaning there is pain. If on the other hand, the client could have noticed those thoughts and feelings that were showing up inside of them and paused to remember why they were willing to experience this pain, what they were working toward, they may have had the space to choose a different or more workable behavior, such as attending the session with you and being honest about their relapse experience, rather than reacting automatically to that drive to escape pain. And if we as clinicians ignore the real immediate benefit of escaping pain and fail to explore different ways to act when pain shows up, we are dooming our clients to a pattern of experiential avoidance that takes them further and further from who and what matter to them and forever labeling them "a failure." So even when behaviors show up that seem obviously harmful or a clearly "bad" decision, remember that every behavior has a function. Work to understand what function that behavior serves for your client. And talk with your client about the real short-term benefits. It is often a relief for clients to know that you do not label them as "stupid," or "a failure," or "never going to change," instead acknowledging that in the face of pain trying to escape or avoid or control that experience is perfectly normal, validating that difficult struggle, and noticing with them that while it provides short-term relief it's just not working for them overall.

FUSION

The opposite of defusion, *fusion*, happens when clients believe or take literally their private experiences, such as thoughts, feelings, sensations, memories. They buy into them or take them to be Truth with a capital T. Their thoughts are their reality and fate all tied into one. This can be problematic because people who take their private experiences to be literally true are no longer sensitive to the outcomes or consequences of their behaviors. Instead, they believe that the outcome will always be consistent with their beliefs, which leads to a narrowing of the available behaviors they can engage in because they are restricted by their own strong beliefs in their private experiences. For example, a person with chronic pain may think "I can't exercise" when presented with the opportunity to do anything active and as a result of buying into that thought will decline as they believe that they literally are unable to exercise. Whereas a person who recognizes that thought is language, a string of words, produced from their mind and can make space for that thought may make the decision to engage in an activity based on various contextual factors, such as how their body is feeling that day and whether they can modify the activity to fit their abilities. If clients take literally the idea that they cannot exercise, then their only option is to say no, whereas they actually have many options based on the context of the situation.

Clients may often find themselves fused with thoughts related to their abilities that restrict their options. As a clinician, watching clients in this situation can be a frustrating experience. Have you ever found yourself in a metaphorical tug-of-war with a client trying to problem solve how they can better engage in the life they want to live and they continue to respond with "I can't do that because of X" or "that won't work because of Y" or "I tried that once and it didn't work so why would I try again?" Rather than wear them down into making a half-hearted attempt at a behavior they believe will not work because they are fused with the thought "I can't," why not instead shift your focus to helping your client make space, or defuse, from that stuck (fused) thought? **Meeting clients where they are and approaching their fused thoughts as a skill or process for them to practice rather than a battle of wills may not be less work, but offers a much more lasting and satisfying outcome.**

INATTENTIVE TO THE HERE-AND-NOW

The opposite of awareness is when a person is not paying attention to the environment and private experiences in the moment and is rather focused on private experiences that involve the past, future, or alternative "what if" realities. They do not pay attention to what is happening right here, right now. Humans spend the majority of their time in their heads rather than paying attention to the world around them. This skill actually increased their chance of survival in the past; it was adaptive. Think about it: for the majority of our lives we are not faced with immediate threats to our survival. Of course vulnerability varies, and people in extremely dangerous situations must be more vigilant. These environments tend to create an extended fight, flight, or freeze state that can develop into hypervigilance, insensitivity to environment (everything is a threat), and significant health consequences from chronic stress. But for those who are lucky to be in a safe-enough environment from a survival perspective, it would be a waste of resources to always be attending to the current environment.

Instead, your mind uses that energy to rehearse potential future dangerous situations, examine past experiences to learn from them and make sure they do not happen again, and explore experiences others have described to learn from their mistakes. If we were out on the Sahara or deep in a forest with many predators, lack of food and shelter, and potential enemy groups, spending that much time and energy anticipating and learning may have been necessary to survival. **Today, however, because our minds cannot distinguish private from observable behaviors, we become preoccupied with things that cause a similar response without the life-or-death consequences.** We spend all day thinking about the things that could go wrong if we went on a date with that person from our office, or the rejection we could face if we tried to make new friends, or the physical pain we could experience if we tried going for a walk at the park. This does not mean we must be attentive all the time, there are situations in which it may be functional to go into our minds—planning your schedule for the week or rehearsing an important conversation in your mind may be working towards being a hardworking and organized employee or an attentive partner. However, it is important that our decision to be attentive to the here and now or to be in our heads is actually a choice based on what is consistent with our values rather than a reaction to something that shows up.

SELF-AS-CONTENT

The opposite of self-as-context is when a person views themselves as the content of their lives; they do not distinguish themselves as separate from their experience. This *self-as-content* is especially problematic when people get stuck on who they "ought to be" or who they "once were" and they don't see themselves as a persistent observer to their changing experience. This tendency is understandable to a large degree because our society relies on roles and expertly categorizes people based on their abilities. Often when people experience changes, such as entering retirement, becoming a parent, or sustaining an injury that limits the ability to do a role the same as before, they face difficulties adjusting when they are fused with their self-as-content rather than noticing that they are the observer of all of their experiences and are not tied to any one role or set of abilities. Similarly, clients can become fused with their diagnostic label: "I am depressed," "I have borderline personality disorder," or "I am an obese person."

Although diagnostic labels can be helpful for categorizing symptoms (and insurance claims), they can hinder therapy when a client takes a label as their identity, believing that is all they are. Just like with a person who is newly retired and feeling the loss of a major role held for a large part of their life, a person going through therapy may feel uncertain or begin to question who they if they are not that label. Working with clients to notice themselves as the observer of their experiences rather than the content does not diminish the importance those roles or thoughts or labels have had in their life, especially if those roles were a significant source of value in their life, such as a meaningful career. It is simply allowing for a new perspective where the person can choose how to respond in a given context - independent of any label, role, or thought that may arise.

DISCONNECTION TO VALUES

It is difficult to get where you want to go if you have no idea what your destination is. **Without a clear set of values, therapy can be difficult because both the client and therapist are unsure what the client is working toward.** The opposite of connecting to your values can come in many forms. It can be a lack of values, poorly clarified values, or values based on societal norms rather than a thoughtful reflection on what is truly meaningful to that person as an individual. For example, a client could have been engaging in a pattern of experiential avoidance for so long that they are completely off-course and turned around and have no idea what a meaningful life would look like since they have not experienced it for a while, if ever.

Clients may also have vague or unclear values that make it difficult to connect committed actions to or to be able to tell whether they are living life according to their values. This may occur when clients come up with an answer quickly without taking any time to pause and reflect on who or what is truly meaningful to them. Similarly, clients may acknowledge values that they think they should value because society or their culture or upbringing suggests they should value, such as "helping others," "honesty," or "religion or spirituality." Now, we are not saying that a person cannot have a value that is also consistent with their culture or societal norms, but rather it is important to be clear when discussing what they want their life to be about that there are no right or wrong answers. In therapy we may focus on a few important values, but that does not mean those are the only things a client may care about, however, their other values may not be something that is guiding how they live their life right now. Being able to help clients clarify who and what matter most to them or acknowledge that their values have changed can be one of the most important interventions in ACT.

DIMINISHED ENGAGEMENT WITH LIFE

The opposite of engaging in values-based actions is a person who engages in experiential avoidance, which does not move them closer to who and what are important to them. Instead, they are doing things in reaction to painful private experiences and are motivated to avoid or limit their exposure to that pain. We often hear a narrative of "I'll do X when my pain goes away" when a person is not acting in accordance with their values. Experiential avoidance does not always mean not engaging in an action. For example, staying late at work every evening is an active behavior, but may not be working toward the value of being a loving parent or spouse. It is not so much what the person is doing, but rather whether that action is taking them toward or away from who and what are important to them. Taking that same example, if that person's value was to be a hardworking employee or personal growth, spending extra time at work may be servicing those values.

CLINICIAN CASE CONCEPTUALIZATION WORKSHEET

We have included a conceptualization worksheet using the hexagon model with guiding questions for each process. You can use these questions to inform your thinking about the clients you see in your practice and use the blank spaces inside the hexagon to keep track of things your client says or does in session including behaviors that they report outside of session. Note that this case conceptualization sheet seeks to answer basic questions about problematic behavior such as "In what way is this client attempting to avoid/escape their experience in problematic ways?" This behavior would be an example of experiential avoidance you may be listening for in a session. There's also strengths-based conceptualization questions that seek to have you explore clients' values and the behaviors they currently are or wish to be engaged in that could assist them in growing a meaningful life with a rich connection to their values.

ACT CONCEPTUALIZATION

Present Moment
Is this client present with their experience? Are they stuck in the past or future?

Values
Who and what is most important to this client?

Commitment
What behaviors is this client already doing or could they be doing to move toward who and what is most important to them?

Acceptance
In what way is this client attempting to avoid/escape their experience in problematic ways?

Defusion
What thoughts, sensations, memories, or feelings does this client take as literal?

Self-as-Context
What stuck stories does this client have about themselves?

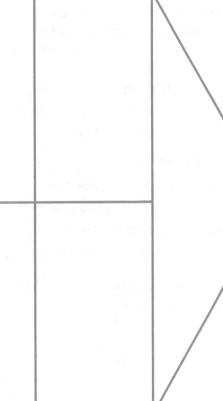

A CASE CONCEPTUALIZATION EXAMPLE

In the following composite of a client we created, you will read about Bill's story. As you read, pause to notice and identify processes of psychological inflexibility. We will walk you through some general questions for conceptualizing Bill and his presenting problems as well as juxtapose ACT conceptualization with some common theoretical orientations to show you where they overlap and where they diverge.

Bill's Story: "Look, I'm here because I have problems. I drink way too much, and I'm terrible at relationships because I'm a loser: I'm ugly and unhealthy. I'm ugly on the inside too. I'm a pervert and it disgusts me, but I can't stop. I can't be in a real relationship, I'll just screw it up like I have every other relationship I've ever been in. Instead I just hook up and have one-night stands. It makes me feel gross, but I keep doing it. I feel so disgusted with myself that I eat a ton of junk food and then end up taking a bunch of laxatives. I need help and I can't change on my own. I just can't bear being lonely anymore. I hate myself and everyone else does too. No one talks to me or wants to hang out with me. I'm completely alone. Can you help me?"

General Conceptualization Questions

The following is a brief list of conceptualization questions that a therapist may ask, regardless of clinical orientation to assess what is happening in a client's life and what they might be struggling with.

- Why is this person behaving this way?
- What does this person think about themselves?
- Why does this person respond to me like this?
- Why is this person having difficulty in various areas of their life?
- What is preventing this person from living the life they want to lead?

It is important to demonstrate and acknowledge how all models generally ask useful conceptualization questions that can aid in developing a picture of what is happening in a person's life. In addition to these general questions, each orientation asks its own theory-specific questions that help to build a case conceptualization consistent with that model. Here, we include conceptualizations from different orientations. You may find it helpful to notice what historical information is sought in further clarifying a conceptualization of the client and the unique direction that each conceptualization goes with Bill's story.

A Psychodynamic Conceptualization

"Bill's mother, while loving, was extremely undependable. For example, she frequently forgot to pick him up from school. As an adult, Bill has drinking problems and difficulty believing that his friends and lovers will be consistent in their relationships with him. Bill must be helped to see that this difficulty may have stemmed from his out-of-awareness fear that people, especially romantic partners in his adult life, will behave as his mother did."

In our opinion, the psychodynamic conceptualization is helpful as it explores Bill's history and looks at what events in Bill's life could have shaped his behavior. It's clear from reading this conceptualization that the therapist values the antecedents that led up to Bill's current problems and theorizes that Bill's formative years are influencing his behavior today. A limitation with this conceptualization is that we are currently unaware of how the behaviors that Bill is reporting as problematic are currently functioning in his life, how they work for Bill, how they are maintained, in what way are these behaviors being reinforced, and how we can practically help Bill break the current pattern of behaving in which he is stuck. A more explicit behavioral plan for Bill that prescribes what he can do today, tomorrow, and the next day could be integrated by this therapist to adopt an ACT-consistent approach.

A Cognitive Conceptualization

A typical problematic situation for Bill is that he has just had sex on a first date. Lying in bed, he has automatic thoughts: "I'm so ugly. She's probably thinking this was a mistake. She will never want to see me again. I might as well get up and leave now." Emotionally, he feels sad, and his behavior is to leave abruptly (probably appearing unfriendly, at best, to his date). His automatic thoughts are, "I'm too fat. No one wants me." He then feels sad, binges, and takes laxatives. The treatment plan is to reduce Bill's depression through helping him change automatic thoughts connected with unlovability and actively schedule socializing. Alternative behaviors to binging, testing assumptions about being rejected, and developing assertiveness skills will be a focus.

We like this cognitive conceptualization with its analysis of how Bill's painful private experiences (self-deprecating thoughts and feelings of sadness) influence his problematic behaviors. Scheduling time to socialize and seek out alternative behaviors to problematic ones as well as a focus on skills training from this conceptualization would be helpful from our perspective and congruent with the ACT approach. However, the cognitive restructuring activities that include testing assumptions and changing automatic thoughts are not consistent with ACT as the foundational theory of language and behavior underpinning ACT, RFT, does not support an eliminative agenda (the ability to remove or replace private events), but rather is additive (creating additional relational frames). Further, through continuously focusing on unpleasant private experiences in session by talking about them, analyzing them, or exploring their validity with the intention of eliminating or attempting to refute them could inadvertently reinforce that relational frame.

Take for example the classic White Bear experiment from everyone's intro to psychology or social psychology class in college: in order to not think about a white bear you must first think about a white bear to know what it is so you can know what it's not. The practice of cognitive restructuring allows us to shift our attention or distract us from unpleasant internal experiences, but it does not eliminate those experiences; they always come back. For example, Bill may feel especially hopeless if the restructuring activities do not reduce or eliminate the recurrence of these painful thoughts and feelings. In ACT, we would instead seek to help Bill increase his acceptance of painful thoughts and feelings, and defuse from the stuck stories that his mind tells him in order to increase his flexibility in the presence of those painful private experiences with the goal of helping Bill create space to choose behaviors that are more workable for him, perhaps behaviors that might move him closer to his values regardless of whether painful thoughts and feelings are present.

A DSM-Conceptualization

F33.2 major depressive episode, recurrent, severe; Rule out bulimia nervosa; F60.6 avoidant personality disorder; E66.9 overweight or obesity; Multiple relationship failures.

We appreciate the disease model assessment of the DSM because it provides the context of the current symptoms and gives us an easy way to research and communicate generalities about Bill's presenting problems. This conceptualization, however, doesn't explain Bill's problematic behaviors in the context of his life. Instead, it simply focuses on clusters of symptoms that tend to hang together and how people with these clusters generally behave or feel. We also fear that the process of identifying people by symptoms and labels could potentially reinforce their self-as-content, creating more language around what they can and cannot do because of their diagnosis rather than the actual contextual factors of the present moment. Additionally, diagnostic labels can potentially reinforce our own fused stories we have about clients similar to Bill; we can begin to view all clients with a similar diagnosis as the same, rather than understanding the function of their specific behaviors in their unique context. This tendency becomes especially problematic with client populations that have severe diagnoses associated with high relapse rates or resistance to treatment, such as addiction and substance misuse issues, narcissistic personality disorder, or borderline personality disorder.

An ACT Conceptualization

Relationship and intimacy, both romantic and social, matter a great deal to Bill. When painful feelings of heartbreak or thoughts of rejection show up for Bill, he engages in several avoidance behaviors, such as drinking, which in turn appear to trigger a painful cycle of behaviors resulting in feelings of loneliness and frustration, and physical arousal or feeling horny. In reaction to these private experiences, Bill regrettably texts his friend Krista to hook up, who reacts in frustration, eliciting feelings of embarrassment in Bill, which he tries to escape further by going to a local fast-food restaurant and eating food he otherwise would not eat. Ultimately, Bill reports feeling fat, and it's at this time that he may end the cycle by being home alone or taking laxatives. Our plan is to help Bill see this cycle he is stuck in that takes him further from a life filled with romantic and social intimate relationships, bring more awareness to the painful private experiences that evoke these problematic behaviors, and invite Bill to accept those painful thoughts and feelings so he can engage in behaviors that he would choose for himself, specifically behaviors that bring him closer to his chosen values: his health, his family, his friendships, and a meaningful long-term romantic relationship.

In the following hexagon model we include the adverse of each of the processes presented as we perceive them from the session with Bill.

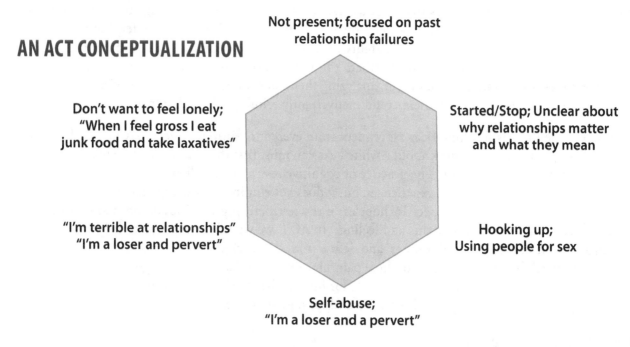

AN ACT CONCEPTUALIZATION

Not present; focused on past relationship failures

Don't want to feel lonely; "When I feel gross I eat junk food and take laxatives"

Started/Stop; Unclear about why relationships matter and what they mean

"I'm terrible at relationships" "I'm a loser and pervert"

Hooking up; Using people for sex

Self-abuse; "I'm a loser and a pervert"

Of note, the hexagon model showing Bill's psychological inflexibility processes only focuses on pathology that would not exclusively be helpful in our opinion because we want more information about Bill such as who is important to him and what behaviors does he want to be engaging in if not the problematic ones he listed. From an ACT perspective, we're not only looking for problematic behaviors and the private experiences that may be painful where we could implement acceptance and defusion practices to help Bill with his most painful experiences and problematic behaviors, but we also seek to reinforce the behaviors Bill wants to grow toward in his life. Our overall aim is to help Bill move toward the life he wants to live, whatever that looks like to him.

Another way to view Bill's narrative from an ACT approach is to use the conceptualization worksheet we showed you earlier in this chapter. Here you will find one filled in as if it were a session note, tracking each of the processes with Bill and noting what the therapist observed in session.

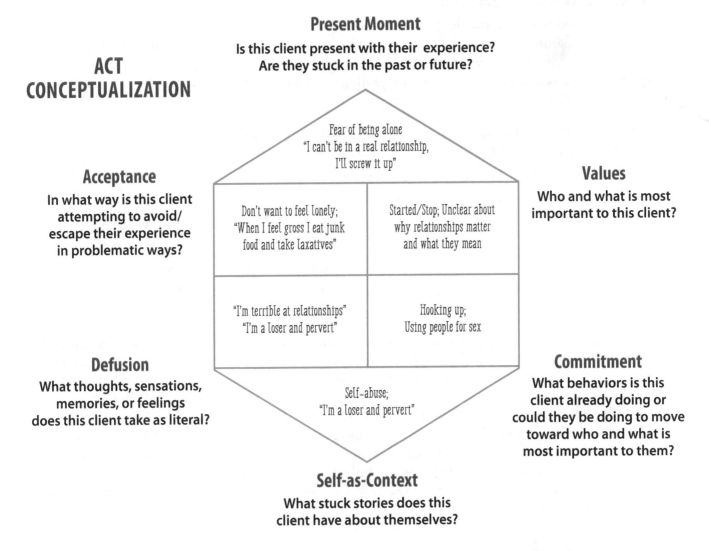

ACT CONCEPTUALIZATION

Present Moment
Is this client present with their experience?
Are they stuck in the past or future?

Fear of being alone
"I can't be in a real relationship,
I'll screw it up"

Acceptance
In what way is this client attempting to avoid/escape their experience in problematic ways?

Don't want to feel lonely;
"When I feel gross I eat junk food and take laxatives"

Started/Stop; Unclear about why relationships matter and what they mean

Values
Who and what is most important to this client?

"I'm terrible at relationships"
"I'm a loser and pervert"

Hooking up;
Using people for sex

Defusion
What thoughts, sensations, memories, or feelings does this client take as literal?

Self-abuse;
"I'm a loser and pervert"

Commitment
What behaviors is this client already doing or could they be doing to move toward who and what is most important to them?

Self-as-Context
What stuck stories does this client have about themselves?

To assist you in creating your own conceptualizations of your cases, we recommend using this conceptualization worksheet and the Life Map (see Chapter 3 for an introduction to the Life Map). The Life Map is a helpful jumping-off point to begin an ACT case conceptualization because it can be completed while delivering treatment to Bill. The therapist can use the Life Map in session with Bill to demonstrate the focus of the work: to grow behaviors that move Bill toward who and what matter most to him. The conceptualization worksheet can be filled out following the session by referencing the Life Map to identify areas of psychological inflexibility and inform your treatment plan moving forward by highlighting which processes should be trained to help this specific client improve psychological flexibility.

If we were to go with Bill's story alone, the information we have about Bill is mostly information that gets collected in the bottom left quadrant of the Life Map, Bill's painful private experiences: heartbreak, loneliness, frustration, embarrassment, the thought "I'm a loser," and feeling fat and horny. We also have some behaviors Bill reports as problematic that we would organize in the top left quadrant: "I drink too much," "I just hook up and have one-night stands," "I eat a ton of junk food . . . take a bunch of laxatives." If we were to begin filling in Bill's story without prompts or being directive, we would only have half the equation, the left side of the Life Map. We are missing Bill's values, who and what matter most to him, what qualities he wants to embody in the way he behaves in the world, and what behaviors would move him in that direction. A strong case could be made that what hurts Bill the most also matters the most to him: relationships both romantic and social. **It is often the case that on the flip side of pain we find our values.**

ACT Conceptualization Questions

The following questions are a sample of what we typically might ask in session with a client when we're seeking to clarify our conceptualization of a client. Please note that they are not a verbatim representation of how we wish you would bring ACT as an approach to your work. **Instead, use these questions to inform how you might begin to listen to your clients and ask guiding questions to better conceptualize the psychological flexibility model.**

- What thoughts, feelings, sensations or memories do you struggle with the most?
- What have you tried before and how has it worked?
- What is the toll or price you pay in attempting to get rid of this pain?
- This struggle hurts for a reason. What about this is important to you?
- When these painful, thoughts, feelings, sensations or memories show up, what do you do?
- In that moment, what would I see you do if I were there?
- What is it like to be present with your pain here and now, even just talking about it?
- If you weren't busy trying to escape and avoid your pain, what would you be doing?

Using conceptualization questions relevant to ACT with Bill, we probe deeper and ask, "When these painful thoughts and feelings show up, what do you do next?" He tells us about drinking when he feels heartbroken and lonely. We then ask, "And what happens after that?" He tells us that drinking leads to more feelings of loneliness and when he's a little buzzed from the alcohol, he's also horny and frustrated. And again we ask, "What do you do next? If I was there and could see you, what would I see you do?" Bill tells us that he picks up his phone and texts his friend Krista, asking her to hook up. And when we ask Bill, "Then what happens?" He tells us about feeling embarrassed and says, "I'm a loser." And yes, once more we ask Bill what he does then, and that's when he tells us about going to his local fast-food restaurant where he will "eat junk." And finally we ask what happens and Bill tells us about feeling "fat" and taking laxatives. Asking these questions allows us to create a functional analysis of Bill's pattern of behavior and understand what is reinforcing this cycle.

FUNCTIONAL ANALYSIS

As we have mentioned many times in this book so far, our aim is to understand the function of a client's behavior and transform a pattern of responding so that when painful stuff shows up, their behaviors function to serve what matters most to them, the life they want to lead, rather than serving to escape painful private events that provide short-term relief at the expense of long-term movement towards their values. Just as it is important for us as clinicians to understand the function of Bill's behavior, it is important for Bill to understand how his behavior currently functions so that he can begin to recognize on his own how it works and what maintains it. We want to train this skill in noticing the function of behaviors in clients so that no matter what context arises they are able to identify for themselves what the function of any given behavior is and then choose how to respond based on what is workable for them or what matters most to them.

To achieve this, we ask Bill to give his current, reported behaviors three separate ratings: short-term effectiveness, long-term effectiveness, and move-you-toward-the-life-you-want effectiveness. We do this for behaviors in the upper left quadrant to acknowledge both their short-term effectiveness in escaping painful experiences and long-term unworkability in bringing him closer to the life he wants to live. We put a checkmark ($\sqrt{}$) beside behaviors that work and an X for behaviors that do not work.

A functional analysis is traditionally presented by separating a behavior or something someone does into three parts: the antecedent event, the behavior itself, and the consequence of that behavior. The antecedent event, meaning what happened before the behavior, in scientific terms is called the discriminative stimulus. A stimulus is anything in the environment that influences a behavior, for example when your phone rings. A single stimulus might have many different functions: The ringing might be a stimulus event for you to answer the phone or for you to check your call display to see who is calling. A discriminative stimulus operates the same way but it's *discriminative* because it influences the occurrence of an operant response (a behavior that is modified by a learned outcome or consequence).

In the example of the phone ringing, you respond to the stimulus event by answering the phone, unless your ringtone plays loudly while you're in a theater and then the discriminative stimulus causes you to quickly grab your phone and turn the ringer off because of the environment. The announcement to please turn off all cellular devices, your experience in the past of being hushed or looked at with disapproval when your phone has rung has shaped your behavior: You're supposed to turn off your ringer at the theater. This three-term contingency can also be separated in an ABC model: A for antecedent or what happened to elicit the behavior, B for behavior or what the person did, and C for consequence or what happened as a result of the behavior. Harking back to Chapter 1, operant conditioning is when a behavior is shaped by consequences (reinforcement or punishment).

Functional Analysis with Bill

Let's use our understanding of functional analysis to see how it works in the case of Bill, paying specific attention to which stimulus events are an antecedent trigger for behavior and where discriminative stimulus elicits behaviors based on contingencies of reinforcement or punishment (stimuli that lead to specific behaviors based on outcomes shaped in a particular context).

The following therapist-client dialogue is an example of how to use the Life Map to perform a functional analysis in session on Bill's behavior in a way that not only helps the clinician understand the function of Bill's behavior and what maintains it, but also helps Bill understand the process through which he can begin to observe his patterns of behavior and see whether the choices he is making are helping him move toward or away from the life he wants to live.

Therapist: I understand that a lot of what we've talked about in this diagram is painful for you, but I don't want to make a mistake here and make all of this painful stuff that shows up in the lower left for you the enemy of our work.

Bill: What do you mean?

Therapist: Good question. Rather than talk about it, could I show you?

Bill: Yeah, go ahead.

Therapist: Okay, in the short-term, so think immediately, does drinking help with your feeling of heartbreak and loneliness?

Bill: Ha! Yes, definitely. [Smiles.]

Therapist: Exactly! So I'm going to put a checkmark beside drinking because it helps you feel better in the moment.

Bill: But that doesn't last long.

Therapist: Yes, I get that. Hang on though, let me come back to that in a moment. So how about texting Krista, does that help you feel better in the short-term?

Bill: What!? No! Look, I don't want to be that guy. She gets pissed at me when I do, and I know I'm not supposed to. She thinks I'm a pig for doing it.

Therapist: Yes, I get that. When you're drinking though, you talked about feeling buzzed, feeling horny and frustrated. Imagine just being there in that moment and reaching for your phone to text Krista and asking her to hook up. Before she even texts back, does that bring some relief to feeling horny and frustrated?

Bill: Oh, it definitely makes me feel better. We've hooked up in the past, so there's always that chance in my mind that she's going to say yes and want to come over. You know?

Therapist: Okay! Now we've got it. So in that moment, just texting Krista actually helps you move away from those feelings?

Bill: Yep. I'm embarrassed to say it and I want to stop, but yes.

Therapist: I understand, and we're going to work on that. In fact that's why I'm showing you this. You continue to do these behaviors because they work in the short-term. It would be unfair of us not to acknowledge how your behavior works. So let me try one last one, eating junk. When you feel embarrassed because Krista has just blasted an angry text back to you, telling you not to talk to her, and then you have the thought "I'm a loser," does eating junk food help move you away from that?

Bill: Oh yeah! Come on, they're open 24/7. I go down, order a double cheeseburger with a Diet Coke, light on the ice, and sink my teeth into a juicy, hot burger. That makes me feel all kinds of better.

Therapist: Perfect. That's exactly what I was looking for. All of these behaviors work in the short-term to help you feel better. You already alluded to it, but let's go through each again in the long-term. How do these same behaviors work in the long-term to eliminate these painful thoughts and feelings, to move away so that they never show up again? Let's start with drinking.

Bill: Nope. No way, I drink now and feel better, but tomorrow morning the same loneliness is there waiting for me.

Therapist: Okay, I'll put an X to show it doesn't work long-term. And texting Krista, eating junk, how do those work in the long-term?

Bill: No for both of them. In fact they make me feel worse, both of those.

Therapist: Ouch, they make you feel worse. Let's get a little more information about that. Drinking when loneliness and heartbreak shows up in your life, does it move you closer to the life you want to have? All the behaviors you listed over on the right of your Life Map?

Bill: Absolutely not. I probably shouldn't be drinking then at all.

Therapist: Okay, that's great that you can notice that right now. And what about texting Krista to hook up when you're feeling horny and frustrated, does that move you closer to the type of life you want to have?

Bill: Hell no. I don't want to be doing that at all.

Therapist: One more, eating junk. Does that bring you any closer to who and what are most important to you?

Bill: Not at all.

Therapist: I can't take that off the table, I can't make drinking, texting Krista, or eating junk any less delicious to you in the short-term. They work, that's why you keep doing those behaviors. Here's what I can do though: give you tools to help you get better at seeing heartbreak, loneliness, horny, frustration, embarrassment, the thought "I'm a loser," and feeling fat before they get you to react and try to avoid or escape them. We can strengthen your connection to who and what matter most and work on skills so that you can slow down, feel what you're feeling, but that allow you to choose what you do next. Sound good?

Notice how the therapist's attitude toward Bill and his problematic behavior is not one of judgment or confrontation. The therapist assists Bill in analyzing the function of his behavior: How does it work in the situations that it happens? Even when Bill protests, insisting that it doesn't help or is wrong, the therapist doesn't seek to reinforce what may potentially be fusion on Bill's part but instead refocuses on the function of the behavior. Ultimately, the conversation ends in workability: How do the problematic behaviors function to grow Bill's life toward what he values? The therapist does not at all evaluate Bill's behaviors themselves or dictate how they function, the therapist continually asks Bill, training him to analyze the function of his own behavior. This exchange is truly anti-oppressive as the therapist holds knowledge in this position and respectfully assists Bill in implementing a functional analysis but does not play the role of the expert. Instead, the therapist invites Bill to connect with his experience and use it as a guide.

On a personal note, as ACT practitioners ourselves, we have had lengthy conversations about our own values as clinicians: respect, anti-oppressive practice, radical feminism, and an allegiance to a strengths-based perspective. We have found that ACT has at times invited us to be more directive therapists but not confrontational or practicing from a position of the expert, knowing better than our clients.

TREATMENT PLANNING

You may be curious what comes next: How would an ACT therapist subscribing to a circular model, seeking to increase psychological flexibility, structure sessions? How would a therapist decide what process to focus on and when? These questions are both good ones to ask. The approach we suggest is to first read this book fully in order to get a sense of how to integrate the six core processes into your work flexibly and how to track those processes in your clients so that you know when each may be efficacious. Chapters 5, 6, and 7 focus on just that, the flexible use of multiple processes in a single session or conversation with a client to target specific process issues.

What follows is an outline of what works for us in terms of treatment planning and creating a noneliminative agenda. We practice ACT from the functional contextual point of view discussed in Chapter 1, meaning our treatment planning does not look different for specific clinical concerns: anxiety, BPD, depression, weight loss, OCD, trauma, diabetes management, and so on. Instead, each session is guided by how clients present in each session and informed by the functional analysis we do. Therefore, even clients presenting with the exact same symptoms may have a different therapy experience because their patterns of avoidance or the processes they would benefit from targeting are different.

In the therapy room across all or most of our clients, however, there are some similarities. For starters, we attempt to practice tight stimulus control by making the therapeutic context, our offices, the place where we practice to not be a part of a client's relational network of problematic behavior, where instead we focus on what matters to them and help them move in that direction. Some clients may have no idea how therapy might benefit them or only have television show references of lying on a couch and sharing every problem they are experiencing. With this learning history, they might use the therapist's listening ear to continue the process of engaging in problematic behavior, such as air their grievances about loved ones, complain about unfair situations, or have someone to commiserate with. Other clients may have extensive histories of therapy and may come into your office with equally strong beliefs about what therapy is.

Given that they have found their way into your office, it is likely that what they have tried in the past has not worked or not provided sustained changes and so you want to be sure to communicate what therapy with you is and is not, and set the stimulus control early on that in this room this is what we focus on. We don't mean for this to be an offensive view of some clients' agenda in attending therapy, instead we want to pause and understand the function of both their behavior and ours in creating a context for valued living or experiential avoidance. We do this through being highly directive ourselves, introducing a noneliminative agenda in our informed consent, and using tools like the Life Map to make salient our case that therapy is an opportunity to learn how to grow repertoires of behavior with acceptance.

Beginning Phase of ACT

In a first session or first few sessions, we orient clients to what our therapeutic work will be about and socialize clients to ACT. Specifically we introduce our therapeutic contract and use it as a tool to develop acceptance around the idea that therapy will be about growing client repertoires of behavior in the presence of painful private experiences rather than symptom reduction. If this idea seems daunting, read on—you will see many examples in this book of how to create a contract with clients about acceptance. Furthermore, there is no explicit need to begin with a specific process. Therapists fluid with this process-based way of working with clients will quickly spot opportunities to hear problematic narratives in a session of being fused with a thought, some self-content, or a disconnection to values that the therapist can begin targeting with ACT's six core processes in that moment.

A typical first session, including a single session working with a new client, regardless of presentation, might be structured something like this:

- Beginning with an ACT informed consent or a brief exercise such as the Life Map to describe the therapeutic contract, the therapist describes a noneliminative agenda (not focused on symptom reduction) relevant to the client's life, assisting clients in understanding the role of acceptance in letting go of or leaning into their painful experiences with the ultimate goal of engaging in commitment behaviors. We would begin to introduce the idea that regardless of what clients may be experiencing, they can be flexible in what they do so they can more easily connect with their values, their unique hopes, goals, and desired outcomes, and choose workable behaviors.

- The therapist facilitates a conversation or exercise undermining unhelpful experiential avoidance using acceptance and defusion processes to demonstrate how instances of avoidance function as a short-term solution resulting in a long-term loss of contact with the clients' specific reinforcers, the values in their life. Think, for example, of a client who avoids taking prescribed medication in order to not have to think about a diabetes diagnosis, but at the long-term expense of uncontrolled blood glucose levels. Or a client who avoids driving to reduce in-the-moment anxiety at the expense of having a career or spending time with friends because that person cannot travel anywhere. The bottom line is that attempts to control, avoid, or manage unpleasant internal experiences such as thoughts, memories, or emotions in the moment may feel better or safer, but over time restricts what a client is able to do in any given situation (when presented with any social invitation or job interview the client afraid of driving has to say no) and keeps that person from living a life that is meaningful.

- The therapist encourages the client to notice instances of relevant behavior outside of the session based on discrimination between avoidance and control and committed actions in the service of values. This prompt may lead to a discussion of values or possibly a focus on other relevant processes, such as present-moment awareness or acceptance. The point is that we want clients to increase their awareness of their patterns of behavior so we can better understand whether what they are doing is working for them or against them in both the short-term and long-term.

- Ending the first session, therapists may wish to introduce an end-of-session ritual, refocusing therapist and client attention on something positive from the session. The therapist might comment on the client's successes in session, mentioning specifically what the therapist noticed: how the client demonstrated learning a new skill, how the client showed openness to new experiences, how the client had the courage to share something personal and vulnerable with a stranger, or something the client said that the therapist was particularly struck by, perhaps when the client spoke of care for a loved one or commitment to making long-lasting positive changes in life. Alternatively, a therapist may simply ask, "Can we each share what we appreciated about our time together?" to mark the end of the session. Again, practicing tight stimulus control and redirecting from a problem focus to a values focus.

Note that particularly stuck clients, those with a long reinforcement history of experiential avoidance who are not willing to choose acceptance and learn to grow their experience toward values in the presence of painful experiences, might require more than one session to complete the work of phase one. We also feel confident in stating that ACT does indeed work as a single-session model using the preceding phase description, especially using the Life Map as the entire ACT model conveyed in one diagram in a single session.

Middle Phase of ACT

Shifting into the second phase of treatment would ideally build upon the therapeutic contract agreed to in the first session or phase of therapy and introduce processes or exercises specific to the presentation of the client. In this sense, ACT is extremely versatile and personalized with an infinite number of variations in exercises that focus on different processes or the entire ACT model together. There is no one "right" way to begin to approach psychological flexibility. You may develop a preference as you begin practicing, but it is important to always remember we are focusing on what works for the client and what the client needs, so every client's treatment may look different and still be ACT consistent. If you notice yourself always starting with a certain exercise or process, use that as a cue to yourself to slow down and create an ACT conceptualization worksheet (presented earlier in this chapter) to identify what process(es) the client may benefit from and then let that guide your next move. This suggestion may sound vague or abstract right now, but as you move through the book we will clarify and provide multiple examples on how different processes can be used to target different aspects of psychological flexibility. **In this second phase, the purpose of ACT's process-based work isn't to focus on one process at a time sequentially but to instead flexibly address what a client may be presenting within the session.**

- Begin with a brief check-in. The therapist may say, "Last session we did something profoundly new and broke the commonsense agenda of eliminating your painful private experiences. What have you noticed now that you're aware of these two different ways of living, one in which you pursue the life that is most meaningful to you and the other where you attempt to avoid, escape, and control your pain?" Please note that we use the term *painful private experiences* generally in this book, when speaking with clients, we suggest you replace that phrase with the specific content the client experiences as painful.

- Some clients will report successes immediately saying they feel positively about not eliminating their pain but instead being open to doing more. Others will not and with sadness will report that they spend most of their time and have spent the majority of their lives attempting to avoid, escape, and control pain. All feedback is grist for the proverbial mill of clinically relevant information. The therapist attempts to be reinforcing of all experiences positive or negative and highlighting their increased awareness or ability to notice.

- Outlining the perils of fusion and not living in the present moment, the therapist comments on how easy it is to get caught in one's head, living a life that is governed by difficult thoughts, feelings, and painful memories and sensations. The therapist offers an alternative (willingness to experience private experiences in service of meaningful life) and encourages the client to practice formal mindfulness and engage in other activities aimed at increasing the client's psychological flexibility.

- The therapist facilitates a formal mindfulness practice or noticing exercise (see Chapter 6 for specific exercises) and solicits responses without an aim for positive or negative feedback specifically. An important note: clients may at times comment on how "relaxed" or "calm" they feel following mindfulness practice and will begin to appropriate mindfulness practice as a control strategy for relaxation. When these comments show up, it can be helpful to reflect that they noticed feeling relaxed as a by-product of the exercise. We may also point out that sometimes we feel relaxed afterward while other times we may feel exactly the same as when we began and that neither is necessarily correct or desired, but simply another experience we can bring into our awareness or practice of noticing.

- Alternatively, therapists may jump to creating behavior plans rather than focusing on present-moment processes if clients report difficulty in engaging in alternative behaviors to their experiential avoidance. In this instance, therapists explain how reinforcement histories work, how clients are reinforced in some way for their avoidance, escape, and control behaviors, that learning new behaviors is difficult and maintaining them to create long-lasting change is even more difficult. The therapist may use commitment questions, SMART (specific, measurable, attainable, relevant, time-bound) goals, or other exercises aimed at engaging in a broader repertoire of behavior (see Chapter 7 for specific exercises).

After socializing clients to this way of working, we may begin with a brief mindfulness exercise to settle-in and prime clients for therapy as a context to practice skills. Alternatively, therapists may wish to practice tight stimulus control in a different way by beginning with a systematic debriefing of the client's experience using the previous session's processes outside of the therapy room. Each subsequent session, including maintenance and termination sessions, can be introduced in this way.

- Beginning with a brief mindfulness exercise or a debriefing of the previous session's process work, the therapist begins the session with a focus on doing the work of ACT.

- The therapist may return to earlier exercises or skills used in session to reorient clients to the process outcome. For example, if defusion was used in a previous session to help a couple see how they can easily be hooked by their partner with behaviors that elicit fused reactions insensitive to the context of the relationship, the therapist could assist the couple to identify different behaviors they can engage in together congruent with their values. In a later session with the same couple a therapist may use defusion again to help one or both of the partners to recognize a moment of fusion that they self-report or that may occur in the session. The therapist may use the same exercise to demonstrate how fusion is once again eliciting reactions and may use the defusion exercise to focus more solely on one member of the partnership, assisting that person in understanding how their behavior works in that instance and look at specific alternative behaviors.

End Phase of ACT

In the final sessions of ACT, whether it be maintenance sessions or terminating therapy, therapists may wish to focus on consolidating the new behaviors clients have learned and implemented during the middle phase of treatment. This may be done in a number of different ways. For example, the therapist might review topics discussed throughout treatment and encourage a generalization of skills or exercises to new problems in the client's life or perceived upcoming problematic scenarios. Furthermore, ending therapy may be difficult for clients if it reminds them of a learned history of difficulty in ending relationships or issues of grief. Some clients may have little or no history of ending relationships and this ending phase of ACT may elicit a deficit in their own repertoire that could come with its own complications including grieving.

- The therapist celebrates client's successes, describing specific instances where the client demonstrated in-session skills and reported out-of-session use of skills.

- The therapist might share personally what was notable about this client's journey in doing the work, moments where the therapist felt excited about changes the client was bravely making or a moment where something the client said in-session touched the therapist personally in an emotional way.

- The therapist might review objectives and agendas from previous sessions, outlining how the work of therapy has addressed these challenges uniquely. This is also an opportunity to consolidate learning by reorienting clients to processes, ways of thinking about problems and hopes, the functional perspective of behavior, and reinforcing a repertoire of using the processes out-of-session.

- Therapists may assess for issues of grief that may come up as termination approaches asking, "What has it meant to say goodbye for you in the past?" Depending on the client's reactions to terminating therapy, it may be helpful to use relevant common core processes to address termination.

- In maintenance and in termination, therapists would be apt to ask, "What upcoming problems or future hurdles do you see yourself dealing with and how might you use what we've done here to make those situations more workable?" to prompt clients to anticipate future barriers and identify learned strategies for managing difficult or complex situations.

We have provided you with the three phases of ACT to outline how sessions may be structured with the hope that it will help you in imagining what this work could look like in your own practice setting and how you might integrate ACT and plan sessions with clients. In the next three chapters, we describe the six core processes of ACT with different populations, presenting therapist and client dialogues, sample scripts of what to say to clients, specific exercises to do, and helpful worksheets to facilitate the doing of ACT.

We don't wish to belabor this point but please remember, **ACT is a flexible, fluid approach built on processes.** We hope that you will read on with interest and curiosity rather than taking the aforementioned phases and the following techniques, exercises, and handouts that follow as a new rule for how to do ACT. The best ACT work is done when you yourself can be fluid and flexible in your integration of ACT and use its six core processes in a way that is unique to you, to your voice as a therapist, and to your practice style.

Chapter 5

Practicing Openness:
ACT for Anxiety, Panic Disorder, and Obsessive-Compulsive Disorder (OCD)

Early on in your journey learning ACT you may experiment with using a Life Map in session to introduce ACT into your practice or you may think about how to start having conversations that are relevant to a noneliminative agenda, creating a therapeutic contract of acceptance and connection to values with your clients. The six core processes, however, may still seem lost to you. Another helpful way to view the six processes is to break them into three main chunks: combining acceptance and defusion, present moment and self-as-context, and values and commitment—an adaptation of Strosahl, Robinson, and Gustavsson's (2012) three-pillar model of ACT: Open, Aware, Engaged. Here we have included a depiction of the hexagon model with its six processes divided into the three main parts.

Present Moment

Acceptance		Values
OPEN	**AWARE**	**ENGAGED**
Defusion		Commitment

Self-as-Context

Starting from the left side of the hexagon, we can combine acceptance and defusion processes, labelling them as one: open. As we move through life we can begin to close ourselves off from experiences we do not like to have, such as painful thoughts, feelings, sensations, or memories. As discussed in prior chapters, this behavior can lead to a narrowing of one's life until our world is revolved around avoiding, escaping, or eliminating these unpleasant experiences and contexts that evoke them, otherwise known as experiential avoidance. Essentially, acceptance and defusion promote an openness to private painful experiences; our aim is to open ourselves and our clients up to all our experiences.

Viewing the acceptance and defusion processes together acknowledges all of our private experiences and encourages leaning in and interacting with these private experiences in ways that create new relationships with what has long caused us suffering. Once we are open to all of our experiences, we can then begin to become aware of patterns of responding or rigid rules or stories about ourselves that are not helping us work toward the life we want to live. In the center of the hexagon, we combine present-moment and self-as-context processes to form this awareness.

Awareness as a unifying pillar brings together not only our interactions with our sensory experiences, but also the effects that our private experiences can have on us, shedding new light on influences that may have otherwise gone unnoticed or been occurring automatically. We can also begin to view ourselves as the observer of our experience, seeing difficult thoughts, feelings, sensations, and memories as content, separate from the self who witnesses those experiences. Once we are open to our experiences and aware of patterns of responding and our own unique perspective as the observer of our experience, we can then begin to interrupt those automatic reactions to private experiences and choose to engage in behaviors that bring us closer to who and what matter.

The right side of the hexagon represents this engaged component while combining values and commitment together. This unification brings together what matters most in life with the actions that move one toward that life, paralleling the importance of both valuing someone or something and acting in accordance with that value. Openness and awareness are helpful pillars that unify four unique processes that focus on our private behavior and help to highlight what is important to us through bringing us in direct contact with our pain, rather than prescribing avoiding or moving away from it. The pillar of engaged creates a unique true north that can be a beacon to guide our behavior when we are not trapped by our own minds. **In ACT we work hard to develop concrete, measurable, observable actions tied to our values.** This chapter will focus on openness processes of acceptance and defusion, while Chapter 6 will present awareness processes of present moment and self-as-context, and Chapter 7 will explore engaged processes of values and commitment.

ACCEPTANCE

Acceptance and defusion operate to create an overall idea of being open to the range of private experiences we have. Often when people are experiencing painful private experiences like strong emotions that they feel are unpleasant, they not only try to close themselves off to those emotions, but also close themselves off to any experience that could potentially elicit painful private experiences, thereby restricting or narrowing their life. Take for example a newly retired healthcare worker whose anxieties have turned to crippling fears. Over time they may have limited their driving and now do not drive at all to avoid symptoms of anxiety, which may work in the short-term to relieve the physical sensations of a panic attack and worrisome thoughts about car accidents, but in the long-term this behavior has begun to limit their life. They are now missing social events because they cannot drive to meet friends for coffee or make it to their favorite yoga class. In behavioral terms, we could say their repertoire (the things they do) has become narrow, and they now engage in few behaviors and limit the number of things they do. Again, this works in the short-term to seek relief from painful private experiences, but limiting one's life in this way may have two effects: reducing or cutting-off connection to valued life domains and potentially reinforcing the behaviors of restricting or narrowing life due its short-term effectiveness. The anxiety always comes back and with each attempt to avoid it, it grows stronger in the face of behaviors or contexts that elicit anxiety (e.g., every time they avoid driving, the next time they try to drive their anxiety will be even greater).

In ACT we target the problems of restricting or narrowing one's life with acceptance and viewing an accepting stance toward painful private experiences as a process that we seek to increase and reinforce in clients. Being able to successfully track when a client presents with experiential avoidance in session or being savvy to when they report problems of experiential avoidance outside of session is a useful skill and can offer opportunities to practice willingness in the face of painful private experiences. Think of experiential avoidance as a class of behavior that involves clients avoiding, attempting to escape or control unpleasant private experiences, and the situations that could elicit those experiences. Acceptance becomes a logical intervention at that time as it acknowledges experiential avoidance as a short-term solution while simultaneously acknowledging that nothing works to rid oneself of painful private experiences permanently. To illustrate what experiential avoidance looks like in session and how acceptance may be used to address problems of avoidance, we describe how a client presenting with panic disorder would be conceptualized in this model in the next section.

ACT with Panic Disorder

In the following therapist and client dialogue you will read about a woman who is actively avoiding a public place in order to minimize the potential of having a panic attack. This behavior is a completely logical and rational attempt on her part to control private experiences of panic in the short-term. However, from a functional perspective, reacting to her fear by believing it and becoming fused with the thought, "If I go, I'll have a panic attack," is getting her stuck in the long-term, narrowing her repertoire and further limiting her contact with the reinforcers in her life that truly matter to her. She finds herself missing out on valued areas of life because of her control agenda that is based on a desire to not feel panic.

Therapist: I know this is a hard time of year for you.

Client: [Looks away.] Yes, the worst.

Therapist: What would be important for us to talk about right now? What could we focus on that might make a difference?

Client: Well, my family celebrates Christmas. I want to give my daughter a great Christmas but her pathetic mom can't even leave the house.

> These two questions are early attempts in a session to evoke this client's values and to prime a conversation about committed actions rather than experiential avoidance.

Therapist: Her pathetic mom. What does it do for you when you say that aloud?

Client: [Sighs] It doesn't.

> This therapist may be picking up on a fused statement from this client, echoing it back and asking about the consequence of this is a gentle early beginning to defusion in session with a client.

Therapist: No way, come on. What just happened there?

Client: I'm hoping you'll not make me talk about leaving the house.

> This therapist's style is to dig deeper, asking about that specific comment and looking to understand more about how it functions in the current context.

Therapist: Thank you for being honest about that with me. Is calling yourself a pathetic mother another way you keep this problem at an arm's length? Kind of like, maybe if I put myself down then my therapist won't bring up this painful stuff?

Client: Yes. Like last year, before I started therapy I just made a shopping list and gave it to my mom and my sister. They went to the mall for me and did all my shopping. They picked up all the presents. I gave them the money but they did the shopping.

This therapist outlines how becoming fused with this thought can have outcomes, especially in this context of talking with a therapist. The therapist describes a potential experiential avoidance strategy and checks in with this client to have her assess how it works in this situation.

Therapist: Is that important to you? Going to the mall and buying gifts?

Client: Yes, my daughter loves Christmas. It's such a big deal in our house, waking up early and opening presents, doing the whole special breakfast and playing under the tree.

The therapist attempts another values intervention by asking if what they are talking about is important to this client. This could also be viewed as another attempt to come back to the core of what is important to this client, evoking what is most important in this moment for her to talk about.

Therapist: And what would it mean to you to go the mall and buy gifts yourself?

Client: I want to. I really want to. I don't want to be this parent. The shut-in who never leaves the house. But I can't go to the mall. There'll be so many people. I'll have a panic attack. I can't handle it.

Attempting to clarify again what is it that this client values about this specific behavior.

Therapist: Right, if you avoid going to the mall, you get to avoid panic. Just like if you call yourself pathetic maybe you'll throw me off of bringing up something that's difficult for you. And what are we missing out on by not talking about this?

Client: [Quietly.] My daughter.

This therapist attempts to integrate openness processes of defusion by exposing the long-term outcome of avoidance strategies by asking what is being missed out on, potentially something this client values by engaging in experiential avoidance.

Therapist: So you push this panic away by avoiding places, staying in, and there's a promise to that. The promise that you'll feel better but before you know it this pushing away has a cost. It costs you your connection with your daughter?

Client: Ugh, it so does. You know it has infected everything in my life.

This therapist uses the feedback from the client and does not assume to know the outcome of experiential avoidance. The therapist reflects what they perceive is happening with this client and finishes by asking if it costs her a connection to someone she values, her daughter.

Therapist: It has and that's why I'm not going to push away. Would that be okay?

Client: Yes, please.

> We applaud this therapist's interaction of joining with this client empathetically and creating a context of choice in session, explicitly stating that the therapist will not engage in experiential avoidance and asks the client if that is okay.

Therapist: So let me ask, would you be willing to work on going to the mall but not because I want you to have fears and panic but because going to the mall is about your daughter, it's about shopping for the gifts you want to buy. Your fears and panic might show up, but avoiding them hasn't moved you closer to the life you want, it's bought you time in the short-term, brought a little relief, helped you to avoid having a panic attack, but that has come at a cost.

> This therapist effectively captures the noneliminative agenda, encouraging the use of defusion and even touches on committed action behaviors in this summarizing of what their work could be about with this client.

Client: I like that idea. It's about her, not me. I've been making it about me, but she's my whole life.

This exchange between therapist and client achieves a number of technical moves focused on increasing this client's openness to experience in a brief conversation. First, the therapist asks what would be important to talk about, seeking to elicit early on in the session what might be valued by this client that could be worked on in the session. Almost immediately the therapist noticed a fused thought the client had about herself as a "pathetic mom" and the therapist asked about it, seeking the function of that behavior. Pay particular attention to the fact that the therapist does not dictate "that's a fused thought" or immediately jump on pointing out how unhelpful the thought is. Instead, the therapist is curious about thoughts of being a "pathetic mom." The therapist then draws a parallel between the client calling herself a "pathetic mom" and other attempts to avoid experiences.

This parallel creates a brief discussion in which the therapist validates this client's attempts to avoid or control her experience and soon asks, "What are we missing out on by not talking about this?" Once again this question relates to values, and indeed this client states that what she cares about is her daughter. The therapist, however, framed the question in asking what the cost of this experiential avoidance is, exposing that this client values her daughter and that although the avoidance and control strategies work to keep panic at bay, they limit something valuable: her connection to her daughter. The dialogue ends with an acceptance question from the therapist: Would the client be willing to experience panic and fear for her daughter? This question helps to highlight that we are not asking clients to experience painful private events without a reason, we are only asking if they are willing to come into contact with painful experiences if in doing so it helps them move closer to the who and what that matter in their lives.

The conversation with this client would continue to focus on strategies about what to do next, specifically what behaviors she could be doing instead of avoiding panic attacks. Perhaps the next steps with her would involve exposure explicitly focused on going to the mall to buy her daughter gifts and experiencing the thoughts, feelings, sensations, and memories that occur in an effort to expand her repertoire of committed actions even in the presence of her panic symptoms. We'd like to encourage you to read on in this chapter about how to assess for avoidance, control, and escape strategies in clients. The second half of this chapter (defusion) will address how to get clients engaged in doing something other than the problematic experiential avoidance behaviors (the hooks worksheet). However, readers seeking to immediately find useful tools in what to get clients doing next will find multiple worksheets and explanation of how to establish and reinforce new behaviors in Chapter 7.

Acceptance Worksheets

We know that having conversations like the preceding therapist and client dialogue that seamlessly tie in acceptance processes with assessing for experiential avoidance is not easy, especially when you're just beginning to learn ACT and experiment with it. Perhaps you're seeing if ACT can fit with you, with your style as a therapist and your practice with the populations you treat. To assist you in facilitating conversations about avoidance, escape, and control strategies that may be problematic, we included a worksheet that we find helpful. Most often, we give clients this worksheet at the beginning of treatment or early on. Sometimes we will send it home with them to be completed after their first session. We recommend using this worksheet early in treatment, whether with a new client or introducing it now with a client with whom you want to begin integrating ACT into practice. Specifically, this worksheet will help both of you identify the problematic behaviors of experiential avoidance, the painful private experiences and avoidance, control, or escape behaviors you will target with acceptance.

This worksheet provides a structured way to begin a conversation about the problems with avoidance, escape, and control of painful private experiences. We especially favor the "Your Avoidance & Control" worksheet because it validates painful private experiences as having a real effect on clients' lives and justifies avoidance behaviors, not as pathological or crazy, but as a logical, rational attempts to rid themselves of what they don't want to think, feel, or remember. For some clients, talking about what they do to avoid, control, or escape their painful private experiences is difficult to do or they may simply have a hard time identifying specific behaviors. Many people are pathologized for their problematic experiential avoidance behaviors or other relief-seeking behaviors such as substance abuse, sex, withdrawal, eating, and other strategies.

Often times clients visit our practice with a lot of shame and painful self-content about the behaviors they have been doing, especially when their thoughts, feelings, sensations, and memories may be somewhat out-of-awareness or where they may have developed long-standing repertoires of avoidance but cannot explicitly identify what may be triggering their experience (e.g., individuals with histories of trauma and especially those with dissociative problems). A useful worksheet you may wish to use as an alternative (is the Escape Avoidance & Control Strategies worksheet on the following page) assesses for specific behaviors that clients may be engaging in to escape or control their experience.

YOUR AVOIDANCE & CONTROL

Begin by listing the thoughts, feelings, sensations, and memories you most wish to avoid, control and escape in your life. Then list the things you have been missing out on due to avoidance and finish by listing what you have been doing to control or escape what you don't want to experience.

1. EXPERIENCES I'D LIKE TO AVOID, CONTROL AND ESCAPE ...

THOUGHTS OF

FEELINGS/EMOTIONS

PHYSICAL SENSATIONS

MEMORIES OF

2. NOTICE YOUR EXPERIENCES

What has trying to avoid the above painful thoughts, feelings, sensations and memories cost you? What have you ended up missing out on in your life due to attempting to avoid the above?

3. WHAT I DO TO CONTROL OR ESCAPE THE ABOVE

What do you do to control or escape the above painful thoughts, feelings, sensations and memories?

ESCAPE
AVOIDANCE & CONTROL STRATEGIES

THINKING

- ☐ Worrying
- ☐ Dwelling on the past
- ☐ Questioning yourself
- ☐ Blaming yourself
- ☐ Blaming others
- ☐ Blaming the world
- ☐ Thinking "it's not fair"
- ☐ Thinking "if only"
- ☐ Fantasizing about suicide
- ☐ Suppressing or pushing away thoughts
- ☐ Imagining escaping your job, school or family
- ☐ Analyzing yourself

DOING

- Isolating ☐
- Eating ☐
- Self-harming ☐
- Arguing or complaining ☐
- Drinking alcohol or caffeine ☐
- Recreational drug use ☐
- Misusing prescription drugs ☐
- Physically acting out or fighting ☐
- Hooking up or being sexually promiscuous ☐
- Shopping or spending money ☐
- Movies, tv shows, video games ☐
- Saying no to opportunities ☐
- Calling in sick to work ☐

WRITE YOUR OWN

Write down strategies not listed on this worksheet that you've tried...

WHAT WORKS?

Go back through the strategies you checked off and wrote down and underline the strategies that have permanently removed your painful thoughts, feelings, sensations, and memories (meaning you no longer experience them anymore). This is not an exhaustive list, we've provided a space for you to include your own thinking and doing avoidance strategies, remember everything listed on this worksheet is neither good nor bad. The focus is on understanding what you have tried and whether it's working.

Which Life Would You Choose?

We have a specific exercise that can be helpful in bringing together the information you are collecting in session with clients about their experiential avoidance behaviors—perhaps using the two previous worksheets eliciting avoidance, control, and escape strategies—that also clarifies a noneliminative agenda. We often introduce this experiential exercise early in treatment and we call it "Which Life Would You Choose?" This exercise is about demonstrating how willingness to experience pain functions in the service of a value. This exercise invites clients to imagine two alternate realities and ask which they would choose. Imagine for example a client with generalized anxiety disorder who tells you they're suffering with constant ruminating thoughts, worries, and describes engaging in problematic planning behaviors. **Using ACT's functional perspective, you look at the function of these behaviors and with your client determine that they go above and beyond what is workable in the moment.** Furthermore, you uncover that these behaviors are all in an effort to avoid feelings of anxiety or thoughts that they are going to "mess up." This client may even report to you that they feel stuck with what to do next. In this moment, you may be curious about bringing openness processes into your work with this client but may not be sure how to bridge the topic. This is an opportunity for you to contrast the perils of experiential avoidance with the long-term potential outcomes of acceptance.

To set up this exercise, we first ask this client to imagine someone in their life that they care about, someone in their life that they could imagine going through the same thing that they are currently going through. This could be a child, partner, or a close friend; the idea is for them to identify someone they really care about that they could imagine going through a similar experience. For clients who have children, it is often easy to set the exercise up by saying, "Imagine your daughter grows up and she comes to you one day and says, ' I've been having a lot of anxiety, I'm constantly worried about my relationships, my finances, my career. It seems like my mind never stops running. It feels horrible. I spend all this time planning and trying to set up my life in a way so that nothing bad happens and I never fall behind, but it's just too exhausting and I find myself running in circles.' Can you imagine that?"

Once we get them to imagine that scenario, we set up the two realities, "Now recently I've been invited to the super-secret therapist society and they have given me two magic pills to share with my clients. If you choose the blue pill everything you are struggling with, all the thoughts and feelings, and sensations of panic, anxiety, fear, and all of the memories and experiences that you have struggled with for so long are wiped from your mind, but there's a catch. By taking the blue magic pill you would be rid of all of your pain, but that also means when your daughter comes to you, that person in your life who really matters comes to you, and is telling you all these painful things that she is experiencing day in and day out and you have to tell her 'Sorry, I have no idea what you're going through. I really don't know how to help you because I've never experienced anything like that before in my life.' Now on the other hand if you take the red pill, all your painful experiences, thoughts, feelings, memories, and sensations are still there, but when your daughter comes to you and explains everything she's been going through, you can sit with her and look her in the eye, maybe hold her hand, and tell her that you're here for her, tell her that you understand what she's going through, and that you love her and will be there for her through this difficult experience. Which life would you choose?"

At this point of the exercise clients will often joke and ask if they can have the blue pill for just the day or just a minute to see what it feels like, but they will invariably say of course they would choose the red pill so they can be there to offer support and help and be compassionate toward that person in their life who matters to them. It's in that moment that we pause and really slow down the session to see the clients and acknowledge what an incredible thing they just said. "Let's just pause here for a moment and feel the full impact of what you said because you're laughing and you're saying of course I'd choose the red pill, but notice how incredible it is that you would be willing to experience all of this pain that you've been experiencing for a long time so you can be there for someone you care about. That's powerful! I mean just hearing you say that, to make that choice, really touches something in me [pause] and that right there, that choice that you just made is what willingness is all about. It's being willing to sit with an experience of pain, lean into it, and let it be there so that even when it shows up you can move forward and connect with the people and the things that matter to you, like your daughter. It means being willing to sit with that feeling of anxiety or panic and instead of sitting down to spend your whole evening planning out every last detail or walking through every scenario of what could go wrong and coming up with plan A, B, and C. You instead choose, in that moment when that anxiety shows up or your thoughts are racing, to turn and sit down for dinner with your family or call your best friend on the phone or go to your daughter's soccer game. Willingness is not giving up or giving in. It's powerful and compassionate and represents all of the love you have for yourself and for the people and things that matter in your life." This opportunity can provide a powerful way to connect on a meaningful level with your client and tap into the powerful impact of acceptance. It is just one way to approach this concept of openness with clients. The second half of this chapter will focus on the other process of openness: defusion.

DEFUSION

Defusion becomes a focus of our clinical work when clients are fused with their experience. Fusion happens when a private experience, such as a thought, memory, sensation, or feeling is strongly believed or taken literally. An example of fusion is often seen in clients experiencing anxiety where they might report, "I can't do things that other people can do" or someone suffering with a history of trauma says "I am broken" and buys into this belief about themselves so strongly that they believe it is literally true. This can be problematic because it limits what clients are able to do. If a client is fused with the thought, "I can't handle a panic attack, it's too overwhelming" then that person will do everything in their power to avoid a panic attack since they literally believe they can't handle it. In ACT, we seek to identify not whether those thoughts are believable and steeped but what is their function. How does the thought work in a given situation. In most contexts, believing in (being fused with) these thoughts limits a client's life. They do less of what matters to them and may find themselves as a result of fusing with these thoughts engaging in experiential avoidance—trying to escape or avoid painful private experiences.

We refer to any experience that impacts our behavior as a *hook*. Sometimes being reeled in by a hook can be helpful, such as seeing an ad for a book on the craft of writing, recalling how much you value creativity, and committing time each day to writing that novel you have always dreamed of writing. But sometimes getting drawn in by hooks can be problematic if it leads to reacting or behaving in ways contrary to your chosen values. For example, you may see an ad for a book on the craft of writing and have the thought, "I'll never be a good writer. What's the point in even trying? I'll just fail anyways." In reaction to that thought you may stop writing or tell yourself that you do not care about your value of creativity, or you may even put yourself down, talking back to your thoughts and telling yourself how terrible of a writer you are. In that instance, the thought that popped in your head after seeing the ad was a hook and influenced your behavior. Sometimes, hooks can be easy to spot, but when our clients are caught up in their own stories or have difficulty identifying their private experiences, it can be challenging.

ACT with Obsessive-Compulsive Disorder

Introducing your clients to the concept of hooks is easily achieved when you understand that the point of the hooks exercise is to facilitate a client's experience of seeing how their behavior can be impacted by private content (fusion). In the following therapist and client dialogue, a woman struggling with obsessive-compulsive disorder is introduced to the concept of hooks, and the process of noticing her private experiences and how they impact her behavior.

We find that using metaphors experientially in the room, bringing them alive with examples and having clients participate in them is helpful. The metaphor of hooks specifically is one we use regularly and we've provided a hooks worksheet here to help you begin to use this metaphor in your practice if you choose. Our goal with defusion is to get clients to look at their private experiences from a new perspective or interact with their private experiences in a new way. For example, using a metaphor, altering language around how we talk about fused thoughts, such as "So your mind is having the thought that . . . ," and asking clients to describe what their private experiences feel like in their body through shapes, colors, or similes (e.g., heart beating as fast as a stampede) are all different ways to defuse from our experience.

Client: I just can't leave it, I know I'm not supposed to and that it makes my OCD worse but I have to check, I'll have a panic attack if I don't.

Therapist: You know what we call that in the biz?

Client: No, what!?

Therapist: A hook!

Client: A hook?

Therapist: Yes, like a fish hook. Check this out: That thought works like a hook because when you buy into it, when you bite it, you get reeled in: hook, line, and sinker. It has you stuck doing all these things that you don't want to be, like checking. Is that what you would have chosen for yourself?

> The therapist playfully socializes this client to the idea that a thought can work like a fish hook. This is an effective way to bring a client's attention to the process of defusion.

Client: [Smiles.] No way. It's brutal when my OCD hooks me.

Therapist: Exactly. You don't get to choose the life you want when you're hooked, like doing a bunch of interesting things you'd prefer to do: connecting with your husband or playing music, doing something you'd enjoy that makes your life richer.

> Completing the analysis, the therapist makes clear that fusing with a thought—or in plain language using the metaphor of fish hooks, biting a hook—has consequences. The outcome of fusing with this thought or biting this hook for this client is that her behavior is impacted.

Client: It's like I'm a hostage to my mind.

Therapist: Right. I feel that in my own experience, but here's the deal, do you get to choose whether you have hooks or not?

> We like this therapist's sparse use of self-disclosure, reorienting this client to her own role in working with painful private experiences such as fused thoughts.

Client: Um . . . no. They're just there.

Therapist: That's exactly my experience too. And when they show up, it's hard not to bite them. But let's just say in our work we train you to notice your hooks so that you can see them. This might seem silly but imagine you and I are fish, swimming along. You're really good at noticing hooks and I'm not. I see something off in the distance that looks delicious and I go to bite it but you know it's a hook, what would you do?

> The therapist reinforces the client experience and comes back to the metaphor, focusing on the chain of action in the presence of the hooks, essentially reorienting the client to the focus of therapy being on her behavior, what she does next in the presence of painful private experiences.

Client: [Smiling.] Ha! I'd push you out of the way and be like "NO! It's a hook!!!"

Therapist: [Laughing.] Okay and remember, we're fish so would we examine the hook for any distinguishing marks, see who manufactured it? Maybe take it back to the lab and analyze what materials it's composed of? Better yet, trace the line back and see who dropped it here, maybe a parent or childhood bully? Put up signs and caution tape, create hook awareness month?

Client: Absolutely not.

Therapist: You got it. You'd probably say something like, "Hey, if you're hungry I know a place where there's some delicious kelp!" And we'd just swim on and not think twice about it. So what if that's what we made our work about, focusing on noticing hooks, not getting rid of hooks or figuring out how to rid ourselves of them, but instead learning how to work with them?

Client: Sure, but I don't know how to do that.

Therapist: I understand and that's my commitment to you. To bring practical tools to the table where we can practice noticing so that you can see your hooks and learn how to choose what you do next in the presence of them.

> This therapist uses humor in interactions with this client to outline the many strategies that could be used in a moment of discovering painful private experiences. Note that readers may choose to alter this metaphor or use something in their own repertoire or office that suits this exercise better.

> The therapist focuses the metaphor on what the client does next, orienting her toward her own role in the presence of fused thoughts. Perhaps not taking thoughts as literal content and choosing to do a different behavior in their presence.

> The therapeutic agenda is clear with this statement as the therapist encourages choosing in the presence of painful private experiences, not living without them.

Client: I like that, choosing what I do next because I haven't had control over this anyway.

Therapist: So, what are the chances, leaving here today, that you'll notice your hooks?

Client: Really high, I'm definitely going to be noticing them.

Therapist: Good and remember, it's about what you do when you see them, because if you can see your hooks that's when you have the freedom to choose what you do next.

Know Your Hooks Worksheet

A helpful way to break down the process of defusion and help clients identify their problematic fusion (hooks) is to use the "Know Your Hooks" worksheet included here. It allows for a simple way to not only look at what happened in any given situation, but also identify what could have been done differently, including noticing the hook and using defusion or acceptance exercises to loosen the proverbial grip a private experience may have. It's also a useful way to prepare in advance for what values-driven behavior a client may wish to engage in when a hook shows up instead of reacting to private experiences and reverting automatically to experiential avoidance.

We typically introduce the "Know Your Hooks" worksheet to clients in the beginning of therapy after we have socialized them to a noneliminative agenda, focusing on acceptance of painful private experiences rather than avoidance (see Chapter 2 for more about an ACT informed consent). We use this worksheet to demonstrate the impact that our painful private experiences have on us. Note that although we talk about painful private experiences, all private experiences can hook us. In ACT we are only concerned with problematic hooks that do not work to bring us closer to the life we want to live. We often refer to painful private experiences here because painful sensations, memories, emotions, and thoughts are what client populations attend treatment to work on with us.

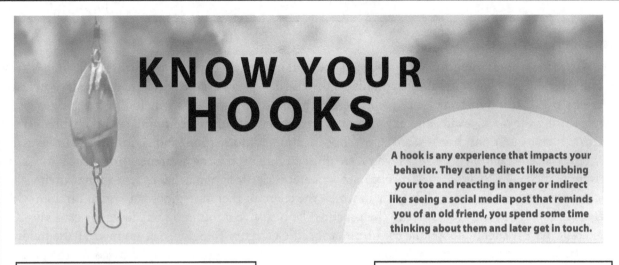

KNOW YOUR HOOKS

A hook is any experience that impacts your behavior. They can be direct like stubbing your toe and reacting in anger or indirect like seeing a social media post that reminds you of an old friend, you spend some time thinking about them and later get in touch.

1. WHAT HAPPENED?

Write down a situation where you did something problematic. What did you do?

2. PAY ATTENTION

Write down what private experiences like thoughts, feelings, memories, or sensations showed up for you and triggered problematic behavior.

3. IS THAT A HOOK?

Ask yourself if that private experience is a hook for you. Here's how you can tell: did it impact your behavior in a problematic way? If so, write down the name of that hook: e.g. my anger hook, sadness hook, etc.

4. PREPARE

The person that you want to be. What would they do when your hook shows up? Would they bite it and react? Engage in those same behaviors? If not, write down what you would choose to do differently.

5. NOTICE YOUR HOOKS

Noticing your hooks is a life skill. You don't get to choose whether you have hooks or not but you can choose how you respond to them and how you interact with your hooks.

ACT Improvisation

Another way to incorporate defusion into in-session and at-home practices with your clients is through what we like to call "ACT Improv." We, the authors of this book, have also created a card deck that we believe augments your learning of ACT and increases your ability to use the skills in this book by including three categories of cards representing the open, aware, and engaged categories described at the beginning of this chapter. Among these cards we have questions, brief exercises, psychoeducational information, and actions that can be used in a variety of ways. For example, therapists who have difficulty incorporating awareness processes into sessions or who want to challenge themselves to incorporate a greater variety of approaches in session may invite clients to participate in five minutes of ACT Improv in which the client or therapist chooses a card at random within the category related to aware processes and then spends the next five minutes on whatever the card says. Or a therapist could have a client choose one card from a specific category to practice at home over the following week. Similarly, a therapist may set aside a few minutes every session to pick one card based on the processes they are touching on that day.

We don't mean for this to sound like a shameless plug for merchandise—we both truly believe in sharing only the most useful tools that we create. In an effort to practice full disclosure and give you, our reader informed consent, we do receive royalties from sales of the card deck. Therapists can also get this same spontaneous improv-like effect through creating their own cards to use with clients or developing a list of exercises, questions, metaphors, and so on as they continue to build their own ACT repertoire and challenge themselves to pick something new each week to try to incorporate into sessions where appropriate. As you begin to further develop and expand your practice of ACT, it can be easy to fall into a rut where you have the same handful of metaphors or exercises or ways of introducing processes that you use with every client. Incorporating some variety and spontaneity into your practice, while unnerving at first, will over time make you a more flexible therapist, sensitive to the ACT approach. ACT Improvisation can also be used with the topics of the next two chapters: awareness of experience and engaging with life.

Chapter 6

Awareness of Experience:
ACT for Posttraumatic Stress Disorder (PTSD) and Borderline Personality Disorder (BPD)

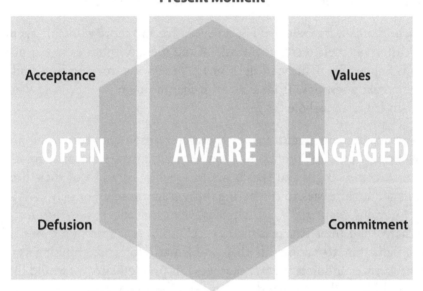

Bringing the acceptance and defusion processes of Chapter 5 alive in our clinical practice inspires us to invite clients to come in contact with their most painful private experiences. When we are open to our private experiences we can begin to increase our awareness of our patterns of responding in the present moment, the here-and-now of the world around us. When we lack awareness, we are anywhere but right here, right now. This awareness of our experience and of ourselves can either become bogged down with labels or it can be limitless. **The potential for flexibility inside these awareness processes is an important point.** Fostering contact with the present moment—where clients can learn to view themselves as the context of their experience or the observer of their experience—can create a touchstone in session in which the therapist continually comes back and draws attention to the here-and-now without overutilizing eyes-closed mindfulness exercises or other more traditional forms of meditation. We want to highlight this point because present-moment exercises can often fall into the eyes-closed, quiet, seated category.

A potential pitfall of relegating present-moment processes to formal eyes-closed mindfulness is that clients do not see the widespread applicability of coming in contact with the present moment. From a process-based approach, we can begin to train present-moment awareness into every interaction so that clients can use their own awareness to draw themselves out of their private content—the mindedness that so easily lends itself to inattention to the here-and-now and elicits an automaticity in behavior. Without focusing attention on the here-and-now, clients get trapped in rigid repertoires of responding and are not free to make choices based on their values but instead are governed by their minds.

USING THE PRESENT MOMENT IN SESSION

Focusing on behavior change makes for a more workable therapeutic contract in that observable behaviors are within the realm of a client's control, whereas manipulating or controlling their private experiences is far more difficult and can have dire outcomes. In ACT, we encourage clients to focus on their own experience of painful situations. For example, when a client reports to you that their "brother-in-law is an asshole," we might empathize and validate their frustration but more importantly, we focus on what happens for this client when that thought occurs to them. We focus on what they most struggle with, what thoughts, feelings, sensations, and memories show up when they have the thought "My brother-in-law is an asshole" in the therapy room as well as in the presence of their brother-in-law and work to identify what they would like for their behavior to be about in these situations. As therapists, we examine how we might best set this client up for successful behavior change in the presence of someone who elicits painful experiences.

Contacting the present moment in session can be an evocative and more workable agenda to approach painful experiences than focusing on their presence outside of the therapy room as it is a potential future situation whereas the session is happening right here, right now. A therapist working in a confluent manner with the ACT approach might evoke a response from a client in that moment saying, "And what is it like right now to tell me your brother-in-law is an asshole?"

The many ways in which a client might answer the present-moment reorienting are welcome in an ACT approach. When working from this process-focused way, all answers are grist for the proverbial mill. For example, if the client becomes angry and speaks about specific instances of their brother-in-law's perceived misgivings, we would gently shift back to contacting the present moment or may even ask a defusion question, harking back to the previous chapter: "What happens when this anger shows up for you? What would I see you do next?" Alternatively, if the client tells us they feel indifferent speaking about their experience of their brother-in-law, we might shift to asking, "Is that problematic for you, thinking your brother-in-law is an asshole?" If the client's answer endorses the fact that, yes it is problematic, we would likely do some values and commitment work, probing further, "What do you want to be about with your brother-in-law? What kind of an in-law do you want to be?"

The point we wish to underscore is that encouraging clients to bring their experience into the present moment is a useful way of working with their painful experiences and makes for helpful therapeutic conversations that involve influencing behavior rather than helplessly battling experiences that are out of the clients' control. The utility of present-moment–focused work does not end at bringing experiences into the present, but also can be used effectively for interpersonal problems; the therapist applies a use of self in session to facilitate meaningful conversations about interpersonal functioning with clients.

ACT with Borderline Personality Disorder

In the following therapist and client dialogue, the therapist uses cues in session during a typical conversation with a client to train present-moment processes. In this exchange, we show you something slightly different from the typical mindfulness, guided imagery, or hypnosis induction that one might usually conceptualize for using awareness processes in session. In the following example dialogue, the focus of the intervention is using the interpersonal therapist-client context in which therapists invite clients to contact the present moment and view themselves as the context of their experience in the therapy session. Note that this is not an intervention we recommend introducing without a sufficient therapeutic alliance established. To further demonstrate the effectiveness of focusing on the interpersonal context, the dialogue presented here occurs with a client suffering with a diagnosis of borderline personality disorder who has reported a history of severe difficulty in interpersonal relationships with friends, family, and other people important to them in their life.

Therapist: I can see this is painful for you to talk about.

Client: [Tearfully.] It is. I'm sorry, I don't know why I'm crying.

Therapist: I'm right here with you. Pause for a moment and just feel that. What's going on right now?

Client: I just feel so pathetic.

> The therapist attempts to reinforce this client and attempts to bring their awareness into the present moment.

Therapist: And what is that like to say, "I feel pathetic" here with me?

Client: [Laughs and looks away while crying.] Oh, it feels great. You know, nothing like balling my eyes out.

> Once again the therapist orients this client to the present moment.

Therapist: Wait, what just happened there? I asked what it's like to say, "I feel pathetic" and you just kind of laughed, looked away, and cracked a joke.

Client: Yeah, I don't know. I just feel awkward I guess.

> This therapist keenly observes a change in this client's behavior and without judging or inferring what the behavior is about the therapist uses awareness processes, potentially also pulling on defusion, to be curious about the change in behavior.

Therapist: I think I get that. It's hard to be vulnerable in front of someone. Isn't this exactly what we talked about though?

Client: [Looking up.] What do you mean?

> The awareness-focused intervention appears to have been successful and this therapist draws a parallel between the client's in-session behavior with the therapist to their self-reported out-of-session behavior with other people.

Therapist: When we first started working together you told me relationships are hard for you. You said being borderline means you're not good at relationships and you've made great strides here in this room and elsewhere in group treatment, and yet just then when I tried to connect more deeply with you, I noticed you cracked a joke.

Client: Yeah, I guess I did.

> This therapist is careful to reinforce the client's in-session successes and attempts at improving their behavior before offering a potentially cutting observation.

Therapist: Is that something you find yourself doing? Someone starts to get close and you crack a joke or use that sense of humor you're famous for?

Client: [Groans aloud and makes eye contact with therapist.] Yes! I have to stop because it is ruining me. Everyone thinks I'm okay until I'm not. Then they think I'm crazy because I get so upset and start hurting myself.

| The therapist asks questions focused on the function of this client's behavior, again not assuming to already have the answer but to instead be curious about how the joke-telling behavior may be working for this client. |

Therapist: Just as you said that and shared how difficult this pattern of behaving is for you, I felt much closer to you. What is that like for you to hear me say that?

Client: I don't know . . . good. I mean it feels good to hear you say that.

| The therapist is quick to reinforce and check-in with this client's experience of their self-disclosure, asking what it was like for the client to hear the therapist share a self-disclosure. Once again, it bears repeating that the therapist assumes that the client does not know how their own behavior is functioning for them. |

Therapist: And what about now. Can you take a step back and just look at this exchange between you and me. What is it like to be here and see that?

Client: It's sad. I don't want to keep doing this. Like I just said, it's ruining me.

| This therapist draws on a self-as-context intervention, which may prove to be helpful, reinforcing this client's new behavior of sharing vulnerabilities. Alternatively, this therapist could have recapped what just happened in the session and focused on new learning with this client. Regardless, the therapist's in-session behavior would be focused on reinforcing this client's in-session behavior, encouraging their continued attention. |

Therapist: And to see yourself saying these things in this room, telling me this is ruining you. How do you feel about that person in this room suffering?

Client: I feel sorry for them. Suffering with this is hard.

| This therapist implements a more advanced understanding of self-as-context through the use of perspective taking, inviting this client to see themselves from an outside perspective. |

We know this script is short and idealized, our minds tell us that you, the reader, might be thinking, "Yeah . . . that's not how my clients would respond." And you're not wrong! In our estimation, we have similar conversations to the previous dialogue with our clients because of our efforts in setting up an informed consent, priming clients to have difficult conversations while we slowly introduce them to ACT's six core processes. After a few sessions of socializing clients to this way of working, we are able to introduce evocative present-moment–

focused exercises like the preceding one. **We find that making ACT practical and useful is not about asking existential, complicated questions that lead to abstract discussions. ACT involves you, the therapist, being willing to ask these questions with genuine curiosity and doing so in a pragmatic way that trains your clients' attention and models this position yourself.** Notice that the therapist in the preceding dialogue comes back to the present moment again and again. This return is purposeful. We do not expect you to mimic this style or memorize verbatim the scripts to do ACT. Each of us has our own therapeutic style: Where Tim is humorous and often directive, Jessica is compassionate and enthusiastic, each bringing our own voice to ask questions and do exercises that invite our clients to take this new perspective. We challenge you to attempt this in your practice using the present moment to influence your moment-to-moment interactions with clients in session.

The Therapeutic Relationship as the Context to be Present

Working on moment-to-moment interactions that are happening in session is incredibly important as we highlighted before that the only context we have any control over is the one happening right here-now. Your office or the environment in which you conduct your work with clients, as well as your face, voice, and presence, is a context. Using your newfound knowledge of ACT's present-moment processes, you can make yourself and the therapeutic relationship you bring to your clients a context for training awareness. This may involve you learning a new set of skills that seem uncomfortable at first. It was that way with us as well, but over time it comes with a lot of benefits. Training the therapy room as a context for awareness means that we continue to redirect clients to the present moment, asking them to focus on now, where now means this very moment in the therapy session. Attending to in-session present-moment processes means that the therapeutic work you do will change from largely talking about what happens outside of the session to working with private experiences now, in the session.

Once clients are successfully socialized to awareness processes, specifically paying attention on purpose, using noticing skills to observe private experiences, and viewing themselves as the context of their experience, we then invite them to more formally practice mindfulness. Transitioning from using awareness processes in session or talking about noticing in session with the Life Map to formal mindfulness and meditation practices can be bridged with a discussion on how clients can sharpen their awareness skills through a practice called mindfulness. This transition is often easily achieved by guiding a brief mindfulness of breath exercise, demonstrating the utility of learning how to slow down and pay attention to experiences on purpose. If you have clients who shy away from the word *mindfulness*, you may want to substitute or connect it to concepts such as "noticing" or "focusing" to underscore that you are now going to more formally train the practice of noticing and focusing attention on the present moment that you have been informally doing throughout therapy.

MINDFULNESS OF BREATH SCRIPT

The following mindfulness of breath script is the first formal mindfulness exercise we facilitate with clients in session. Typically, we introduce this exercise by saying, "A lot of what we have been doing is about increasing your awareness, your ability to catch your private experiences and notice them, sort of catch them in flight before they dominate your view of the world and take over so to speak. In my estimation the best way to sharpen your noticing skills so that you can pay closer attention to your experiences and choose what you do next is to practice, to practice here in this room with me, to practice at home so that you can get better at noticing."

MINDFULNESS of BREATH

—

I'm going to invite you to close your eyes if it's comfortable for you. If not, maybe allow your gaze to drop and let your vision soften its focus.

Take a breath on purpose. Feel the belly expand as you inhale and collapse as you exhale. Really feel that movement in your body.

Notice how the chest lifts as you breathe in and drops as you breathe out. See if you can focus your attention to stay with the movement of your breath in your body.

Inevitably distractions will arise, whether it's a sound, a sensation in your body like your nose itching, or tension in your body. Whenever distractions arise, notice them. They're inevitable. Come back to your breathing, really pay attention to the sensations of your breath.

On your next inhale, notice that there's a space between inhales and exhales. You breathe in and there's a brief pause, almost as if your body knows when it's full of air, followed by an exhale. See if you can catch that brief pause.

On your next inhale, breathe in, feel that pause, hold it for a moment and breathe in a little deeper, like taking an extra sip of oxygen, topping up the lungs with air, and then breathe all the way out. Notice what that feels like in your body.

Repeat that at your own pace a few times. Breathing in, feeling the pause, taking an extra breath in, and exhaling all the way.

Still breathing here, allow your distractions to come: thoughts, sensations. And allow your distractions to go as you bring your attention back to the breath as you notice your mind becoming distracted.

Before we end this exercise, just take a brief moment to notice what it feels like to be in this moment.

Still with your eyes closed, bring your attention back to the room you're in. Notice the sounds in your environment and the sensations of the chair underneath your body.

Bring a little motion into the body, wiggling the fingers, rotating the wrists, maybe rolling the shoulders up forward and down, moving the head from side to side, bringing some motion into the neck, allowing your body to wake up and meet this moment.

And when you feel ready, gently allow your eyes to open.

What did you notice?

We like to send clients home with a sense of what to do, actual behaviors we want them to engage in. These mindfulness exercises are the specific practices they can use out of session in their daily life to increase their engagement with the processes we target in session. To make it more concrete, instead of simply saying "practice mindfulness at home every day," we may practice a specific exercise in session and then provide the client with a printed script of the exercise or allow the client to audio record us doing the exercise in session for them to listen to at home. This way they leave the session with an actual exercise to practice rather than a concept to approach. When it comes to practicing mindfulness, we've had mixed successes with clients following through at home through various sources, such as mindfulness mp3s, recording the therapist guiding mindfulness, and sending links to videos instructing mindfulness exercises. In our experience, providing a handout reiterating what mindfulness is and how it can be done is useful.

The following handout helps to bridge the work done from the therapist's office out to the home lives of clients. Remember, in ACT we seek to increase contacting the present moment as a process not just mindfulness as a traditional meditation practice. This process is especially represented on the sample handout "How to Practice Mindfulness" in which we recommend noticing one's experience during simple activities that may typically be taken for granted and can be performed while paying attention on purpose: washing the dishes, eating, and more. The idea is to increase formal mindfulness practice in activities we are already doing every day, and by pairing a daily task with mindfulness we can more easily incorporate the practice of noticing into our everyday lives.

HOW TO PRACTICE MINDFULNESS HANDOUT

Here is a sample of a handout you can give to your clients so that they can bring mindfulness practices home with them and use them as a process in their own lives, not simply a new method, technique, or as an outcome—"feeling blissed out" and the like.

HOW to PRACTICE MINDFULNESS

Mindfulness is a practice. It's something we work toward and do with repetition to master in our own repertoire of skills. One doesn't simply finish being mindful or check it off a list like " mindfulness, done for today!" Instead, understand that mindfulness is a state of mind that you learn to cultivate in your daily life, and you can return to it over and over throughout the day. One of the early pioneers in bringing mindfulness to western health practices, Jon Kabat-Zinn (1994) defined mindfulness as paying attention (noticing), on purpose, in the present moment, nonjudgmentally.

Our hope is to present you with a mindfulness practice that increases your ability to simply notice your private experiences. You can then use your new mindfulness skills to practice creating a distance between you and your painful private experiences through noticing thoughts, feelings, sensations, or memories that would trigger you to engage in problematic behaviors.

It means we focus on the paying attention on purpose—noticing! Even if judgments show up for you, our recommendation is that you notice them too. For example, take a look around the environment you're in now; do you see anything that you cannot judge or affix some evaluation to? We'd wager that you likely can't.

Noticing is the skill we seek to increase and that means you can work on your noticing skill (paying attention on purpose) many times throughout your day without needing to close your eyes and focus on your breathing, buy a meditation cushion, or attend a yoga class. Take a few moments out of your day to try one or more of the following:

- Take a breath on purpose, wherever you are, whatever time it may be. Notice the sensations of your breath in your body, and the rise and fall of your chest and belly.

- If you're driving or commuting, turn off any distractions like the radio, song, or podcast you might be listening to. If commuting, put down the game you might be playing, book you're reading, or whatever else you might be doing. Notice what you see, the quality of the light entering the space you're in, the rumble of the seat underneath your body, sounds you can hear, the temperature of the air on your skin.

- When eating, take a moment to slow down and eat purposefully. What flavors do you notice? Take in the smell and texture of your food. Take your time to eat and just notice what that experience is like.

- Even now as you're reading, go slowly with an aim to pay attention and notice your experience. You may notice yourself getting distracted as you read. See if you can pay attention to that and see where your mind goes.

During your morning routine: brushing your teeth, washing, getting dressed, go slowly and pay attention to your experience. What do you notice as you spread toothpaste on your toothbrush? Pay attention to the sensations as the toothpaste makes contact with your teeth or tongue.

As you learn to practice mindfulness, you may find judgments show up. For instance, as you become more familiar with how your attention moves around, you might become frustrated with yourself. Even that is an opportunity to notice your experience: what thoughts and feelings show up for you as you notice your attention moving on to something other than what you're doing in the moment? And remember: every moment is an opportunity to be present.

The ability to bring one's awareness to both private and public experiences in any context and learn to engage with the present moment in day-to-day life is invaluable in creating sensitivity to contexts. Take for example a client diagnosed with posttraumatic stress disorder (PTSD) who experiences hypervigilance, fear, and symptoms of anxiety, such as heart racing, sweating, and flashbacks. This client, in an attempt to avoid these experiences, often stays at home and rarely goes out. If this client values connecting with others, but activities they would commonly do to demonstrate that valued connection such as going out to the movies or a crowded restaurant are no longer in their repertoire, they simply don't go. When asked about not going to the movies, the crowded restaurant, and other similar contexts that might connect them more closely with their values, they describe unpleasant internal experiences that they would work to escape. Through a functional analysis with this client, they find that they will more often than not find themselves not engaging in values-consistent behaviors due to the fear of these sensations arising. Instead this client will act in ways to control or manage these symptoms. This is not inherently pathological, it makes rational, logical sense that this client would work to escape their most painful private experiences by limiting what they do.

Through awareness processes we can begin to train this client to notice their physical sensations, thoughts, memories, and feelings with curiosity through the use of their observer self such that they can start to notice that their mind is having the thought, "I'm not safe here, I must leave," rather than be fused with that same thought and believe it to be true. Similarly, instead of being lost in their head replaying past traumatic memories or thinking through potentially future dangerous situations and escape strategies, this client can use mindfulness practices of engaging all of their five senses similar to the preceding worksheet to bring themselves back into the present moment when they otherwise would be sucked out of the present and into their mind. By engaging the five senses, the client may draw their attention to the smell of popcorn at the movie theater, or the sounds of their friends laughing at a restaurant, or notice the taste or texture of their food.

This exercise may seem like a simple one, but being able to increase sensitivity to the context they are in and distinguish between private and public experiences can help create more space between their private experiences and their response such that when they have the thought, "I'm not safe I must leave," they can choose to leave or they can choose to stay and asked their friend a question, take a bite of their food, or reach out and hold their partner's hand at the movies. This behavior of noticing creates a space for choice and freedom from the reactive automatic response under aversive control.

It is important to note that we are not training this client to distract themself from their private experiences, but rather to engage in noticing them in a different way and in a way that helps them to discriminate between the environment that they are in and what is happening inside their mind so they have more options for how to interact with the world and so those options can be based on what matters to them rather than only trying to escape. The following exercise is another way to train this practice of noticing and looking at our own private experiences, our physical sensations in our body, from a curious stance.

BODY SCAN MINDFULNESS EXERCISE

The following exercise is a favorite of ours to use in group settings, but we have on occasion used this body scan with individual clients who may need additional instruction on mindfulness or who typically try to avoid noticing bodily sensations or who may benefit from evidence-based relaxation outcomes of mindfulness exercises such as a body scan. Readers savvy to Kabat-Zinn's mindfulness-based stress reduction (MBSR) program may be familiar with body scans. The cues we focus on in ACT, however, are somewhat different and encourage noticing of all experiences, including judgments that may arise or frustrations. We don't prescribe to not have certain judgments or to "let go" of experiences, instead we opt to encourage an engagement with that content. After all, it is just that: mental chatter that one can learn to work with.

We often end this exercise by allowing for a long pause and asking, "What was your experience of that exercise?" Or more simply "What did you notice?" There is no wrong answer from an experience point of view (e.g., "that was relaxing" or "I kept noticing cramps in my leg"). Our typical response is "Great!" Or we may validate: "You noticed that showing up and what else? Or what happened next?" We wish to say explicitly that we attempt to reinforce the client's noticing behavior and sharing it with us in session. We don't desire to have a specific outcome of "feeling better" or "that was relaxing," although those may be benefits of a dedicated mindfulness practice.

BODY SCAN FOR MINDFULNESS

Today I invite you to do a body scan exercise with me where we will practice noticing the sensations happening within our own bodies. You may find that you notice areas of tension or relaxation that you weren't aware of or you may find yourself not wanting to pay attention to certain parts of your body that bring you pain. These are all normal experiences. I ask that in serving your own progress and in developing your own practice of awareness that you try your best to notice all of your experiences during this exercise, even those you don't want.

This practice is not about relaxing, or having any expectation or desired outcome, but rather it is the practice of simply noticing your experience. Give yourself permission to feel what you're feeling right now and make space for everything that shows up, even judgments or critical thoughts.

If you feel comfortable, please allow your eyes to close gently, or simply allow a soft gaze on your lap or a neutral spot in front of you.

If you find your mind wandering, traveling to the past or future or a "what if" scenario, or making noise and commenting on the exercise, simply notice where your mind is taking you, listen to the noise, acknowledge it, and bring yourself back to the sound of my voice and the part of your body I am directing your attention to.

Begin by bringing your attention to your breath, to the fact that you are breathing. Noticing the rise and fall of your chest and belly as you breathe in and out. . . . Try not to manipulate your breath in any way. Simply observe the breath, your natural way of breathing. . . . Throughout this exercise you may notice a resistance to doing something that I invite you to. Remember to always choose what is best for you, always having the option of returning to the breath, breathing deep into the belly.

Now gently turn your attention to the top of your head. Notice if you can feel the area just above your head paying attention to any sensation of warmth or coolness. . . . Start here and gently, slowly begin to turn your mind's eye inward and begin scanning down your body, noticing all the tiny muscles in your face. Can you feel any of them tightening with tension or loosening with relaxation? . . . Can you feel the cool air enter your nostrils and the warm air exhaling through the nose as you breathe? . . . Continue down to the positioning of your tongue in your mouth, noticing saliva in your mouth begin to pool as you pay attention, the feel of your tongue in your mouth as you swallow.

Next, lower your mind's eye to the point where your neck meets your head . . . and slowly scanning down to the point where your neck meets the rest of your body . . . paying attention to the sensations there and expanding your awareness to any thoughts or feelings that may arise as you scan down to your shoulders. . . . Breathe into those thoughts and feelings, and with an exhale follow your attention down your shoulders.

If you feel comfortable, bring your shoulders up to your ears and then gently roll them back and down, noticing any change in sensation with the movement.... Slowly draw your attention down your shoulders to the tips of your fingers. . . . Can you feel the point where your fingers end and the air begins?

If you notice your mind has begun to wander, that's alright. That's what minds do. Simply acknowledge where your mind has gone, and bring your attention back to the sound of my voice and the part of your body I am directing your attention to.

Turning your attention to your back, notice your posture and follow the curve of your spine. . . . Feel the points where your back touches the chair. . . . Slowly wrap your attention around to your stomach, feeling how the abdomen expands with an in breath and deflates with an out breath. . . . Moving down to your hips, feel the weight of your body sitting in the chair, the places where your legs meet the chair. . . . Notice any sensations as you move down your thighs, around your knees, to the back of your legs, and finally to your feet. . . . Can you feel any sensation from the soles of your feet? Points where your foot touches the inside of your shoe? . . . The texture of your shoe or sock against your foot? Do you feel any sensation of warmth or coolness?

Gently draw your attention back up your body to your chest and belly, feeling as they expand and deflate with each inhale and exhale. . . . Notice with curiosity if your breathing has changed at all from the beginning of this exercise. . . . Notice your own practice of noticing throughout this exercise.

Begin to turn your attention outside your body to the room around you. Listen to the sound of your breath and to the sounds around you both soft and loud, and near or far away. . . . Listen to the sound of my voice as I walk you through this exercise . . . and in your own time, when you are ready, gently flutter your eyes open or raise your head.

PERSPECTIVE-TAKING AND SELF-COMPASSION

Building on the practice of noticing and expanding awareness, one of the most powerful tools at the disposal of ACT therapists is transforming relational frame theory experiments to ACT clinical interventions. To date, many RFT experiments have focused on perspective-taking, a person's ability to see the world from different points of view (Hughes & Barnes-Holmes, 2015; McHugh, Barnes-Holmes, & Barnes-Holmes, 2004). While important to the advancement of basic science, it can also be an invaluable tool to the clinician. An ACT therapist can use the perspective-taking tools of RFT to train their clients in empathy, compassion for others, and self-compassion (McHugh & Stewart, 2012). Perspective-taking can be crucial in therapeutic settings where clients are especially stuck with interpersonal relationships or encounter a great deal of hurt toward themselves. It is a practical way to increase clients' ability to feel what another may feel or have compassion for their own experience.

The Self in ACT

In ACT the self is constructed from three unique processes: self-as-process, one's awareness of one's experience that is constantly ongoing (e.g., thinking, feeling, sensing, remembering, behaving); self-as-content, the evaluations, qualities, and descriptions that one ascribes to one's self (e.g., "I'm a good partner" or "I'm six feet tall"); self-as-context, one's ability to shift perspectives as needed in a given situation to observe and describe one's experience from a persistent point of view (e.g., seeing oneself as transcending one's experience, observing the content of experience as separate, not one's self).

Considering these processes in establishing a self, we can safely say that in ACT, the self is not static. It's not a thing. The self is an ever-changing process of behaving and framing experiences from a perspective. This notion might seem heady, so bear with us. RFT is essentially saying that in order for there to be a self, that self needs to be engaged in perspective-taking—that is to say, seeing that there is a you, there, right now doing something: even now as you're reading this book. Perspective-taking can be broken down into three main frames: interpersonal (person) relations, situational (place) relations, and temporal (time) relations.

In the following illustration, we have separated the three frames necessary for training the self-processes we have been describing with perspective-taking. The first is interpersonal, discriminating a difference between I-you (e.g., myself and yourself). The second is spatial, discriminating a difference between here-there (e.g., here where you are reading and over there where there's a lamp or some other light or decoration). The third is temporal, discriminating between now-then (e.g., now you're reading and after you'll be eating or drinking).

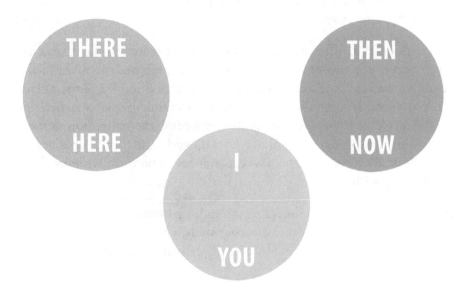

Formally these relational frames are called *deictic framing*. The interesting part about using these perspectives is that RFT demonstrates in order for you to have the experience of "I," there must also be a separate "you" or someone other than "I." Each of these relations can be trained if they are weak, thus increasing one's ability to frame deictically. Through combining these frames, using them clinically to shift between I-you, here-there, now-then, we can create powerful clinical interventions that increase empathy and compassion.

Here we have once more depicted the three frames necessary for training the self-processes, but this time we have overlapped them to demonstrate the interplay between I-here-now and you-there-then.

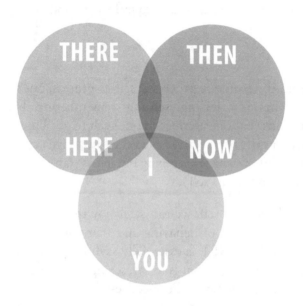

Training Compassion Exercise

Combining deictic frames to create clinical interventions and exercises need not feel complicated or academic like learning RFT! Below we've included a therapist script for a brief mindfulness exercise that involves some guided imagery. Notice how this script uses the powerful perspective-taking tools of deictic framing, inviting clients to experience their self (I-here-now) and to then picture someone else (you-there-then) and to view themselves from the other's perspective.

This exercise may have a number of different outcomes with your clients. If a client has a difficult time allowing themselves to be behind the eyes of someone who has valued and appreciated them, that's okay. You can use what comes up in the present moment to have a conversation about more clinically relevant behavior. Painful private experiences could arise as a result of your client not being able to think of someone, perhaps they were betrayed by that person. You, the therapist, in the present moment can bring their attention to their private experiences of judgment and evaluation, the content their mind comes up with, and use the openness tools from Chapter 5 to foster an environment of allowing those painful experiences to be there without defense even while your client is in the room working with you.

On a technical note, you may wish to read the script through again and pay attention to how the script invites a shifting of perspective. Using these perspective-taking skills, you can introduce exercises like the previous script flexibly or by adapting perspective-taking into practices that are already working for you.

GUIDED IMAGERY

I invite you to picture someone in your life whom you've felt connected with, perhaps someone who appreciated you, someone who saw some value in you—whether it be a caregiver such as a parent, or someone with a special interest in you, including a friend, a partner, or a teacher. Someone who really valued you.

Take a moment to close your eyes and see whether you can visualize them. Picture them as vividly as possible. Take a moment to picture their face, noticing the details of their eyes, their eyebrows. Let yourself see their hair, their lips and their nose.

What is the emotion on their face as they look at you?

Take a moment here and really see them looking at you in this moment. And notice what that feels like for you as you look into their eyes and feel their connection.

I'm now going to invite you to slip your awareness out from behind your eyes and in behind theirs, seeing yourself from behind their eyes. Seeing yourself as someone they want to connect with, someone of value, someone who is appreciated.

What do you feel?

Notice in your body as you're feeling what they feel looking at you and seeing your eyes.

Take a breath here and notice what that feels like.

Perspective-Taking Worksheet

In the interest of making perspective-taking as practical as possible, we have included the "Connecting to Your Future Self" worksheet that is based on the powerful tools of deictic framing. We use this worksheet in session with our clients and also hand it out in groups and have participants use the worksheet in pairs to interview one another. In our experience, this worksheet is extremely helpful as it offers a structure to doing a difficult perspective-taking opportunity: I-here-now communicates with you-there-then in a potentially painful future situation.

The exercise starts with inviting a client to bring to mind a potentially painful situation that they may have to face in the coming days. In session, moving on to the second component of this worksheet, you may wish to prompt them to describe that situation: where they might be, what that place looks like, who is there, and what it feels like to be in that painful moment. The tools of deictic framing are already at work as clients are being prompted to see themselves there-then. The third part of this exercise involves a client here-now, in the session with you, speaking to their future self there-then. You may prompt, "What do you want to say to yourself there, in the future, suffering?" The fourth component is to track how your client makes sense of this exercise, how would they there-then, in this future imagined situation, receive what is being shared with them. Next, the client is invited here-now, in the present moment to take on a posture and tone of voice toward their future and imagine themself in the there-then. Finally, the last component of this exercise invites sharing from the heart here-now that they know it's hard for their future self.

Integrating perspective-taking into your practice may seem foreign at first but we wish to encourage you to use this worksheet to begin experimenting. Furthermore, once you find yourself easily tracking I-you, here-there, now-then deictic frames in action, you may be able to more easily foster a client's successful use of perspective-taking by asking, "Just being here in this moment, what is it like to imagine yourself in this future situation we're talking about that could be painful for you?" Or an intervention more explicitly akin to self-as-context, you might say, "Take a moment here, almost like we could zoom out of this situation. What is it like right now to see yourself here in this room with me hearing the words coming from you about this suffering?"

The bottom line for us in the last part of this awareness chapter is that we wish for you to see that present-moment, self-as-context, perspective-taking activities need not be highly technical, formal practices or laborious interventions that require a significant set up. These awareness processes can be drawn upon in any moment of a session.

CONNECTING TO YOUR FUTURE SELF

This exercise is about picturing yourself in a future situation that could be difficult for you. You may wish to write your responses to each question below. Do your best to really picture yourself in that future situation and communicate with that future version of yourself.

1. YOUR FUTURE

Call to mind a painful situation you anticipate having to face in the coming days...

2. BEING THERE, NOW

What would you see or hear? Can you envision yourself there?

3. SPEAK

Can you here-now, in this moment speak to your future self in pain? What words or gestures can you share with your future self?

4. RECEIVE

How does the future vision of yourself receive those words/gestures?

5. YOUR NEEDS

What tone of voice or posture do you use with the vision of your future yourself?

What might you in the future situation need as you're in pain?

6. VALIDATE

Share from your heart, here-now that you know it's hard, maybe really hard for that vision of your future self.

Chapter 7

Engaging with Life:
ACT for Depression, Chronic Pain, and Couples

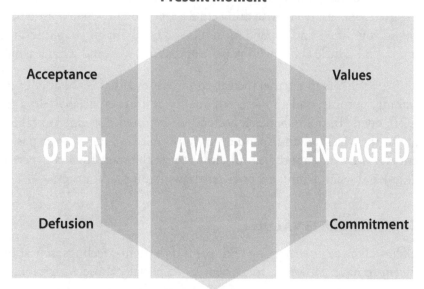

With a better awareness of our private experiences, ourselves, and the context in which we live we can more easily understand how we make decisions to engage in the world. With a willingness to be open to all experiences and an awareness of what we want to be doing in this moment, we can decide to act based on what matters most to us rather than reacting to avoid unpleasant experiences. This decision goes beyond acknowledging our values and extends into the observable world where we create committed actions that each take us a step closer to who and what matter most. That last statement is important because all the accepting, defused, present-moment–focused, viewing the self-as-context, valuing work is about empowering the doing, the actions that move us toward the life we most want for ourselves. It is with this understanding that we introduce conversations about values early in our work, typically in the first session, either through a general conversation about what we are working toward in therapy or through a more directive conversation about who and what matter to the client.

A potential pitfall of establishing the noneliminative agenda that we discussed with creating an ACT informed consent in Chapter 2 is not having sufficient clarity in what one might do if not busied with the work of attempting to avoid, eliminate, and ultimately escape painful private experiences. Here is where tight stimulus control on the part of the clinician comes in. We don't mean to sound overly technical, so please allow us to unpack this statement. Your office, the environment you work in, you yourself as the therapist become a context. You, not unlike us, the authors, may idealize your therapeutic relationships as helpful and strengthening to your clients, not coercive or aversive. Practicing stimulus control means that you can intervene early on in your assessments or therapeutic conversations to create a context that is a stimulus event about growing one's life toward meaning and an improved quality of living. Notice that the context we describe is not a stimulus event to complain, vent, wish away, or espouse the innumerous ways one's life could, should, or ought to be improved. We do not wish to create a caricature of psychotherapeutic settings or relationships. We simply want to describe that without our intervention clients may be socialized through past therapy experiences, television shows, or cultural references to view the therapist's office as a place to go to engage in more of these experiential avoidance activities.

Armed with this understanding of building a therapeutic context consistent with the ACT approach, we act as soon as possible by asking questions that focus on exposing clients' values early on in therapy, often in the first session. In almost every initial session, you would likely hear us first explain and sign the informed consent and then quickly move to saying: "Thanks for taking care of that initial bit of paperwork. Before we really get started, one of my favorite things to do is get to know you a little bit outside of the context of what's going wrong in your life. I find I spend most of my day talking to people about what's going wrong in their lives. Could you tell me a little about who you are and about who and what are most important to you?"

This early attempt to prime clients to the therapeutic context as one that is about engaging in life and growing behavior toward meaning, purpose, and an increased quality of life is especially relevant with mandated client populations such as offenders. In our experience, offenders are often not eager to take an hour or two out of their week to talk about their feelings and spend even more time looking at their past transgressions. But no matter who the client is or why they are there, our aim is to set the stage for a conversation about what we are working toward (values) and what painful experiences show up on that journey.

WHERE THERE IS PAIN, THERE IS VALUE

In our experience, clients come to us struggling with painful thoughts, feelings, sensations, and memories that they largely do not want to have. However, some people—especially those with a long reinforcement history of rigidly following rules, avoiding painful outcomes, and generally not contacting long-term reinforcers—may have a difficult time answering a seemingly obvious question such as, "Who and what are most important to you?" In these cases, it behooves us, the helping professionals, to listen closely to what hurts our clients the most and to explore the inside of that pain. With curiosity and a careful sensitivity, we likely will find our clients' values inside or connected to that hurt. Their reinforcers, their values, or said more simply as "the who and what that really matter" to our clients is often directly connected with what hurts them the most. Caring deeply about being in a supportive partnership or being a loving parent makes one susceptible to the pain that comes with losing that relationship or making mistakes as a parent. We worry that this may read as a pessimistic message rather than one that seeks to dignify our hurts; pain only appears in relation to values. In short: it hurts because it matters.

ACT with Chronic Pain

We're providing you with an example dialogue between client and therapist in which a client may be challenging or quickly begins talking about their desire to eliminate painful experiences or posits how life would be better without painful experiences. Although this exchange at first makes quick work of acceptance processes, notice that this exchange has a focus on values. Pay special attention to how the therapist explores what the client's attempts to avoid pain have kept them from as a way to help identify what really matters to the client. The following dialogue occurs with a client who presents with a severe chronic pain condition.

In the preceding exchange, acceptance processes were utilized early in the conversation, facilitating openness to experience where the therapist points out the lack of workability in avoiding pain. It is important to note that sometimes this is a larger conversation as some clients are highly fused with the idea that their pain can be eliminated and believe they have just not found the right doctor, medication, or procedure. In those instances

Therapist: Before we get started talking about what has brought you in to work with me today, I'm curious to get to know you outside of what is going wrong in your life. Would you be willing to tell me who and what are most important to you in your life?

This is an early attempt on the therapist's part to engage this client in their values, curiously asking about what they value.

Client: I'm a retired gunnery sergeant and I was injured on my third tour in Afghanistan and since then I've been screwed. I'm always in pain, always. Do you have any idea what that's like? This is my living hell. Pain is an enemy that never retreats and this is my life now, fighting a battle I will never win because they've tried everything from pills to different pills to injections.

Therapist: [Slowly.] I don't know if I can imagine that. The words you just said: "my living hell" really struck me. What is the cost of this hell, what toll does it have on your life?

The therapist's early attempt to connect with this client's values may appear to have failed at first. However, listening closely in painful moments for vulnerabilities that are tenderly connected to values enables the therapist to purposefully slow down their speech, empathize, and ask about the cost of a living hell.

Client: [Tearfully.] My wife and my little girl. I'm not myself anymore. I left strong and unafraid, now they just get this empty shell of a man.

Therapist: And what does that look like if I was there? What would I see you doing?

Client: Nothing! I wake in pain and take muscle relaxants because they help take the edge off, then I'm in a fog until it's time to take my pain meds, I stay in bed and I hear my wife and daughter get up, get ready for the day. I might stream a show or old movie on my tablet. When my daughter's home from school, I'll have gotten out of bed twice and that's it. We usually have dinner as a family but I'm in such a miserable mood, my wife and I fight. I'll sometimes just stay in bed.

Although the client presented with what sounds like some self-fusion or self-as-content, in this early intervention the therapist seeks to clarify the behaviors that are happening; a compassionate approach to bringing this client's attention to their self-content would have also been a workable intervention.

Therapist: I don't mean to ask an obvious question but is that problematic for you?

The therapist assumes nothing and assesses for what may be examples of experiential avoidance.

Client: Yes, I can't keep living my life like this. This isn't a life.

Therapist: What do you want to be doing?

Client: I don't want to have this pain. I want to get back to my life like it was.

This question is again an attempt to draw on committed actions and values. The therapist here focuses on what behaviors this client would like to be doing if not engaged in the earlier described problematic behaviors. We may already have a hint that his wife and daughter are important to him, but again, the therapist does not make any assumptions.

Therapist: Yes, and you've been trying to avoid pain. With the mobility that you have, the life you've got left, what do you want to do?

Client: I know every night after dinner my wife washes the dishes and looks out the window at the sink. It overlooks our yard where our little girl plays. I want to walk up behind my wife and wrap my arms around her and kiss her on the neck.

This could go either way, someone experiencing high levels of pain with some difficult fusion around the self and being limited could react in anger in response to this question; however, we trust this therapist has built a sufficient rapport and asks this question with genuine respect and compassion.

Therapist: [Smiles.] That's beautiful and sounds like a significant change. What else do you want from this life?

Client: I want to go out and just be with my little girl, even if I can't play ball with her like I used to. I just want to be there with her so she sees her dad.

The smiling may be reinforcing along with the validation acknowledging the significance of the change. The therapist presses forward, asking for additional commitment behaviors. For clients who have difficulty identifying any behaviors that are consistent with what matters to them, it may take a few more gentle probing questions.

Therapist: It sounds to me like your wife and your daughter are important to you.

Client: They're my world.

Again, the therapist assumes nothing and offers a pause for this client to explicitly author his values.

Therapist: I can tell. Let me ask you one last question about them. The type of father you want to be to your daughter, the type of partner you want to be your wife—what kind of quality do you want to bring to those relationships?

Client: [Tearfully.] Loving. I want them to know I love them.

We again recognize that this question asking for this client to elect the qualities they most wish to be about in their life could go either way. However, an encouraging therapist with a genuine style often evokes meaningful content.

Therapist: I really like hearing you say that: "They're my world, I want them to know I love them." I wonder if this is what our work can be about, your wife and daughter. Not how to get rid of pain, I can tell you've tried that, been trying really hard for a long time, and you haven't been successful. You've unfortunately

Reinforcing this client's connection to their values, the therapist shares something personal about enjoying hearing this client speak about his family. Furthermore, the therapist concretizes the therapeutic contract of a noneliminative agenda by making explicit the pursuit of values over attempts to escape.

discovered no one has that answer for you. Instead, what if we learn how to hold onto your pain, maybe even lean into it so that we can find a life worth living. We can discover ways for you to do the things that bring you closer to the loving husband you want to be to your wife and the loving father you want to be to your daughter.

you may want to ask clients if they are willing to try something different with you and acknowledge that they can always go back to their old attempts to eliminate pain, but point out that from what they have said, from their own experience, this has not been a workable endeavor.

In the preceding dialogue also notice the therapist's persistence in drawing on this client's values. That's no mistake or happenstance; the therapist in that exchange evokes something emotional but not for emotions' sake or because therapy must be done tearfully or ACT is dependent on provocative exercises. The therapist listened closely to this client's pain and drew on what that pain is connected to. Just as someone who dearly loves their partner finds news of their partner's terminal illness heartbreaking, so too is pain permanently linked to what matters the most. **An apt metaphor is that of a coin: what hurts us the most is the flip side of what matters the most to us.** It is in walking with clients to this painful place that the therapist can also find what is most precious to them and what they cherish most in this life.

VALUES CARD SORT TASK

A values card sort task can be helpful for identifying and clarifying who and what are important to a client quickly and eliminate responses that may be based on trying to look or act a certain way to either fit in with society or avoid judgment from you, the therapist.

There are many values card decks available on the Internet or contextualscience.org (the organization for ACT) that you can print out and cut into cards, or if you like you can make your own on the computer or handwritten on index cards. Basically, values cards are a series of words, generally adjectives or phrases (honest, helping others, creative, etc.), that represent a broad range of potential values people may have.

When you begin a conversation with clients about values, even those who can identify some values often have not spent a considerable amount of time thinking about what in life they value, what they want to be about. I mean when was the last time you sat down to think about who and what matter to you or the type of qualities you want to represent your character? It is not something we often take time for in day-to-day life.

We generally set up a values card sort task by saying, "We have been talking in therapy about spending less time caught up in our thoughts, and more time engaged in the who and what that matter to you—what we call 'values.' I know you've already told me a little about what your values are [or I know you've mentioned having difficulty identifying your values] and I was wondering if you would be willing to go through an exercise with me that will help to clarify what your top, say three to five, values are so we have a good idea of what we are spending our time working toward. I like to keep it to three to five values because if we have too many that we are focusing on, we tend to get pulled in too many different directions and it is difficult to move forward. This does not mean that those are the only things that matter to you, simply what you are focused on right now. Would you be willing to try this exercise with me?"

Once they agree to participate, you take the stack of cards and emphasize the rules of the card sort task: "This stack here does not represent all of the values a person could have, but it is a good starting point. I am going to read aloud and hold up each card for you, and you will decide whether it is a value of yours by saying, 'Yes,' 'No,' or 'Maybe.' As you go through the card sort you may start noticing thoughts saying, 'You should say yes because you're supposed to care about helping others, or [therapist's name] is going to think something is wrong with me if honesty is not a value of mine.' That is completely normal. When those thoughts show up, notice them, and remember the goal of this task: to identify what your top three to five values are right now. Saying 'No' does not mean you do not care about something, only that it is not a priority in your life right now, and that is okay. There are no right or wrong values. Remember, we are interested in what your values are, not what culture or society or even I deem valuable, only what is important to you, what you want your life to be about. Ready?"

Go through the cards once separating them into Yes, No, and Maybe categories. Then put the No stack aside and go through the Yes and Maybe categories again, this time only allowing clients to say Yes or No to them. If needed, go through the Yes stack a third time, reminding the client that the goal is to get down to three to five values. It is important to note that this does not mean three to five cards; sometimes depending on the card stack, themes emerge, such as "helping others," "spirituality," "learning," "relationships," and so on. If you notice these themes emerging ask the client if it is okay to put a few cards together on the table or ask if one card goes together with another card and listen to the response. Sometimes clients may note specific reasons why those cards are different to them. Make sure to listen. At the end of the task, you and your client should have a solid idea of their values, which can help guide what behaviors to focus on. What they will engage in or not.

FINDING MEANING

Conversations with clients about who and what matter most to them are fruitful early ways of looking at their values. You can ask additional follow-up questions that further explore clients' individual values, for example, "What qualities do you most wish to demonstrate in pursuit of being a. . . ." We end with an ellipsis because the outcome is virtually infinite: father, mother, son, daughter, professional or employee, citizen, neighbor, and so on. In the previous example in which a man suffering with chronic pain talked about his wife and daughter mattering to him, we asked what qualities he most wished to have toward them and he explained how he wanted to be a loving father and partner. We consider this a further success in understanding his values. You may also surmise that what the therapist was doing in that dialogue was inviting this client to engage in hierarchical framing where meaning was sought even in the presence of painful experiences (asking what qualities you want to bring) and how they connect together to organize behavior congruently toward some values (his daughter and wife).

Facilitating clients' ability to express deeper meaning and qualities of their values can be difficult for many reasons including clients' own lack of reinforcement history in contacting their values and acting on them, demonstrating considerable deficits in their behavioral repertoire. This deficit can be especially prevalent in marginalized individuals who have been victim to oppressive systems, abuse, and other contextual factors that have operated to limit their contact with reinforcement. In all such instances where a client may become stuck—citing that their world is not organized in a way that allows for a committed action—connecting to their unique values and finding meaning in their lives, a powerful clinical tool at the therapist's disposal is using hierarchical framing to promote a connection and eventual commitment to values even in the presence of aversive stimuli (typically one's most painful private experiences) allowing for a helpful transformation of stimulus functions (i.e., painful private experiences no longer serve to limit behavior). Said less technically, painful events show up and there are ways that you can promote a client to do something that is a valued action even in the presence of the pain. Said more poetically, in sorrow we can elect to let love stand.

COMMITMENT QUESTIONS

We have developed four engaging questions that promote valued actions even in the presence of painful experiences. As a tip, we present the four questions to overlap with the four quadrants of the Life Map in a useful way. (For an introduction to the Life Map, see Chapter 3.) In our experience using ACT with clients, commitment questions came about as a natural evolution of using the Life Map that increases the Life Map's usefulness throughout treatment by continually coming back to it. To begin, each of the four commitment questions correspond with a section of the Life Map targeting different clinically relevant topics in clients' lives: their values, the painful thoughts and feelings that get in the way of them moving toward their values, the behaviors they engage in when painful private experiences show up in their lives, and finally what behaviors they wish to be engaged in to move toward their values.

The intention behind commitment questions is for them to be asked by clients every day. Clients score themselves each day on a rating scale that they choose or that you agree to in advance: for example, a scale of

1 to 10 where 1 means no effort at all and 10 means maximal effort, or using smiley faces, neutral faces, and frowning faces to note the outcome of the question. Commitment questions keep the focus on the clients' behaviors: what they do or say. This point is important because when writing a Life Map, we put clients at the center of map and these questions keep them there. Through engaging in these questions, therapy quickly becomes about what they do to act on each of these areas of their lives.

Let Go

Letting go is about the problematic behaviors our clients tend to engage in to move away from painful private experiences. These behaviors are found in the top left quadrant of the Life Map. After clients identify a problematic behavior they want to do less of or reduce, they have a commitment question related to what they identified or wrote down: "Did I do less of or reduce a problematic behavior I want to let go of?"

Accept

Clients often ask us what to do about their painful private experiences. We believe this commitment question quickly cuts at the core of *what* to do. First, we ask a client to identify a painful private experience that they most wish to accept or make peace with. We like using the "make peace with" language because the word *accept* can be difficult for some clients, especially those with a history of being told to "get over" their experiences. Having established the specific private experiences to accept or make peace with, the commitment question asks: "Did I choose to accept or make peace with my painful experiences?"

Grow

Asking clients what behaviors they want to see grow in their lives to improve or maintain what is important to them seeks to identify the specific behaviors they could be or currently are doing to move toward their values. We feel including the word *maintain* is important because there may be invaluable behavioral repertoires that you and your client wish to reinforce and not take for granted or see extinguished. The commitment question for this category of behavior is focused on doing, what clients say or do: "Did I grow my life toward improving or maintaining who or what is important to me?"

Connect

Relationships are hard work but rarely is that caveat offered with sound advice. The "connect" category of behavior is about just that, the who and what our clients wish to forge new or deeper connections to. And once this has been established, the commitment question asks: "Did I forge a new or deeper connection to who and what are important to me?"

COMMITMENT IS ABOUT DOING

Our hope is that these commitment questions will have a clear utility. Remember, commitment is about the doing of behaviors. Even though the Life Map may list values in its bottom right quadrant with behaviors listed above them that move one toward those values, you can use these commitment questions to assist your clients in thinking about values in different ways. For example, a young woman married to an abusive spouse may wish to forge a deeper connection with her children and simultaneously experiences anxiety about the abuse she suffers from her husband. She reports shielding her children from the abuse by hiding it to the best of her ability. The therapist asks the commitment question, "What do you want to do to see your life grow toward your children?" The young woman reports wanting to leave her husband. Therapists skilled in domestic violence and intimate partner abuse know that this conversation can be a delicate one. ACT's ability to draw on this young woman's values to find strength is paramount to the approach. The therapist asks, "What gets in the way of you leaving him?" She responds by sharing her insecurities and self-stigmatization around "giving up." The therapist's analysis assumes nothing. This young woman may be staying because she's not willing to have the painful thoughts and feelings that arise in leaving her husband, or perhaps she has never given up on anyone before in her life; this may be a new repertoire of behavior, ending her relationship. The ACT therapist comments, "It sounds like insecurity and self-stigmatization controls the outcome of what you do next." The young woman agrees and speaks at length about how she wants to model the right kind of relationship for her children. The therapist then asks, "Are those insecurities and self-stigmatizing thoughts what you would choose to accept if it meant you were more easily able to choose what you do next?"

COMMITMENT QUESTIONS WORKSHEET

Facilitating behavior change is hard work. Remember, the temporary relief-seeking, away-moving behaviors that most of our clients present with work for them in the short-term, which is why they continue to do them. If their environment, the context they live in, was set up to create positive behavior change, they likely would have done it already. In fact, behavior change that moves clients toward their values may be hard, feel unpleasant, or seem downright impossible. Remember, they come to you with narrow, rigid repertoires of responding, and often times they have such a long reinforcement history of that aversive control that moving away from what they don't want to feel and their estimation of what is possible in their own lives have become limited. It is here that we hope you will use the commitment questions worksheet.

The engaging questions may seem like a simple venture into facilitating committed actions, but don't underestimate their relevance. The ACT approach is about broadening clients' behavioral repertoire (what they do) in the presence of aversive stimuli (typically their most painful private experiences). Through answering these questions, clients are learning to both come into contact with unpleasant private experiences and identify behaviors they can engage in even when that stuff shows up. The following tracking sheet can be used in conjunction with the commitment question worksheet to facilitate clients' scoring of their commitment questions daily.

You may wish to make your own tracking sheet, but we find the one on page 96 useful as a handout for clients scoring themselves over the course of a week. The commitment question tracking sheet is overlaid with the Life Map so clients can score their behaviors based on each commitment question category listed: connect, accept, let go, and grow. This tracking sheet makes easy work of keeping track of clients' progress weekly. If you see clients less frequently you can still use these tracking sheets, you may simply wish to send a client home with more tracking sheets. Alternatively, we have had some success in having clients track their scores by emailing them daily with the expectation that no intervention, feedback, or processing will occur until their next session in which we review their scores with them in session. In these instances, the daily tracking and emailing of scores is a way for the clients to increase accountability and keep themselves committed to the process.

POWERFUL QUESTIONS
TO CLARIFY THE LIFE YOU CHOOSE

Ask yourself: Are the answers you wrote important in your life? Will moving toward these help you to be the person you want to be?

LET GO

What are problematic behaviors I want to do less of or reduce in my life?

GROW

What behaviors do I want to see grow in my life to improve or maintain who and what is important to me?

ACCEPT

What painful experiences in my life do I choose to accept or make peace with?

CONNECT

Who or what in my life do I choose to forge a new or deeper connection to?

COMMITMENT QUESTIONS

Score your commitment questions for each category every day on your tracking sheet. Ask yourself each question and score each individually. Use the next worksheet to track your answers.

Did I do less of or reduce a problematic behavior I want to let go?

Did I grow my life toward improving or maintaining who or what is important to me?

Did I choose to accept or make peace with my painful experiences?

Did I forge a new or deeper connection to who and what is important to me?

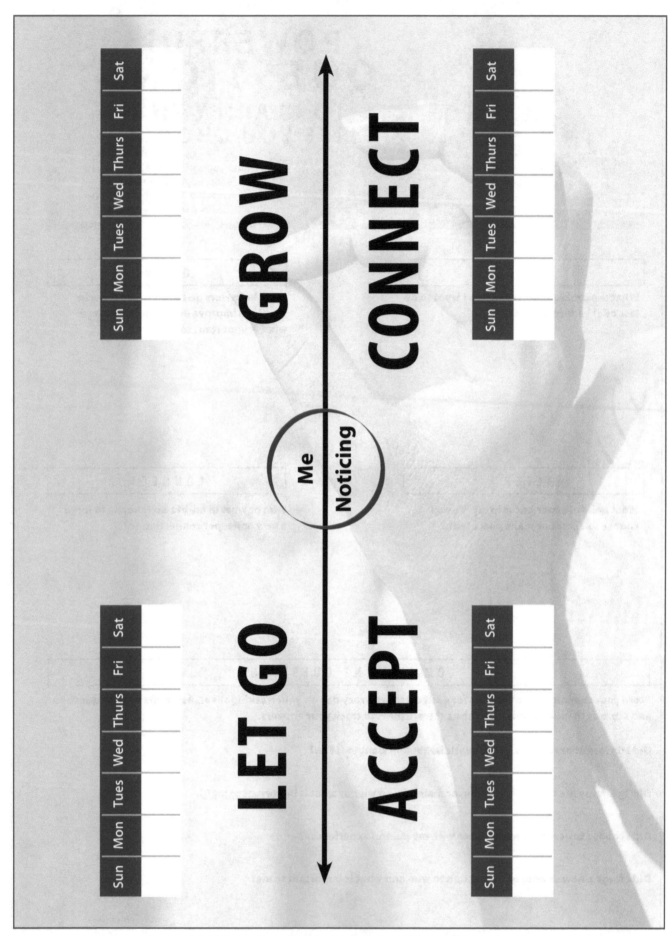

Sun	Mon	Tues	Wed	Thurs	Fri	Sat

GROW

Sun	Mon	Tues	Wed	Thurs	Fri	Sat

CONNECT

Me / Noticing

Sun	Mon	Tues	Wed	Thurs	Fri	Sat

LET GO

Sun	Mon	Tues	Wed	Thurs	Fri	Sat

ACCEPT

ENGAGED MINDFULNESS

One of the behaviors you may encourage your clients to engage in in their daily lives is a regular mindfulness practice. A helpful way to encourage clients to practice engaging their use of present-moment process in the world outside the therapy session is through a more active mindfulness practice that involves practical considerations in how one might plan to behave. In the following exercise, clients are able to expand their mindfulness practice to outside the therapy room broadening present-moment awareness as a skill that is initially modeled in therapy, but is used with everyday life. We offer two different scripts here for how you might present this idea to clients. First, a mindfulness of avoidance and committed action exercise invites clients to observe themselves reacting to their painful private experiences and then observe their experience of connecting and acting on their values. The second exercise, mindful walking, focuses on a daily task completely taken for granted and encourages training present-moment processes in a task as commonplace as walking. Both of these exercises are designed to be highly practical, engaging even the most skeptical of clients who may not see the utility of mindfulness of breath or other mindfulness exercises.

Two Ways of Being Mindful Exercise

A useful way of making contact with one's values without being as explicit as in earlier exercises while still drawing a distinction between two forms of behavior—a life spent governed by painful private experiences and one that is led by a connection to values—is achieved in this simple mindfulness exercise. It exposes two different ways of being in the world. The following script encourages clients to see themselves reacting to painful private experiences in one instance and picturing themselves acting on their values, living the qualities in their life that are important to them in the other.

We frequently end this exercise, coming to open eyes in a moment of silence in the room, by asking "What did you notice?" Oftentimes clients will comment on how good it felt to picture themselves being the person they want to be. We frequently prompt, "And what was it like being there and seeing yourself behaving that way?" Regardless of the answer, we seek to create a clear discrimination task here by asking, "And the other way of being, your reactive self, what was it like to picture yourself there behaving that way?" From these questions we are not seeking a right answer. Instead, the task draws on the powerful tools of perspective-taking (see Chapter 6) to create an on-the-spot taste test between behavior that is governed by painful privates experiences from a reactive standpoint and contrasting that behavior with a life organized by values and the qualities one most wishes to live in one's life. Each of those directions *feels* different. This exercise seeks to expose that difference while demonstrating what the experience of a life guided by values may be like.

TWO WAYS of BEING MINDFUL

Throughout this practice I'm going to guide you to bring your attention to different areas of your life. If you find yourself distracted, take a breath, notice your distractions, and come back to the instructions. Let's begin with our practice.

Breathing here, notice the sensations of breathing in your body. Notice how the belly expands on an inhale and collapses on an exhale.

Really stay with the movement of breath in your body. Inevitably distractions arise. Your job is not to avoid distractions but to notice them. You will have distractions. Take a breath on purpose when you notice distractions and come back to the movement of your breath.

I'd like to invite you to picture yourself interacting with someone who is important to you, maybe at work, school, volunteering, or at home. Imagine yourself there with whomever may be there and imagine you are being pushed around by your thoughts, some hooky thoughts that show up for you. Really see yourself hooked by your thoughts.

How do you react to them, how might you behave in those moments? What does the expression on your face look like? See yourself there with that look. What does the tone of your voice sound like? What does the posture of your body look like? Really see yourself in this reactive state of mind, reacting to your painful thoughts, feelings, sensations, or memories, and see how it impacts your behavior. Really picture yourself there. Take a breath and notice what it feels like to observe this version of you, to see your reactive, hooked self.

Let's go ahead and come back to the present moment. Breathe and let go of the image of your reactive self. Take a breath and notice the sensations of your breathing in your body.

I'm now going to invite you to picture yourself again interacting with someone who is important to you at work, school, volunteering, or home. But this time I'm going to invite you to imagine yourself connected with what is important to you in life, acting on those values and qualities that you want to be about. Really see yourself in that situation, living those qualities that matter most to you.

What does your face look like? What is the look in your eyes in that moment? What does the posture of your body look like? Really see yourself there and breathe it in. This version of yourself is deeply connected to these areas of your life that you wish to connect more deeply with and grow your behavior toward. What is it like here to observe this version of you?

Take a breath here and notice how that feels. Allow that image to pass as you come back to this present moment. Feel the sensations of the chair you're sitting on supporting your body. Notice the sensations of the breath. When you are ready, bring some motion into your body, whether it's a wiggle of the fingers, a rotation of the wrists, rolling the shoulders up forward and down, or gently bringing motion in the neck as you turn your head from side to side.

Mindful Walking

The following mindfulness script is a client favorite. It takes the present-moment processes of Chapter 6 and makes them applicable to the world outside the therapy office or a time where one might sit down and take time in a quiet space to practice mindfulness exercises (e.g., the body scan). The following exercise is about clients keeping their eyes open as they experiment with purposeful attention, noticing their experience as they engage with the world while walking.

MINFUL WALKING

As you begin to develop your mindfulness practice, you may notice yourself becoming narrow in your view of what mindfulness or present-moment awareness is—believing that it is always an eyes-closed exercise or done in a seated position in a quiet room. But mindfulness, being mindful or simply aware of the present moment, is an approach to engaging with the world and yourself, and as such has no limitations on how it can be done. So today, I invite you to join me for an alternative way of experiencing and expanding your mindfulness practice: mindful walking.

[For those who are unable to stand and move using a wheelchair or similar device, make sure to alter the language used when the exercise refers to standing or feeling their feet on the ground to instead focus on the different sensations of their bodies in their chair, focusing on areas of sensation, as they move forward.]

Begin in a standing upright position, if comfortable, bringing your shoulders up to your ears and then gently rolling them back and down. Notice your breath expanding your chest and belly with each inhale and releasing with each exhale. Before moving, simply notice your intention to walk mindfully, bringing full attention to the sensations of both your body and the world around you.

First, notice your feet in your shoes and the points where they touch the inside of your shoes. . . . Begin to walk at a slow, leisurely pace, feeling with each step your heel touching the ground first and then the rest of your foot rolling down into the floor, followed by the sensation of your heel lifting from the ground, leaving the pad of your foot and toes the last part touching the ground. . . . Pay attention to the places on the bottoms of your feet that touch the ground as you walk, not trying to change or alter your pace or step in any way.

Practice simply noticing your walk for a minute or two.

Turn your attention to the sensations against your skin: Is there a breeze or heat pulsing against you? Do you feel warm sunshine or cool breeze or wet rain? Notice the different sensations and temperatures. Do you feel a difference between exposed skin and skin hidden beneath clothing?

Practice simply feeling different sensations for a minute or two.

Next, look around you, noticing the colors, textures, and shapes you see. . . . Allow your eyes to linger on anything that interests you and then continue on to the next, constantly observing all the details of your environment. . . . If your mind begins to wander or chatter about what it sees, simply notice that and return your attention to the sights around you.

Practice simply seeing what is around you for a minute or two.

Now, allow your ears to open wide, picking up the sounds of your feet taking each step. . . . Notice the sounds nearby and those far away. . . . Can you hear the different volumes and tones in the sounds around you? Notice both the separate distinct sounds and how they all sound together.

Practice simply listening to what is around you for a minute or two.

Finally, bring all of these experiences together: your feet in your shoes taking each step, the sensations along your skin as you walk, the different sights around you, and all the sounds you hear both near and far away. . . . Notice too any thoughts or feelings that arise as you practice, acknowledging these as part of the experience of observing and turning your attention back to your walk. . . . When safe to do so bring your body to a stop, noticing how your body feels at rest, scanning the body down to your feet in your shoes. . . . Feel the pace of your breath flowing in and out . . . and notice your intention to pause your mindful walk.

Helping people connect with mindfulness practice as part of everyday life, as a behavior, can help transform the notion that mindfulness is an exercise for quiet rooms with eyes closed, sitting in stillness. Instead, we describe a broader viewpoint that mindfulness is one way to practice being present and engage with the world through all our senses. It is about taking it out of the therapy room and into the client's life outside of the time you spend together.

ACT WITH DEPRESSION

So far we have focused a lot on ACT's unique approach to the new ways one can interact with private behaviors because they tend to be the concepts that people are the least familiar with or that take the most time to settle in and shift perspective. But it is important to remember that at its core ACT is a behavioral approach. ACT is considered a radical behavioral approach because it views private events as behaviors, but we would be remiss if all we did was help you to understand the processes of private events. Outside ourselves, there is a whole world to engage, often a large world that our clients have been actively trying to avoid. The whole reason we train clients to be open to all their private experiences, to become aware of how they interact with those private experiences, and to identify unworkable patterns of behavior is so that clients can begin to slow down and notice how their behavior functions in a given context and then choose how they want to behave based on their values. We are working toward helping clients engage in a life meaningful to them.

Take, for example, a client struggling with depression who isolates, sleeps all day, is largely apathetic toward life or any activities they once enjoyed, and has a lot of stories about how "things will never get better" and "there's no point in trying." Across many theoretical orientations, therapists, for various reasons consistent with their approach, encourage clients to begin to reconnect with the world and the people in their life, otherwise known as behavioral activation. Some may even use the phrase "follow your feet" to emphasize that rather than waiting for emotions or thoughts or a particular situation to change before they begin engaging in the world, clients should start doing those things first. You could even phrase it as "follow your feels," the idea of engaging in the world based on what is important to them, meaningful to them, evokes any level of excitement even if it's not at the same level as it has been in the past.

Working with private events can provide strategies for clients to use when their minds get really loud as they start to do things that matter to them with the understanding that as functional contextualists, we are working toward a picture of functional living. Going back to the example of the client with depression, our outcomes are not a decrease in a depression score or a self-reported improvement in mood; our outcomes are functional, observable behaviors that a client identifies for themself as what their life would look like if they are living according to their values. That can be different for each client. Two clients with the same depression presentation may have different behavioral outcomes they are working toward: one may want to reconnect with family and friends, and begin to set goals related to social interaction via texting, calling, or meeting in person people who are important to them, while the other may want to connect with the activities they formerly enjoyed and so they set an intention to ride their bike at the park once a week or take an art class at a community center or enroll in open mic night at a local bar.

The point is that both are creating goals and acting on those behaviors that function toward living consistently with their chosen values. Taking time at the beginning of therapy to identify what clients' lives would look like if they were living according to their values is a helpful way to identify specific behaviors to target. Clients may initially fall into an eliminative agenda and begin to talk about their wonderful future selves free of unpleasant feelings and their minds empty of painful thoughts. One way to redirect toward observable behaviors is to ask them, "If I could see you living a meaningful life, if I could somehow watch you as if I were watching a movie (in a noncreepy way), what would I see you do? Who would you be interacting with? Where would you go?"

A word of caution: It is important to pay attention to the function of behaviors within the therapy room as well. Many times, focusing on private events and developing flexibility around how clients interact with their minds are completely functional and appropriate goals. However, at other times, continuing to focus on private events can be a form of experiential avoidance. Have you ever worked with a client who spent so much time preparing for how to handle a particular situation that they never actually put themselves in that situation because they did not feel "ready"? Or a client who spent a considerable amount of time planning for Plan B that they never follow through with Plan A? These examples indicate how the therapy room can be another context in which clients contribute to their own avoidance behaviors. As therapists it can be easy to get caught up in the content of the session, the painful stories our clients have, the difficulties they've overcome, and the resulting painful thoughts, memories, sensations, and feelings they're left with. It can also be easy in those moments to inadvertently reinforce a client's avoidance without realizing it, because if we only listen to the content of the dialogue, it may appear that we are working on important issues. If we take a step back, however to pause and notice the function of the behaviors, we may see a different pattern form.

For that reason, it is important to incorporate specific, measurable outcomes as process measures from session to session and a way to determine when clients have met their functional goal set at the beginning of therapy. Throughout this chapter we provided examples of how to help clients connect with or clarify their values. As we mentioned earlier, bringing values conversations into the earlier sessions can be an important aspect of treatment planning and deciding what outcomes we are aiming for. When you get to the place where a client has clear, consistent values they identify as important to them and what they want to work toward, the next step is to develop specific observable behaviors that are in line with those values. We may say something to a client, such as "If we think of our lives as a journey where our values are the direction we are headed, we can begin to imagine ourselves on a long stretch of road heading north with mile markers along the way. Our values are a direction and can never be completed or reached or checked off as done. Instead they are a process of moving forward. The behaviors we do along the way, along that journey, that are consistent with our values can be checked off or met; they are the mile markers along the way." This simple yet effective way differentiates values from committed actions. Values are the direction while committed actions are the mile markers or landmarks or rest stops we pass on the journey.

Continuing with that metaphor, sometimes our clients aren't even facing north. Sometimes they are turned around and speeding south, so working on what the next mile marker is may not be workable. Sometimes our work involves turning around and heading back north, and that can be a process in itself. Usually the easier way to turn ourselves around is not to spin quickly and start rushing in another direction at the same pace as we were heading south. We first need to recognize that we're headed in the wrong direction, stopping to take a look around and find out where we want to turn, and then taking a few steps of approximation to slowly turn ourselves toward the direction we want to be headed. Understanding where our clients are in this process is important; it can help influence which processes we begin to focus on to build up enough skills or create a different perspective or develop flexibility around alternative options of engaging with our minds and with the world. We want to meet clients where they are and build from there. They are the only ones who understand their journey and their direction, and through analyzing the function of their behaviors using the Life Map and with your guidance, they can begin to turn around or start moving forward.

Wherever clients are on their journey developing the ability to set specific observable goals is necessary in order to measure progress. In this case, we are not reinventing the wheel. Simple behavioral strategies, such as behavioral activation and goal setting that you may already be familiar with can be the best approach. The first question in developing any goal is to ask your client, "What value is guiding this goal?" It can be easy for clients to get distracted by many different activities or actions they want to do, so taking time to clarify what the value is first can ensure that the goal is taking them in a valued direction rather than to another avoidance strategy. Also, if clients have large or complex goals, it can be helpful to break down the goals into small pieces: "If you were to work toward this goal, what would be the first step or action you would need to do?" For clients with depression, the first steps to going back to work may be getting out of bed, showering, and putting on clean clothes. These initial steps can sometimes seem demoralizing to clients because it reminds them just how far away their goal is, but it is important to recognize and reinforce that these are steps toward the life that they want to live and a necessary part of their journey. Reinforcing clients for any behavior change, even if it is simply doing less of an avoidance behavior, is necessary for continued progress. And reminding yourself and your clients that as long as they continue to take these steps forward, they will reach their goal, can help keep them moving forward when the journey seems too long.

SMART GOALS WORKSHEET

You may already have worksheets or homework assignments that you use, but we have provided two of our favorites here because we find them to be the most helpful and hope they may be of use to you. The first is a "SMART Goals" worksheet that helps clients set specific, measurable, attainable, relevant, and time-bound goals. This worksheet can be helpful if a client has a vague or broad goal that they need to refine into an actionable task. Creating the context for slowing down and working out steps to a desired goal will increase the likelihood that the person completes the goal as they know what completing the goal will look like—it is specific and measurable.

S M A R T GOALS

Living a values-driven life involves getting out of your head and stepping in to the world. What will your next step be?

1. SPECIFIC

Write down your goal. Remember this is a behavior you want to begin doing — make it as specific and detailed as possible.

What steps will you take to help you reach your goals?

2. MEASURABLE

How will you track this goal? How will you know when the goal is met?

3. ATTAINABLE

Is this goal possible? Do you have all of the skills and resources to complete this goal? If not, how can you get them? Who can help?

4. RELEVANT

What value is this goal connected to? Why does this matter to you? Will this take you toward the life you want to live?

5. TIME BOUND

Set a due date and once you reach it, pause to review. Did you meet your due date? If yes, what is your next goal? If not, examine SMART goal steps to see where modifications need to be made. If you felt stuck, fill out a Life Map. And REPEAT!

I will reach my goal by:

Note that we do not assume in ACT that committed actions will by default be reinforcing to a client. We understand that patterns of avoidance, escape, and control are most likely reinforced in our clients' repertoire, exposing problematic patterns of behaving. For some clients, coming in contact with long-term distal reinforcers such as values might seem abstract and not at all rewarding at first. It is with this knowledge that we created a further adaptation of behavioral activation tools.

PURPOSEFUL STEPS WORKSHEET

The second worksheet is similar to the "SMART Goals" worksheet but it does have some specific differences. The "Purposeful STEPS" worksheet uses a STEPS acronym that mirrors the idea of clients taking steps toward the life they want to live. Like SMART goals, it contains an emphasis on specific, observable, measurable goals, but the worksheet also cues the client to identify the value underlying goals at the top of the worksheet. The last action in the acronym is to identify potential barriers, both private and observable, that may get in the way of their goal, prompting clients to come up with solutions in an effort to prepare for perceived barriers and avoid setbacks. With any behavior change, we want clients to meet initial success and find the idea of working toward their values rewarding, rather than punishing. By spending time to ensure the committed action is connected to one of their values and to anticipate any setbacks, we are increasing the probability of a successful first step.

PURPOSEFUL STEPS

Living a values-driven life involves getting out of your head and stepping in to the world. What will your next step be?

MY VALUE IS:

1. SPECIFIC

Write down your goal. Remember this is a behavior you want to begin doing — make it as specific and detailed as possible.

What steps will you take to help you reach your goal?

2. TRACKING

How will you track this goal? How will you know when the goal is met?

3. END DATE

Set an end date and once you reach it, pause to review. Did you meet your end date? If yes, what is your next goal? If not, examine your STEPS to see where modifications need to be made. If you felt stuck, fill out a Life Map. And REPEAT!

I will reach my goal by:

4. POSSIBLE

Is this goal possible? Do you have all of the skills and resources to complete this goal? If not, how can you get them? Who can help?

5. SETBACKS

What barriers, both private and observable, could potentially arise that would get in the way of you reaching your goal? What can you do to prevent setbacks?

We hope that these worksheets help your clients connect with the steps they need to take to move in the direction of valued living. We also hope they provide a clear understanding of when that next step is met.

Even though this book has primarily focused on ACT as an approach with an individual, we wanted to give you a taste of what an ACT approach looks like outside of the typical individual adult client. You got a taste of that in Chapter 3 with Life Map in groups. Now, in the rest of this chapter and the entire next chapter we will expand that understanding to ACT with Couples, ACT with Children and Adolescents, and Training Parents. It is our hope that at the end of this book you feel comfortable with the processes of ACT and the foundational skills and theory and are able to apply it to any population you encounter as you continue to be flexible and open no matter the context.

ACT WITH COUPLES

Integrating the ACT approach to work with couples is easy. As a note, we will discuss ACT with couples as a way of working with two people in an exclusive romantic relationship, although we have experience using ACT with nonmonogamous couples and have found it effective as well. We do however wish to give you a caveat: The evidence for ACT with couples specifically needs to be developed. At the time of writing this book, few published studies are available and those that are published have small sample sizes demonstrating the effectiveness of ACT with couples. We've placed this section, "ACT with Couples" at the end of the "engaged" chapter because in our experience, the same open, aware, and engaged processes we described in Chapters 5 and 6 are done individually with each member of the couple. The same work presented in those earlier chapters will be used with each person in the couple you're working with as a way to identify what each person in the couple brings into the relationship and what values and private experiences are driving their behavior. Simply said, a couple presents as two individuals in a relationship and each person in that relationship may need to do their own work on acceptance, defusion, contacting the present moment, seeing themselves as the context of their experience, and engaging with their values in sessions together as a couple.

We will give you an example of what it means to be working with couples from the functional perspective of individuals in a relationship together, each with painful private experiences and problematic behaviors. Generally, couples present with an issue in their relationship and through looking at the relationship problems that each partner encounters, the therapist surmises that one person is fused with thoughts about their partner and that fusion has severe consequences, the fusion gets them hooked, and the consequence of this hook is behavior that is incongruent with the partner they want to be. In an ACT session with a couple, we focus on that one partner for the moment and assist that individual in doing something in session that might be helpful, perhaps defusion in a way that promotes noticing their private experiences. We then inquire how that thought, feeling, sensation, or memory impacts their behavior and with respect ask, "Is that what the partner you want to be would do?" If the answer is no, we often respond with "We have a name for that in the biz, we call it a hook!" We then, in session with that individual and their partner present and privy to the intervention, conduct an abbreviated hooks exercise (see Chapter 6 for the hooks exercise and worksheet). We may also use the opportunity for the other partner to recognize or become aware of how their own behavior—the things they do and say—impact their partner.

From this perspective of looking at what triggers behavior and what follows, we transition into a conversation in session demonstrating how one partner's behavior can trigger a hook in the other and when that partner bites the hook that just showed up for themselves, it has deleterious effects on the relationship, oftentimes resulting in a vicious cycle of avoidance, escape, and control. We especially see these patterns in couples with reactive behaviors such as yelling obscenities or becoming physically abusive. **In a relationship, both partners bring with them their own hooks.** Working to identify what triggers problematic behavior, how unworkable patterns of interacting are maintained, and what the individuals' and couple's values are will help the therapist develop a functional analysis of their relationship.

Beginning ACT with Couples

When a couple begins therapy, we will often start this session the same way we would an individual session, instructing couples about the limits to confidentiality and having them sign the necessary paperwork before telling them, "I know the two of you have come here for a specific reason in working with me but before we talk about the issues you're struggling with in your relationship, I'd love to get to know the two of you outside of what's going wrong first." Couples have always agreed with this stance and we move forward by asking, "Could each of you tell me what you admire about your partner and what's important to you about being in this relationship?" There are typically engrossed answers from each: if not, that is okay. This question is an early attempt to draw on each partner's values, a way of practicing tight stimulus control in the session, setting the context of therapy to connect around who and what are important, not as the environment to unload about relationship issues or air grievances about the misdeeds of one's partner.

Working Together Worksheet for Couples

We include a worksheet here that we find useful to assist couples in conceptualizing their own role in what is happening within their relationship before we plan the next steps. The worksheet explains that each partner fills out the first section independently, meaning they focus on their own private experience and behaviors. Beginning with "why we matter," the worksheet cuts right to each person's values in the relationship: what it is about the relationship and partner that matters to each person. The second section is completed collaboratively by couples. Using this worksheet in session often lightens the conversation about their behaviors and creates a collaborative environment in which one partner can encourage the other. Furthermore, it encourages couples to broaden their behavioral repertoire together, with one another and in the presence of their own painful private experiences.

WORKING TOGETHER

Start by writing your individual answers to the first section and use that information to create your answers to the second section where you'll plan what to do next.

1. SEPARATELY, EACH PARTNER WRITES

| WHY WE MATTER | WHY WE MATTER |

| WHAT HOOKS ME | WHAT HOOKS ME |

2. TOGETHER, WITH YOUR PARTNER PLAN

What do we want to be doing together to move us toward what matters as a couple? What can we do to support one another when we get hooked? What could each partner do for the other to support them when they're hooked?

Life Mapping Relationships

We have had great success using the Life Map (see Chapter 3) with couples. We demonstrate in this section how we have worked the Life Map into sessions with couples flexibly and creatively, but again we wish to encourage you to not follow it as a step-by-step guide. Instead, bring your own self to ACT, using your own creativity to do this process-based work.

One way we facilitate early discussions with couples about the function of their behavior is by completing one Life Map for both partners, where we depict both of their behaviors and experiences on the same page or whiteboard, often using different colors for each partner to represent individual experience and behavior. The Life Map then becomes a metaphor for all experiences and behaviors that happen in the context of the relationship. In the following therapist and couple dialogue, we demonstrate a creative way of working with the Life Map that deviates from the orderliness of Chapter 3's Life Map.

Therapist: What is important to each of you about being here?

Paul: Maddie is important to me. She's my best friend and I want to get past what's happened.

Therapist: Would it be okay if I kept track of what you're saying with a tool we use called the Life Map?

Paul and Maddie: Sure.

Therapist: Great. A lot of people find it really helpful and I myself find it useful to keep track of what we're talking about as well. I'm going to write down here that Maddie is important to you. [Draws a line horizontally across a page and writes "Maddie" in the bottom right quadrant.] What about Maddie is important to you?

Paul: What do you mean?

Therapist: Well, you said Maddie matters and I'm noticing that it takes a lot of courage to bring yourself into a session with a stranger and talk about your relationship, so I'm wondering what is it that's important to you about getting past what has happened?

Paul: Getting past it. I just can't. It keeps coming back.

Therapist: Okay. [Writes "getting past it" in the bottom right quadrant.] And what is getting past this about for you? What does it move you closer to in your relationship?

Paul: Having trust. I want to be trusting of Maddie.

Therapist: Okay perfect, trusting. [Writes "trusting" in the bottom right quadrant.] And Maddie, what is important to you about being here?

Maddie: I'm really glad Paul is here. Trust is important to me too but just being a better partner, someone Paul wants to be with.

Therapist: Can I write Paul because he's important to you?

Maddie: Yes, of course.

Therapist: [Writes "Paul" in the bottom right quadrant.] And what can I write to capture the type of relationship you want with Paul?

Maddie: Well, trusting also, but love, happiness, excitement!

Therapist: Perfect. [Writes "love, happiness, and excitement" in the bottom right quadrant.] What are the two of you already doing that move you in this direction?

Maddie: We spend time together with each other's friends.

Paul: Hiking and day trips, we do a lot of those things together.

Therapist: [Writes "spend time with each other's friends, hiking, day trips" in the top right quadrant.] That's great! Inevitably there's going to be thoughts and feelings that get in the way of you two being able to move toward what's important to you in your relationship. What are some of those thoughts and feelings that show up?

Paul: Well, obviously thoughts of her cheating on me with this other guy.

Therapist: And that's the core issue you were saying that has brought you to work with me.

Paul: Yes. Like if she's on her phone, I can't help but think she's talking to someone else. She could be shopping, playing a game, I don't know but I don't trust her.

Therapist: Hang on, what does that feel like?

Paul: Suspicion. [Looks at Maddie.] I don't want to feel this way, I'm sorry but I don't trust you.

Therapist: Okay. What thoughts and feelings show up as you see Maddie on her phone?

Paul: I don't want it to be, but suspicion.

Therapist: Suspicion. [Writes "suspicion" in the bottom left quadrant.] What sensations show up in your body when suspicion shows up for you?

Paul: My heart races, my chest is tight, and my face gets hot. I feel like I'm on alert and have to constantly watch out for danger.

Therapist: It's like being on alert and having to constantly watch out for danger. [Writes "heart racing, being on alert, watch out for danger" in bottom left quadrant.] Got it. And if I was there with you when you see Maddie on her phone and all of these painful thoughts and feelings show up for you, what would I see you do next?

Paul: [Looks away and grabs his own hair.]

Maddie: He blows up.

Paul: I don't blow up.

Therapist: Hang on, hang on. Maddie says you blow up, and Paul you don't agree with that, but if I was there, what would I actually see you do, Paul, or hear you say?

Maddie: It's an interrogation.

Paul: Yes, I get mean. I get mean and defensive. I ask Maddie a lot of questions about who she's talking to or what she's doing.

Therapist: Okay, thank you. That's helpful for me to better understand the things you do in that moment. [Writes "blow up, get mean and defensive" in the top left quadrant.] So, Paul's saying "suspicion, a feeling like being on alert, blowing up, get mean and defensive" is what happens for him. In that moment what shows up for you?

Maddie: I just feel really defensive too. I think the biggest part of why we are here is because we go over and over what I have done. I am sorry. I've told him a thousand times I'm sorry. [Sighs.]

Therapist: So, is that what you do next? You apologize?

Maddie: Oh yes. I just shut down and won't even look at him. I'm in this horrible mindset.

Therapist: And what do I see you do?

Maddie: I won't look at him. I look away and am quiet, then apologize later.

Therapist: It sounds like a vicious cycle between the two of you. [Draws semi-circles from painful private experiences in the bottom left quadrant to the top right quadrant and from that same behavior in the top left quadrant to a private experience in the bottom left, repeating.] Paul sees you on your phone and gets reactive; you pick up on his attitude and you get defensive and shut down, try to defend yourself. Do you see this cycle going on here?

Maddie: Yes, I defend myself and we have a huge fight, or I defend myself and we're miserable for the rest of the night.

Therapist: So this cycle keeps going?

Paul and Maddie: Yes.

Therapist: Could we take this a step further?

Paul and Maddie: Yes.

Therapist: The huge fight that you say could emerge from this cycle, do any of these behaviors, the blowing up, shutting down, fighting your most painful feelings, thoughts, and memories help in your relationship?

Paul: Well, the fight exhausts me, and I just think it's not worth it, so I give in.

Therapist: Okay, so at a certain point you get run down by the fight. That helps in the short-term?

Maddie: Well, yes, because we stop fighting, and after a few days we go back to talking.

Paul: And that'll last a week before we're back at it again.

Therapist: Okay, so it could last for days?

Maddie: Maybe a week at the most.

Therapist: So even a week sounds short to me before you're back into this cycle that sounds painful. Am I right?

Paul: Yes.

Maddie: This needs to change.

Therapist: If the two of you weren't so busy getting stuck in this cycle, what would you be doing together?

Maddie: Ugh, remember when we used to have fun?

Paul: [Laughs.] That seems like a long time ago.

Maddie: If this just didn't happen, things would be so much better. We'd be so much better.

Paul: [Looks down.]

Therapist: Maddie, is it all right if I called you on something?

Maddie: Uh, yes. Go right ahead.

Therapist: Am I right in hearing you just put a kind of condition on your relationship, saying you'd have the relationship you want if this wasn't happening?

Maddie: [Looks at Paul.] Well, it's true, isn't it?

Therapist: Slow down with me for a moment. Let's catch what just happened there, because this is how our minds work. The argument is now that this has happened, the relationship you want is no longer accessible to you.

Maddie: Mmhmm. [Nods in agreement.]

Therapist: Could we try to do something different with your pain here? What I mean by that is not being ruled by your most painful thoughts in these situations but instead allowing yourselves enough distance from this history you're both battling with and learning a new way to work with it. Not to put a condition on your relationship [points to the bottom left quadrant of the Life Map].

Paul: I do! I feel like I'm not allowed to be upset. I want to do positive things and have fun with you, Maddie. I just also want to still be allowed to be upset without you shutting down and me feeling like I'm supposed to just ignore everything.

Therapist: That's incredible, Paul. What might it look like if you were able to express being upset and share how you're feeling in a way that embodies these qualities of trusting and getting past this, like you told me earlier?

Paul: I'd actually tell Maddie I'm upset.

Therapist: Okay, and that's a different behavior from when you get suspicious and blow up?

Paul: It's completely different.

Therapist: And what might that feel like?

Paul: [Sighs.] Just easier. Not like I'm desperately trying to fight for Maddie.

Therapist: And Maddie, in that moment where Paul is sharing something tender from his heart. How do you want to respond?

Maddie: [Looks at Paul.] I would love to hold you and tell you I'm sorry without you saying, "What are you doing? Who are you talking to?"

Therapist: Hold on, let's go slow here. You want to hold Paul.

Maddie: [Tearfully.] Yes.

Therapist: And what's that like to take that in right now. To see yourself there as Paul is sharing this painful stuff: He's not trying to choke it down or blow up, no interrogation, he's sharing something tender and you reach out to hold him. What is that like?

Maddie: [Smiles.] Good.

Paul: Really good. That's what I want.

Therapist: I get that. In fact, I feel really positive picturing the two of you in that space. Here's the thing, and this is why I like to write all of this down on this Life Map. [Draws a circle in the center and writes Paul & Maddie Noticing.] This map is all about your relationship. It shows the pain you struggle with and the things you want your relationship to be about. We can't cut off this painful half of the map, it's a part of your experience and history. What I'm hoping to show you is a way of noticing what you're feeling, thinking, and remembering so that you can choose what you do next that works for you.

Although we demonstrate using the Life Map in the preceding dialogue, you could just as easily leave the Life Map out and simply point out the relevant information, the stimulus events that you hear are significant and reflect that back in session, asking your clients if what stands out to you is accurate for them in their experience. We like the Life Map or other ways of visually representing this information because it allows a reference point to return to and to keep track of clinically relevant content in sessions, the target thoughts, feelings, sensations, memories, qualities, and values that are unique to each of your clients.

Conclusions on ACT with Couples and Additional Learning

The most significant clinical insight we can offer in applying ACT to couples from our years of practicing ACT with them is that understanding their values, why they want to be in a relationship, and building the behaviors couples do together, to connect with one another, to move toward the type of relationship they want to have together is important. When working with couples, we touch on patterns of problematic experiential avoidance behavior in the individual; we analyze the vicious cycles that they can get stuck in, but we focus on their values and how to engage them in growing their behaviors toward the type of relationship they most wish to have. We also look at the ways in which each individual can support their partner in doing so as well.

If you have an interest in furthering your reading or training in evidence-based approaches to therapy with couples, we recommend Integrative Behavioral Couple Therapy (IBCT) pioneered by Andrew Christensen and the late Neil S. Jacobson (Jacobson & Christensen, 1996). IBCT combines acceptance and change processes with a behavioral focus that is contextually based, therefore confluent with ACT.

Chapter 8

ACT with Children and Adolescents

As we have emphasized throughout this book, ACT is not merely a therapy encompassing only methods and techniques. Rather ACT is a science based on functional contextualism with an active experimental research program (relational frame theory) that has many useful applications to human development that can in turn be used to create powerful clinical interventions with young people (Coyne, McHugh, & Martinez, 2011; Epkins, 2016). When we reference development, we are specifically referring to how humans grow and learn. From our contextual behavioral science view of the world, development includes the origins of language and fusion, and it includes how children learn and what they learn, whether it's what to fear, how to play, communicate, and create, or the strategies they develop in reaction to painful experiences. Relational frame theory understands language and thinking to be a behavior: something someone does. And it is from this viewpoint that we seek to increase flexibility in young people's private and public behavior, to increase their psychological flexibility.

Let's begin to examine this approach through the developmental lens of a 4-year-old's experience with their world. Around 4 years old, children have an egocentric view of the world, observing antecedents and behaviors and deriving relationships. They often engage in idiosyncratic magical thinking between behaviors or objects and take the world and their experiences as literal. This of course is helpful and has numerous benefits for children exploring the world and learning new ways to interact with people and objects in varying situations. This literality though can also be problematic and lead to suffering based on the context.

From an ACT perspective, the treatment of children involves meeting them where they are developmentally. We cannot begin to help children if we focus on ways of relating to the world and their own experience that they are developmentally unable to do. Their developmental level may pose a number of significant barriers in traditional psychotherapy approaches to the treatment of young people as therapists may get stuck in a child's inability to engage in a complex task such as making sense out of the death of a parent, learning how to integrate painful private experiences from fears or trauma memories into their lives, and working with the painful sensations that arise as a part of a physical rehabilitation or recovery from a surgery or physical trauma. In adapting ACT as an approach to practices with young people, these barriers become workable by using a scientific lens to assess for deficits in perspective-taking, the ability to differentiate between private and public behaviors, or other cognitive operations we may take for granted as adults. And beyond mere assessment of deficits, we can use this scientific understanding to develop interventions that train the appropriate skills and abilities in young people so that we as therapists can be more effective in our work to alleviate suffering.

ATTACHMENT SCIENCE

Attachment science is a behavioral system that works well with ACT's functional contextualist view of the world and is confluent with modern evolutionary science. If you work with young people, particularly children, having an understanding of attachment theory gives insight into the reinforcement of problematic behaviors in young people, specifically, why is this behavior persisting? Attachment science has assumptions that are important to understand: children are motivated to maintain closeness with their attachment figures (typically biological parents, but can include anyone in the role of primary caregiver); children will change their behavior to adapt to their attachment figures and develop patterns of behavior and affect regulation that get their needs met (Slade, 2000).

The assumptions of attachment science have a significant bearing on how we understand problems that occur between primary caregivers and children, and help to promote a functional way of viewing patterns of behavior. For example, we can assume that if children are motivated to maintain proximity to their caregivers for survival and if a caregiver is frightening, traumatizing, or abusive, children will develop patterns of behaving that may function in the short-term but prove unworkable in the long-term or in other contexts. These assumptions and their outcomes are confluent with ACT's functional contextual view of the world, viewing attachment as a class of behavior with operant functions—understanding this pattern of behavior to be a learning history that is reinforced by some interaction with the parent. This interaction is likely negative reinforcement, where a child was able to escape harm by regulating their emotions or learning operantly that their needs would not be met, and therefore their behavior was shaped to meet their needs in alternative ways.

Viewing behaviors through this lens, similar to an adult with a substance use disorder who continues to engage in behaviors that topographically seem like a bad idea (e.g., drinking at the expense of health or family or career) helps us to take a step back from the "this is a problematic, trouble-making child" to an approach of compassion in which we realize that these behaviors, however extreme, serve a valuable function to that child. Attachment science demonstrates how these patterns of behaving over time turn into attachment styles that predict patterns of behaving that generalize to relationships other than that of the primary caregiver, especially relationships with romantic partners later in life and parenting behaviors with one's own children (Ainsworth, Bell, & Stayton, 1971; 1974).

For ACT therapists, the implications for shaping a young person's behavior in attachment relationships are many. First, using a relational frame theory account of expanding relational networks, not eliminating them, we posit that attachment histories cannot be erased. Therefore, new learning opportunities should be offered to young people to assist in the healing of attachment problems. This could be achieved by way of therapeutic interactions, caregiver involvement in therapeutic sessions, and training caregivers to bring the therapeutic skills home to use with the young people in their lives who are suffering. And for those of us who do not work with children, know that understanding attachment science can help us identify patterns of behaving in adults, particularly in romantic relationships, and develop interventions that help that person discriminate between learned patterns of behavior that may have functioned as a young person, but that are not helping them work toward being the partner they want to be here-now.

ASSESSING CHILDREN AND ADOLESCENTS WITH ACT

Before we jump into treatment, we must first assess the needs of young clients, their patterns of behavior and what is maintaining them, and the context in which these behaviors occur. It is helpful to begin your assessment by collecting collateral information about the young client's context: their physical environment, social context, and any relevant history. We recommend meeting with primary caregivers first and asking what are their theories about what is happening with this young person. Furthermore, meeting first with caregivers provides an opportunity to socialize them to the treatment justification for ACT and set the expectation that therapy with you is about a noneliminative agenda. We do this through using the same informed consent as we described in Chapter 1; we encourage a broadening of behavioral repertoires while in contact with painful private experiences.

Assess the Function of Behavior

In our experience with primary caregivers, schools, group homes, and other institutions involved in the welfare of young people, they primarily report problematic behaviors (the topography, what the behavior looks like) with little insight into how the behavior works and what maintains it (its function). This is okay. It's a teaching opportunity for you as a professional now aware how behaviors work in a given situation (functional contextualism) to educate the adults involved in the welfare of a young person you are working with why we focus on the function of behavior and how we work to broaden repertoires of behavior through positive reinforcement. This can help get buy-in early so that when or if you involve the caregivers in reinforcing certain behaviors that they understand the function. You may also wish to employ exploratory questions to uncover functionally relevant events caregivers, teachers, and others may be privy to, specifically the antecedents of problematic behaviors (what happens before the behavior and what historically has happened to trigger this behavior) as well as the consequences of the behavior (what happens as a result of the behavior). Please do not underestimate the relevance of doing so. Far too often the contingencies at play that maintain a young person's behavior are lost in the minutiae of caregiving. Consider the following example.

During a consultation visit to a group home, the staff reported having difficulty in managing a young girl who was engaging in a number of sexually promiscuous behaviors. The young girl was not assaulting the staff or other children in the home but was streaking nude, dancing promiscuously around a shared bedroom nude, and putting on informal strip shows. The staff talked about having a difficult time with the sexual nature of the girl's acting out and inferred potentially frightening sources for this learned behavior, including the girl being sexualized from a younger age by sexually abusive primary caregivers.

It's important to note that while I would later go on to work with the girl individually and help her process her trauma history and focus on regulating her emotions, my first objective was to collect information from staff and respond to the initial issue raised: her acting out behavior in the group home. I did this through asking the group home staff what would happen before these acting out events as well as consequences afterwards. Although no pattern appeared to precede these behaviors, there was a pattern to the consequences: The group home staff would chase her if necessary and remove the other children from the area by having them go to their rooms or to a shared common space in the home. Next, they would remain calm and stop her from streaking or stop her from removing her clothes and have her put clothing back on using a team effort with multiple staff present due to the potentially litigious nature of intervening with a young girl who appears to be hypersexualized. When asked what happens next, the staff reported that they would deescalate the situation verbally, reestablish connection, and redirect her behavior.

While topographically this response seemed appropriate and helpful, when prodded for what redirecting her behavior was in response to the staff were unable to identify what triggered the response; the group home staff would simply have this girl now do something else without an awareness for what triggered the acting out. Through looking at this behavior from a functional contextual viewpoint, I imagined that the antecedent event that triggers the streaking may have originally been apropos of who knows what, however, when it was met with a team approach (which rarely happens in group homes) and therefore lots of staff spending time directly with this young girl, interacting with her, and paying specific attention to her without other children around, I wondered if that attention and individual time was reinforcing for her. Adding to this analysis was the fact that the girl seemed to like the staff quite a lot, enjoyed these interactions following the problematic behavior, and staff members were courteous and professional, kind even.

When presenting this analysis to the staff they looked astonished as they believed they had been acting to reduce her problematic behavior when in fact they seemed to be reinforcing it through individualized attention. Working with the staff, I suggested they modify their behavior to not inadvertently reinforce this young girl's acting out behavior; I encouraged them to intervene as they always have by removing the other children as per their policy, but once the young girl is dressed instead of reinforcing with attention, they simply ignore the behavior and not spend time with the young girl. Following this advice, each shift stopped reinforcing with attention and the young girl's behavior quickly changed, the streaking and sexually promiscuous behavior reduced to, in their words, "almost never."

This example shows how seeking out the specific antecedent and consequence events can be fruitful early in your analysis of problematic behaviors. This example is not meant to make a cartoon of the situation or paint a caricature of group home staff as unaware or uneducated in any way, but rather to demonstrate how the focus of our analysis is on how a behavior works in a given situation, which in this case, suggested that the young girl continued her acting out behavior because it was being reinforced somehow or by something. Uncovering what was potentially reinforcing about the situation to the young girl gave way to a workable strategy whereby the staff could adjust their behavior in a way that was consistent with their protocol, but was not as reinforcing. It could have also been the case that the staff behavior was not what was reinforcing the behavior and the intervention might have not worked to reduce her behavior. That is why it is important to follow through with any behavioral changes because we can only know whether our analysis is correct if the resulting behavioral change actually affects the consequence or outcome. In some cases we can spend considerable energy seeking out what antecedent events triggered acting-out behaviors or searching for alternative behaviors that were reinforcing.

Assess Children and Adolescents' Ability to Identify Private Experiences

Information collection and functional analysis aside, your first interaction with a young client may include a developmentally relevant assessment. As part of that you may wish to know whether the young person you are working with has the ability to tact to private experiences. Said simply, can this young client identify private experiences and label them: "I feel sad" or "My tummy is grumbling, I'm hungry." *Tact* is a scientific term from Skinner's 1957 book *Verbal Behavior* (for more about language and cognition see Chapter 1). We find this assessment essential to moving forward and is an early determinant of what we do next after information collection: Do we need to train this young person to tact to their private experiences? If so, can they identify the clinically relevant content that we wish to target in sessions? If yes, then we begin with training them on more advanced discrimination tasks: noticing. If not, we engage in training exercises to teach children how to effectively tact to their private experiences. Again, we want to make sure to meet the child where they are. Please note that if you're working with young people who are struggling with developmental disabilities or are diagnosed on the autism spectrum, you may wish to seek specific ACT confluent resources such as the PEAK Relational Training System (Dixon, 2014; Dixon, Stanley, Belisle, & Rowsey, 2016) meant to focus on developing skills with individuals who have deficits in their language abilities.

In your practice, you can easily assess for a young client's ability to tact to their private experiences in a relevant way for treatment by asking about their feelings in specific situations. This early assessment can occur directly while working with a young person during either an early interaction or initial assessment. For example, while working with a young boy struggling with fears of anaphylactic shock involving eating at school, you may initially assess for his ability to tact to private experiences by asking, "When it's lunch time at school, what do you feel?" or "What feelings are difficult for you when it's lunch time at school?" Give children lots of time to respond, more than five seconds may be appropriate. If they are not able to identify their feelings or tact to that experience, invite them to remember and picture the events, "So yesterday when you were at school, do you remember being there?" The young boy responds, "Yes." And the therapist asks, "Where do you go when it's lunch time?" And the young boy explains, "Well, I have to go to my cubby first in order to get my bag." And the therapist prompts, "Okay. And then what?" The young boy says, "I eat my lunch." A little more prompting is necessary from the therapist, "Where were you yesterday when you went to eat your lunch?" And the young boy responds, "I eat at my teacher's desk." The therapist emotes with wide eyes a face expressing curiosity, "Oh! Okay, you eat at your teacher's desk. And what feelings showed up inside of you yesterday when it was time to take out your lunch from your bag and eat at the teacher's desk?" In most situations with children 6 years old or older, they are able to describe feelings. Some children cannot tact to these private experiences and this is an opportunity to train them in identifying and labelling their private experiences. Training young people to tact to their private experiences will be presented later in this chapter under the section "Adapting ACT to Children and Adolescents." Alternatively, you may wish to seek out additional resources for assessment, especially with young people suffering from intellectual disabilities, including Dixon, Stanley, Belisle, and Rowsey (2016).

Generalized Operant Behaviors

Once a young client identifies and labels their private experience, the therapist seeks to understand how this stimulus functions in other situations, specifically curious if these experiences have generalized and affected other areas of the young client's life. In the preceding example of a young boy suffering with fears of anaphylactic shock regarding eating at school, the stimulus that elicits problematic behavior is fear of an allergic reaction. It can be important to understand whether fear is present in a specific context or whether it has generalized to other contexts that may be similar, such as other situations where eating may occur: at home, at a friend's house for a playdate, sleepover, or birthday party. Again, all behavior has a function and we do not judge it "good" or "bad" based on its form alone: a young boy with severe allergic reactions fearing eating food at places that are not home in an effort to avoid having an allergic reaction is logical. This reaction is what we would call a generalized operant.

A generalized operant is when a class of responses (fear of allergic reaction) that often don't have the same form (avoiding food, refusing food, not eating, only eating at home) typically have the same effect in certain situations (successful avoidance of feared stimuli). From the ACT perspective, we see this behavior as purely functional. Yes, it can be limiting and problematic but remember, the behaviors do work to avoid, escape, and control. An understanding of what experiences and outcomes become generalized to other situations and possible outcomes are important as it helps create a clear target for your analysis. An understanding of generalized operants in your young client's life is an important beginning step to conceptualizing where things are going wrong.

Conceptualization with Young People

In your first meeting with a young client, you can use the same conceptualization tools from Chapter 4 to analyze who and what are important to them, what they value (play, socializing at school, challenging video games, delicious food, cuddling, creativity), and what cultural and other systemic values influence their behavior. You will of course also need information on what problematic behaviors this young person is struggling with: refusing to attend school, bullying, avoiding places, bedwetting, arguing, panic, and so on.

Children generally have rigid repertoires of responding and binarily organize the world in black and white with little room for grey. They categorize the world into "good" and "bad," "right" and "wrong," and are strongly fused with their beliefs—there's a reason one of the first words children learn is "NO!" Through a *functional* view of the world, we can begin to view children's problematic behaviors as instances of experiential avoidance and understand that a child's avoidance is not exclusively pathological.

In painful situations, human beings regress and their world becomes small, folding in on itself just like a body in fear might curl into itself for protection. In a given circumstance (trauma, stress, anger, sadness), the repertoire of responding gets narrowed, especially for children who already have a rule-governed view of the world and a limited repertoire of responding.

ACT's approach, its processes and theory, works the same with a child as it does with an adult. In our offices, it is not unusual to see us making art or drawing pictures on the Life Map to teach a young client about experiential avoidance. We do this work without any complicated labels or descriptions of what ACT is. Instead, we work to create an ACT-consistent therapeutic agreement with our young clients, a noneliminative agenda that focuses on doing more, not feeling less. Considering the adaptations of art, sound, and games that we can use with young clients in our ACT work, we need to emphasize important distinctions and ways of approaching the model in session that depend on the developmental level of a young client.

ADAPTING ACT TO CHILDREN AND ADOLESCENTS

Using ACT can be a lot of fun as an intervention with young clients because you're not bound by strict methods or techniques; remember, the functional contextual approach is about what works! This gives you creative license to do physicalizing exercises such as using a tug-of-war rope, finger cuffs, and other experiential activities, as well as create art, play music, and many other engaging ways of helping children to learn to interact with and not avoid aversive private experiences while encouraging new behaviors that bring them closer to the quality of life they want. In being creative in your interventions, consider making ACT developmentally appropriate to your client. A young girl of twelve may present developmentally younger compared to a 17-year-old and may, for example, have values focusing around family and peer groups while a 17-year-old may be struggling with romantic relationships. Regardless of who walks through the door, we wish to encourage you to match the complexity of your exercises to the young person's developmental level. Furthermore, using your understanding of the principles of positive reinforcement, challenge yourself to capitalize on your young client's strengths and abilities.

We will guide you through a number of techniques we use in our practice, but remember the focus is always on increasing psychological flexibility, which means many of the exercises target multiple core processes, including all six of them at once in some instances. With that being said, in the following exercises we wish to draw your attention to their structure. In these short activities, the therapist instructs a young client to do something, a specific behavior, in the session, and the therapist attempts to reinforce the young client's participation. Each exercise ends summarizing what has been learned in the session as a strategy to both increase a young person's mastery of the skill as well as encourage the use of the specific behaviors or activities after the session.

Training Children and Adolescents to Tact

The exercises that are presented in this chapter assume children can tact to their experience in some capacity and provide activities for further developing a young person's ability to tact to private experiences, such as thoughts, feelings, and memories. *Tact* is a behavioral term for making contact with or labelling an experience. For example, while you're reading this chapter you may be noticing a grumble in your belly and you tact the sensation saying, "I'm hungry." Or let's say you read a case example in this book that impacts you personally, it brings up a painful image and you feel sadness well up inside of you. You notice that emotion and tact to it with "I'm feeling down and sad." Assessing for a young person's ability to tact to their experience early on is essential in creating a plan for what to do next. There is evidence that training young people to tact is efficacious with children on the autism spectrum (McHugh, Bobarnac, & Reed, 2011), and in our practice we have adapted these experiments to work with children and adolescents who have difficulty identifying their private experiences. Explicitly, training a young person to tact to their experience is about encouraging and facilitating their use of language to describe private experiences, specifically emotions.

We generally begin this training exercise with a young person using a piece of paper and drawing a feeling face using a marker or crayon. The face we draw is a human face with a simple expression: we typically begin with "happy," a smiling face, and "sad," a frowning face. After drawing the happy face we ask, "What feeling is this?" If the child responds correctly: happy or a variation of happy, we say "Good job," give them a high five, or applaud them in other ways to reinforce the behavior. If they answer incorrectly we applaud their attention and effort, "Good try!" We then tell the young client the face is expressing "happy" and we go on to explain how happy might feel: like someone smiling at you and telling you you're special, or succeeding at something like scoring a goal or drawing a picture. We then ask our young client, "When is a time you felt happy?" If this question is difficult or the young client is shy, we interject with something personal or funny: "I was happy when we first met and you told me you like *Star Wars* because I love those movies!" This bout of spontaneity need not be improvised; you may wish to instead share an example from your outside-of-therapy interaction: "I was happy this morning when I took my dog on a walk and she did something funny."

Here we include basic illustrations that we would draw in our practice with young clients: afraid, happy, sad, angry. As you can see they are crude illustrations and simple to do in the moment with your young clients. We recommend you have them draw the feeling face, mimicking you as they tell you about a time they were feeling that way.

Using the feeling faces to facilitate a conversation about what each face is, how that feeling face might be experienced, and discussing a time where that feeling occurred, we then facilitate a game of feelings tic-tac-toe. The premise is the same as tic-tac-toe where four intersecting lines are drawn. In our feelings version, however, each player (the therapist and the young client) chooses a color, we typically use a game like rock, paper, scissors to determine who goes first. The first player draws a feeling face and the other player has to guess what the feeling is. The player who drew the face (first player) then describes a time they felt that way. Your own variations on this game are welcome and are easily adapted to fit the context and development of your clients. We recommend as you go through the game that you maintain the focus on directly training emotional experiences. To advance the game and make it more entertaining, we have included multiple feeling faces that could be used in your therapeutic work.

ASHAMED   **BORED**   **FRUSTRATED**

HURT   **JEALOUS**   **EMBARRASSED**

Here are some additional faces. You may wish to learn and employ these extra feeling faces in your feelings tic-tac-toe or other tacting exercises to increase the difficulty and variability of the faces and emotions in your work. Of course, you can always come up with your own feeling faces and ascribe your own inference of what the face depicts.

The following are examples of a feelings tic-tac-toe game. The players are differentiated by shades of grey, which allows for a different feeling face to be drawn by each player on every turn.

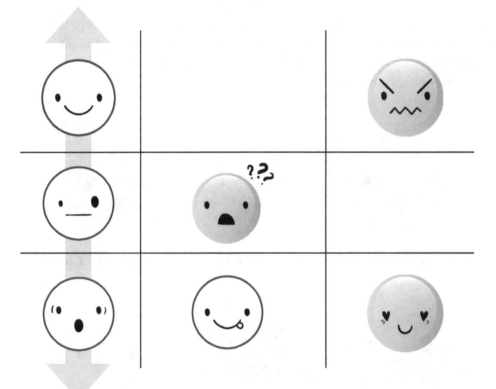

This game was won by the non shaded player, scoring a line in the left column, depicting happy (top left), hurt (middle left), and scared (bottom left). This player added "silly" as a feeling face (center bottom) although it did not score them a win.

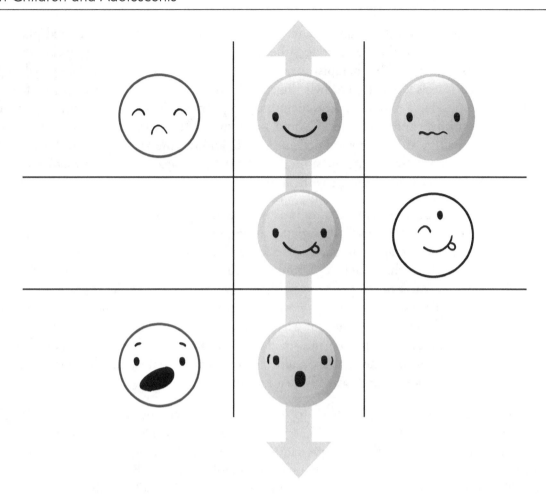

This game was won by the grey shaded player (depicted as the darker grey) by connecting happy (center top), silly (center middle), and afraid (center bottom).

Inside or Outside?

With ACT, we can achieve amazing clinical feats, such as the transformation of stimulus function: taking painful private experiences and transforming their function so that instead of serving to limit our behavior (when painful feeling X shows up, I always do A), we instead connect with our values in those dark moments to create a broader behavioral repertoire (when painful feeling X shows up, I could do A,B,C, etc.) so that we can choose what we do next, perhaps electing to do the things that bring us closer to a vital and meaningful life. However, in order to make this choice for ourselves, we need to engage in a discrimination task at the core of relational frame theory: telling the difference between our private and public experiences. This discrimination task is important to train so that we can become sensitive to our environment and respond based on what functions in a given context rather than simply responding to private experiences that may be insensitive to the context. Over time we can begin to realize that we can engage in public behavior X even when private behavior Y shows up. This discrimination task does not need to be a heady, intellectual pursuit and our favorite way to do so is especially relevant with children. We call it the "Inside or Outside" exercise.

To effectively deliver this exercise you could use something edible such as a raisin or malleable like playdough. In this example, we use brightly colored playdough and sprinkle in some humor. Briefly, the purpose of the first portion of the exercise is to encourage a young client to describe anything that they notice that is part of the outside (publicly observable) world. Some people like to refer to the outside or public world as what is experienced by the five senses: the world that is available to us through taste, touch, smell, sound, and sight.

The therapist begins by inviting the young client to take a chunk of the brightly colored playdough. The young client grabs a handful and the therapist does the same while reinforcing the young client (saying "good job" or smiling may be enough). The therapist instructs the young client to squeeze the playdough in their hands and notice what it feels like between their fingers. The therapist asks, "What does that feel like?" The young client might respond in a myriad of ways including, "Squishy!" The therapist is once again reinforcing, "Right! It does feel squishy!" and continues, "Now I want you to roll it in your fingers and between your palms. See if you can make a ball." The young client does so, and the therapist asks, "And what is that like?" The young client may respond by saying it is "smooth." The therapist again reinforces that response and says, "Great! You noticed that. What temperature is the dough?"

An additional prompt may be necessary and that is okay. The therapist may ask, "Is it cold like ice, hot like a hot chocolate, or somewhere in between?" After giving the young client some time to respond and reinforcing them for their noticing, the therapist instructs, "Now press your thumb into the dough. Then take your thumb out and look closely at the dough. Can you see your fingerprint? What do you see?" A successful answer from the young client is not dependent on them giving an accurate description of the impression into the dough. Instead, it is the young client's noticing and tacting to the publicly observable dough that we are most interested in fostering, regardless of what aspect of the dough they may focus on. The therapist says, "Now bring the dough up to your nose and smell it! What does it smell like?" Playdough tends to have a unique smell, so the therapist may need to use additional prompts. Playfully the therapist says, "Okay, now we're going to put it in our mouths and taste it—just kidding!"

Next, the therapist instructs the young client to set the dough aside and sets aside their dough as well. The therapist will prompt the client, saying, "Let's both close our eyes. Do you remember the color of the playdough? Can you describe it with your eyes closed? And what about how it felt when you squished it between your fingers, do you remember what that felt like? Could you describe that to me while keeping your eyes closed? When we rolled the playdough in our hands and made it into a ball, what did that feel like? Can you imagine that? And what about its temperature? What was the temperature of the playdough like in your hands? Remember when we pressed our thumbs into the dough, what did that look like when you looked closely at where you pressed your thumb? Describe what you saw. And the smell, what did the playdough smell like? Even if you can't describe it well, do you remember the smell?" This prompting is asked slowly allowing the young client time to both think about and describe out loud their experience. Some clients may try to sneak a peek at the dough. For those clients, additional prompting to keep their eyes closed or putting something over the dough to cover it from sight may be helpful.

After going through the questions, the therapist next invites the young client to open their eyes. The therapist can hand the playdough back if they choose, although it may be distracting to the child client for the next moment as the exercise is wrapped up.

Asking the young client—and giving extra time for them to think about this discrimination task—the therapist asks, "When we were looking at the playdough, is that something that happens outside of us that we can see, hear, smell, taste, and touch, or is that something that happens inside of us like a thought, feeling, memory, or sensation like feeling a rumble in your tummy and being hungry?" Remember, it is okay if the young client cannot successfully identify whether it's an inside or outside experience. (The correct answer is that it's an outside experience.) This simply signifies that you will need to focus on this discrimination task and get creative with new interventions to train the inside/outside discrimination with them while reinforcing any attempts at noticing or tacting to their experience.

The therapist follows up and asks, "When we set the playdough aside and I had you close your eyes and remember—what it looked like, what color it was, how it felt in your hands, its temperature, and its smell—was remembering that an outside experience like you seeing my face right now and hearing my voice, or was that an inside experience like thinking about something that isn't here right now like a cat or dog, having a feeling like being happy or sad, remembering something like what you had for breakfast this morning, or a sensation like feeling a rumble in your tummy and being hungry?" Again, it is okay if the client cannot identify the correct answer. (It is an inside experience.) It is additional information that the client may need further training in inside/outside discrimination.

Life Mapping with Children and Adolescents

We think a fair criticism of child and adolescent psychotherapy is that therapists often lack the ability to effect control over a young person's environment that likely is reinforcing problematic behaviors. Critics would say that young people are not as free as adults to choose what they do next with their behavior as they are not able to influence their environment to the same degree as independent adults. One might conceptualize that young people are susceptible to the whim of primary caregivers and the influence they have over a young person's behavior. This is not untrue; however, there are also many situations in which children may benefit from understanding why they do what they do in certain situations. This is where the Life Map becomes an invaluable tool for sharing ACT with young people. For adolescents who believe their lives are controlled by their parents and that they have absolutely no control over what happens in their lives, a Life Map can help them identify that how they act in a given context is entirely their choice. Furthermore, we can use this perspective to educate primary caregivers on how a young person's behavior works in a given context and help plan a reinforcement schedule that encourages young clients to engage in new, nonproblematic behaviors.

We typically introduce the Life Map with illustrations and stories, not by launching into asking questions straight away as we would do with adults as demonstrated in Chapter 3. Incorporating drawing into the Life Map can assist you in telling young people a story about how behaviors function. Typically we use paper or a whiteboard and draw a horizontal line with arrowheads on each side. We label the right side "toward" as we say, "This arrow represents moving toward the people and things we like in life." We then write "away" on the left and say, "And this arrow is about moving away from the things we don't want to experience." We go on to set up this functional contextual point of view saying, "We're going to talk about you today, focusing on who and what matter most to you as well as talking about some of the yucky feelings you might want to move away from. But because humans, people like you and me, are so complex I'd like to show you how this map works using something more simple like a rabbit! Would that be okay?" In our experience we get a resounding "yes" from young people, adolescents included!

Next, we draw a rabbit above the line in the middle of the Life Map and say, "Here's our friend, Mr. Rabbit. What do rabbits like most in the world, what do they want to move toward?" The most common answer we get is "carrots!" Responding with drawing a carrot on the right side we say, "Yes! Rabbits love carrots." We sometimes get different answers like "other rabbits" and we'll typically say, "Yes, we could draw other rabbits over here" pointing at the toward side and we may write "other rabbits" or other answers like "water" or "fun," but we always redirect or point out what a rabbit's favorite food is: carrots. We then describe a situation, "Imagine one night Mr. Rabbit has snuck under a farmer's fence and he's digging up some carrots when all of a sudden the farmer's big dog runs over toward Mr. Rabbit and starts barking!!" We begin drawing the dog in front of the carrot, between the rabbit and the carrot, and ask, "What does Mr. Rabbit do when he sees a dog running toward him and barking?" We suggest waiting for an answer and even describing the story again, pointing at the illustrations you've just drawn to prompt the participation of your young client. Young clients will generally respond with "He runs away!" And we say, "Yes! Exactly. Mr. Rabbit does what rabbits do best and he hops away."

We've included a Life Map here that we adapted in session to be used with a young client. It includes the drawings from the exercise: a line with arrowheads labelled "Toward" and "Away" as well as simple illustrations of a rabbit, a dog, and a carrot.

TOWARD

AWAY

Just as we, the authors, explained to you in Chapter 3 that moving away is not bad, we use this opportunity to describe how Mr. Rabbit's behavior works with young people: "Sometimes, moving away from something scary or a difficult situation is what works best. Even though Mr. Rabbit is now missing out on some delicious carrots, by running away from the dog, he might be going home to his hidey hole where he could have fun with other rabbits or he could escape to a stream where there's no barking dogs and cool water to drink."

The transition to making a Life Map with your young clients collaboratively is now easy having set up how the map works. We begin by asking, "So I assume carrots are not the most important thing in your life?" Our young clients often smile and respond, "No!" We say, "Good! And I assume barking dogs aren't your biggest problem that you've come to talk to me about?" Once again they tell us "no." We finish by saying, "That means you're a lot more complicated than a rabbit, so let's make a map that's all about your life."

We use a new piece of paper or erase the whiteboard and draw a new horizontal line with arrowheads on each side and once again write the words: "toward" on one side and "away" on the other. With this new Life Map free of any illustrations you can now ask your young clients questions to fill in each quadrant beginning with "Who is most important to you?" We often do the writing for our young clients who cannot write the answers themselves or who may have difficulty printing, though we always offer them an opportunity to draw illustrations in each quadrant to represent the answers they give. After we have some representation (written or illustrated) of who is important to our young clients we ask what is important to them. Another helpful prompt is asking questions in relation to whom they state is important to them, for example "You said your dad is important to you. What do you like to do when you're with your dad?" They might respond, "Fun" which is great, another item you can write in the lower right quadrant. You might even ask, "What does it feel like to hang out with your dad?" They may respond "Good," and again you have more to write in the bottom right quadrant. As a technical note, you're not looking to fill the bottom right quadrant as much as you are seeking to assist young clients in tacting to their private experience of what they value. Another way of saying it is that you're teaching them valuing, clarifying who they value and what they value about those relationships.

We then move on to the lower left quadrant by pointing to the lower right quadrant that we just completed and saying, "This is who and what matter the most to you. These are the carrots in your life!" We then point to the bottom right quadrant, "What thoughts, feelings, sensations, or memories get in the way of you moving toward the people and things you want to move toward in your life?" If we get answers that are not private experiences, for example "other kids" or "school," then we ask, "What feelings show up for you about these other kids?" Likewise with "school" we might ask, "What feelings show up at school that are difficult for you?" Even then as we talk about other kids and school, a helpful prompt might be to ask, "And what does that feel like for you when other kids are mean or school is difficult?" You may get answers like "mad" or a thought "I'm stupid," and these answers are exactly the private experiences we are hoping to contact in completing the bottom left quadrant.

Asking about specific behaviors becomes easy when we can point to the lower left quadrant and ask, "What do you do when you have these thoughts and feelings?" We often repeat what is written to focus on the specific experiences written in the bottom left quadrant. Next, we prompt our young clients to describe "toward" move behaviors by asking, "And what would you want to be doing to move toward who and what are most important to you?"

We've included the Life Map here in which a young client drew themselves at the center of their map.

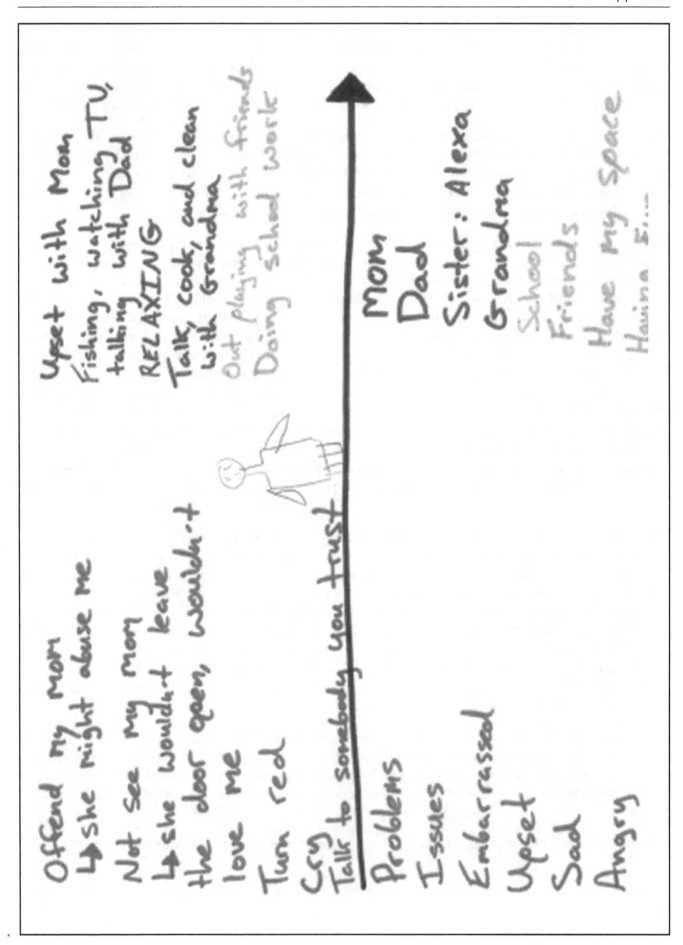

Offend my mom
↳ she might abuse me
Not see my mom
↳ she wouldn't leave
the door open, wouldn't
love me
Turn red
Cry
Talk to somebody you trust
Problems
Issues
Embarrassed
Upset
Sad
Angry

Upset with Mom
Fishing, watching TV,
talking with Dad
RELAXING
Talk, cook, and clean
with Grandma
Out playing with friends
Doing School work

Mom
Dad
Sister: Alexa
Grandma
School
Friends
Have my space
Having Fun

While completing the Life Map with a young person, we often ask, "What does it feel like to move toward?" Answers vary and that is okay, including answers that do not evaluate moving toward as positive. We want to reinforce any responses young clients give as often, like with adults, moving toward who and what matter to them can be difficult or scary. We then ask, "What does it feel like to move away?" And again we may get responses that evaluate moving away as positive, which makes sense given that those away behaviors are being reinforced somehow in the short-term. After asking about each direction, we invite young clients to depict the feeling of moving toward and away with their own illustration. The Life Map on page 132 is a sample from a session with an adolescent boy who was suffering with an intellectual disability. He described moving toward as feeling relaxed and calm, depicting a smiling meditator, legs crossed and arms at rest. When asked about moving away, he used the word *awful* and depicted an angry monster-like character with menacing jaws and arms outreached with claw-like hands.

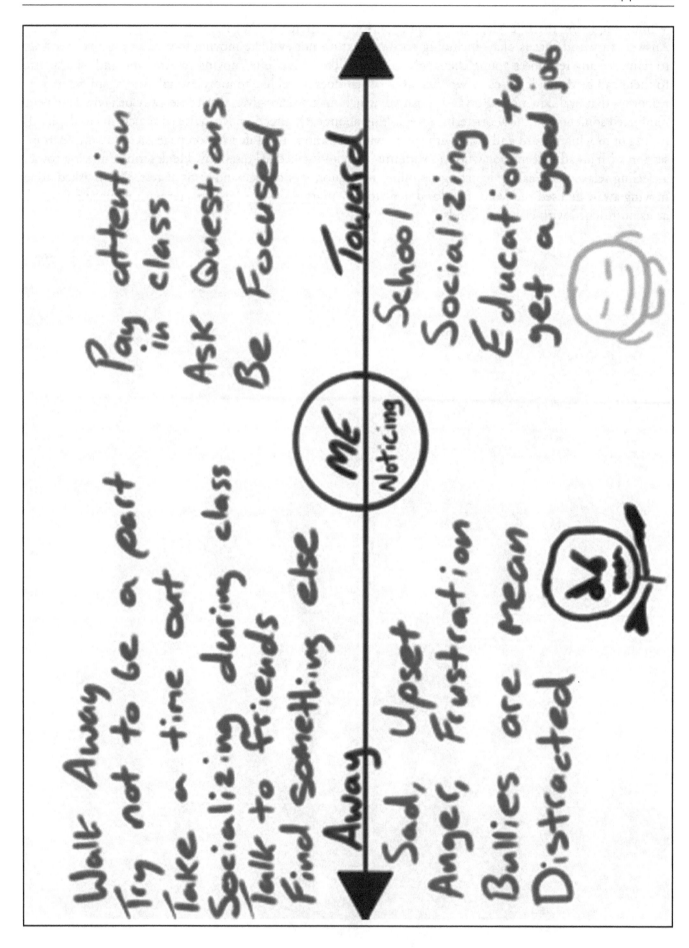

The next step in the Life Map is to pay attention to who is noticing. We have developed reminders to practice the paying attention on purpose or noticing activity of the Life Map. We recommend using a system of reminders for young people to regularly prompt them.

Mindful Reminders

Young people and adults alike are often not in the present moment. This is evident in children's ability to immerse themselves in imaginative worlds or "flow" states. Picture an adolescent completely focused on a video game unaware of what may be happening in the environment right in front of them. Also, picture an adult waiting in line at a grocery store overcome with anxiety and tension, sweating as they think about their upcoming income tax paperwork that is due soon and worrying about completing their taxes in time. The ability to not be in the present moment and to become fused with experiences is extremely helpful, yet it causes many problems in certain contexts. Prompting young people to pay attention to their experience is incredibly valuable and can have profoundly positive effects. Making a young client's private experience conscious to them enables them in the right context to choose what they do next. We use the aforementioned Life Map exercise to demonstrate to a young client the utility of mindful attention (noticing) and the act of choosing what one does next. We then use mindful reminders to prompt purposeful attention.

We have had success with many different types of media: using sticky pads of paper and drawing an image on five to ten sticky notes, sending those notes home with a young client and their primary caregivers to be posted in various locations. Other options include printing and laminating your own mindful reminder images and sending a number of them home with your young client and primary caregiver with double-sided tape or other adhesives.

We instruct young clients and primary caregivers to carefully place the mindful reminders in varying locations where the young client will see the reminder and use it to practice mindfulness. With some young clients we may not use the word *mindfulness* and adapt it to "paying attention on purpose" or "slow down and notice!"

We have had a lot of success with one young client who affixed their mindful reminder to the footboard of their bed. Every day when they woke up they were reminded to practice slowing down and noticing. They would take the blankets off their body slowly and, exaggerating their yawning, they would lift their hands above their head slowly, taking a long stretch. This is an excellent example of what we aim to increase, a class of behavior that's about being mindful. This particular young person also put a mindful reminder in their school lunchbox, at the back of their cubbyhole in their classroom, and one just above the cup that holds their toothbrush in the bathroom at home.

We'd like to encourage you to once again be creative, use varying images on different reminders, try including text such as "be mindful," "b r e a t h e," or "notice!" Adolescents may also benefit from this exercise or may choose to set reminders on their phones at various times throughout the day. No matter what you and your young client choose to select for mindful reminders, the goal is to increase awareness of the present moment, particularly their private experiences.

Fighting Off the Balloons

Once awareness of painful private experiences are established in a young client's repertoire (see "Assessing Children and Adolescents with ACT"), you may wish to transition into this activity to set up the therapeutic contract or agenda. This activity could also easily be used during a first session. Creating a therapeutic agreement with a young client that is about a noneliminating agenda can be quite fun using this exercise "Fighting off Balloons." Although this exercise focuses on acceptance it also uses present-moment, values, and commitment processes. Defusion and self-as-context can also easily be integrated into this exercise.

For this exercise we recommend having balloons and markers on hand. (You may need to inquire about whether your clients are sensitive to latex. We found nonlatex balloons online easily for a low price. We also recommend washable markers to minimize the chance of staining skin or fabrics.) The therapist may already have balloons inflated or may wish to do so in session with the young person. Note, however, that the balloons need to be tied so that they remain inflated. You will not require many balloons but more balloons are more fun in our experience.

The therapist uses markers to write down words on the balloons that represent painful private experiences that your young client is experiencing, for example: fear, worry, sadness, anger, panic, soreness, loss. Alternatively, if the private experiences include memories or painful topics that are difficult to verbalize including preverbal trauma, the therapist can draw images and invite the young client to also draw images that represent the difficult private experiences. With drawing, the images need not be sophisticated. We have had a young client use multiple marker colors creating a blob-like creature and smudging the image on the balloon to further depict its grotesqueness. It is important to be flexible in session and notice what will reinforce pointing to difficult private experiences. The taking stock of painful experiences and articulating them on the balloons could very well be an improvement in your young client's behavior and be increasing their psychological flexibility in that they are already learning a new way to relate to their painful experiences, especially as you, the therapist model being okay with these difficult experiences.

With several inflated balloons now covered in words or decorated with images depicting the difficult private experiences for your young client, the therapist invites them to stand apart from the therapist. Holding up the balloons, the therapist reminds their young client that the balloons represent their difficult feelings, thoughts, sensations, and even memories that they don't want to have. The therapist then says, "Now I'm going to throw these balloons at you, they can't hurt you, they're just balloons but remember what they represent, the scary and yucky thoughts, feelings, memories, and sensations we put on them. I want you to try your best to not let these balloons touch you, you can fight off the balloons, you can do whatever you want, push them away, duck, roll, jump out of the way, but as I throw these at you, I am going to try and talk to you about something important. Will you try this with me?"

The therapist begins vigorously throwing the balloons at the young client, picking up spent balloons after they've been thrown. All the while, the therapist tells the client about something important like a pet the therapist loves very much or a really great movie the therapist thinks the client will like. Allowing a minute or so to repeat, the therapist stops and asks, "What happened?" Listening as the young client talks about fighting off the balloons and running away, the therapist asks, "How hard was that?" Regardless of the young clients answer, the therapist orients the young client to how difficult it is to do other things while fighting off the scary and yucky stuff we don't want to have. Focusing more specifically, the therapist describes observable behaviors, "How well can you eat a piece of pizza while you're fighting off these yucky and scary thoughts? And if I wanted to teach you how to drive a car, can you do that while you're fighting these off?"

The therapist invites the young client to repeat the activity with special instructions, "This time we're going to do something slightly different though, I want you to let the balloons hit you and I am going to talk to you about something important. Ready?" The therapist repeats throwing the balloons at the young client, all the while repeating the same information from the previous round, speaking about something personally important, whether it be a pet or a movie they think the client will like. The therapist may need to remind the young client that fighting or escaping the balloons is not necessary this time around.

After the completion of telling the young client what was important or simply after a minute of this exercise, the therapist asks, "How was that different from the first time?" The young client may answer in a variety of ways. The therapist will again inquire of the young client how difficult would it be to do other things while not fighting off the yucky and scary stuff we don't want to have. Focusing more specifically, the therapist asks about observable behaviors, "How well can you eat a piece of pizza when you're not fighting off the yucky and scary thoughts? And if I wanted to teach you how to drive a car, could you focus on that while you're just letting the balloons hit you and land wherever they may?" This exercise is completed through drawing a distinction between fighting with our private experiences and allowing them to simply be there or touch us, highlighting acceptance through the client's own experiences with both rounds of the balloons.

Working with a Young Person's Inner Storyteller

Young people and adults alike can have problems with fusion to private experiences that can have severe results, especially when the stories involve traumatic events that leave someone with feelings of self-blame, guilt, and shame. We have developed step-by-step instructions for creating a trauma narrative that is a variation of an exposure therapeutic exercise. ACT fits well with exposure activities, especially considering ACT's significant body of literature demonstrating the futility of experiential avoidance and the advantages of practicing acceptance instead. A point of divergence between ACT and traditional approaches to exposure work is that in ACT we do not seek to lower subjective units of distress (SUDS) but instead seek to broaden a young client's repertoire (what they do) in the presence of their painful experiences. An ACT therapist in this exercise would be interested in whether the young client can articulate their difficult experience and not fuse with their thoughts and what else I (the therapist) can encourage the young client to notice in the presence of this painful experience and memory.

During each step of the trauma narrative it is recommended that therapists praise the young client's efforts in producing the trauma narrative. Trauma narratives are created in session with the therapist and are not worked on at home—this may be an important instruction for therapists to give young clients and their primary caregivers. The trauma narrative as described in this book does not include identifying information, such as the client's name.

- **Step 1:** Choose a format that works best for your young client. Using a book with blank pages is one approach that we prefer, however simply using unbound blank or lined pages to write the narrative is also conducive to this creative process. Be creative and give options to your client: drawing, coloring, collage, stickers, scrapbooking supplies, etc.

- **Step 2:** Take a strengths-based approach and begin the narrative with "Something important you should know about me when I was a child is _____." or "One of my favorite memories about myself as a child is _____." Another option may include simply starting with what happened on the day of the trauma, beginning before the trauma happened or what your young client was doing right before the trauma happened.

- **Step 3:** Do not shy away from the trauma. Drawing upon the earlier skills of acceptance and present-moment awareness the therapist has demonstrated that they are "strong enough" to hear and hold the young client's experience, modelling acceptance. Prompt the young client to write about the trauma: "I think now is a good point to write what first happened." The client may shy away from explicit details. The therapist can rely on the therapeutic rapport by asking the client to describe what the client was wearing, where the trauma took place, what the room or place looked like. The therapist can then prompt the client to describe what happened by having the client speak about it as the therapist writes or the client can write what happened, what was said or done, and what the client said in response. Now is good time to stop and review everything that has been written. Next the therapist has the option to come back to the trauma narrative at the next session, to leave some time at the end of the session, or to continue. If continuing, the therapist asks what thoughts or feeling the client was having at the time and what the worst moments or memories of the trauma are. Again, the therapist will encourage the client to include as much detail as possible.

- **Step 4:** After rereading the trauma narrative together, with the therapist check-in and assessing for distress, the therapist asks the client to describe what happened after the trauma: if the young client kept the secret of their trauma, who was the first person the client told or what else happened after the trauma. Now may also be an opportunity to process some of the private descriptions, for example: a young client who believes the trauma was their fault may feel guilty or they may believe there is something they could have done to stop or avoid the trauma.

- **Step 5:** Your work on the trauma narrative now shifts focus to the future, what does the young client hope to get out of treatment, focusing on what will be different about their life that is observable. Think of what behaviors would go in the top right quadrant of the Life Map—the observable behaviors that take the client toward who and what matter to them. This is a good opportunity to discuss relapse prevention and termination, however, these topics may not be reflected directly in the narrative.

- **Step 6:** Share the trauma narrative with parents, partners, or other caregivers. Destroying the trauma narrative is now an option if this is something the young person you are working with elects to do. Through coming into contact with details of the experience and looking at them on paper, the client is practicing an alternative way to come into contact with their traumatic private experiences, which creates more space for the client to choose how to act moving forward when these private experiences show up.

Sexual Abuse Trauma Narrative Worksheet Sample

We offer this trauma narrative sample with fill-in-the-blank sections that some young clients may find helpful, especially those who have difficulty telling their trauma story. The fill-in-the-blank structure of this exercise may alleviate anxiety over telling their trauma story, taking the focus off young clients' telling their story and using this exercise to allow them to simply offer responses. Therapists may elect to have the worksheet printed or written on a large piece of paper or on a whiteboard, reading the exercise aloud and inviting young clients to give answers for the therapist to write in the blanks.

WORKSHEET

BUILDING YOUR NARRATIVE

—

One of the most important things you should know about me from when I was younger is

_____.

When I first started school, I remember that _____.

An important memory I have about school is when _____.

I remember really enjoying _____ and laughing
about _____.

I remember a favorite vacation was _____ because _____.

When I was ____ I was sexually abused by ____ _____.

I remember the first time it happened. The abuser said _____ and I responded
by _____.

The abuser did things to me like _____ and also _____.

During the sexual abuse I felt _____.

The abuse went on for _____.

I kept the secret about being sexually abused for _____ because I was worried that _____.

The first person I told about the sexual abuse was _____.

When I told, I was surprised that _____.

Now my family _____.

If I were to see the abuser, I would _____.

Although when I think about the abuse, I feel _____.

There are a lot of things that cheer me up and make me feel better, like _____ and
_____.

This past year, one of the things I did that I am very proud of is _____.

This is my life so far, and I hope that in the years ahead _____.

After completing the trauma narrative, we recommend the therapist read the narrative aloud from the beginning, including the answers filled in collaboratively, and then invite the young client to read the trauma narrative. We hope this provides one way to practice exposure to painful private experiences in the service of developing a broader repertoire of behavior and creating a better opportunity to choose to move toward who and what matter most.

Take Your Monster with You

ACT presents a unique opportunity to be creative and flexible in your practice. In the following exercise, we use art to facilitate a conversation about being willing to have your most painful private experiences. Note that although it is an art-based activity, therapists may wish to use props to physicalize the metaphor. We suggest that you introduce this exercise while talking to young clients about their behavior, what they do in the presence of their most painful private experiences. Clarifying specifically the difficult thoughts, feelings, sensations, and memories your young client struggles with is a necessary precursor. This exercise aims to increase acceptance and defusion. It also utilizes a connection to values and commitment behaviors in helping a young client to choose acceptance as an alternative to experiential avoidance: avoidance, escape, and control strategies.

We begin by asking a young client to tell us about their painful private experiences, "What does it feel like when that yucky stuff shows up inside of you that tells you not to go to school?" Adding this descriptor to the end of the question—"that tells you not to go to school"—is helpful in our experience because it specifies the situations we are referencing as an attempt to focus our analysis on the specific antecedent to painful private experiences. Using the preceding questions, let's say a young client responds by saying "really scared." We reinforce the client's participation by validating, "Yes, you have a lot of fear around going to school." We then invite the young client to draw what the painful private experiences look like by prompting, "Can you draw a picture of what feeling really scared would look like if it was a monster?" At this point we provide paper and pencil, crayons, or markers and encourage the young client to start drawing. As the young client is drawing, we make a drawing ourselves on our own paper of our own yucky-feeling monster.

Some helpful prompts and questions might include: "If your yucky feelings were a monster what shape would it be?" "And what color would it be?" "How big would it be?" The therapeutic aim here is to increase defusion with these painful private experiences. The therapist encourages engagement with these private aversive stimuli that would otherwise be cause to experientially avoid.

We may comment on our young client's progress during the drawing task or ask questions about the monster, again attempting to reinforce client participation in the session. Once a young person completes the drawing of their monster, we ask them to draw themselves on the same page, showing us how big they feel they are in comparison to the monster. There is no incorrect answer. Some young clients may depict themselves as small in comparison to their monster while others may be an equal size.

Next, we expose the processes of experiential avoidance and fusion in our young clients' lives. We adapt an ACT classic tug-of-war metaphor (Zettle, 2007), asking our young clients if they know how to play tug-of-war. We keep a braided rope dog toy handy in our offices to enact this exercise with young clients. We explain that the things they do to avoid, escape, and control their painful private experiences are like trying to win a tug-of-war with this monster. The problem though is that while it might feel good at first to pull harder and it may feel like they're winning, they never win; the game is never over. We attempt to demonstrate why acceptance would be a deserving long-term outcome by asking, "While you're busy fighting with this monster, what are you missing out on in your life?" If we are holding the braided rope in session while our young client holds the other end, we will pull the rope and invite the young client to pull back, asking, "If I wanted to pass you my puppy to hold and say hi to, could you do that?" Typically a young client answers no and laughs while we each pull the rope back and forth. We then ask, "How well can you go play with your friends and pay attention to them or pay attention in class while you're fighting with your monster?" Some children will drop the rope. Although this is another short-term solution, we point out that the reality of the situation with this monster is that it regularly comes back, antagonizing them to fight. We pose a difficult question that we leave hanging, that is to say we don't answer it for our young clients: "What if instead of fighting with the monster, we could take them with us?" We sometimes will need to use additional prompts or questions, for example asking, "What would it be like to go to school *with* your fears?"

The responses we receive from young people are astonishing. They typically talk about the difficulties in living with their most painful experiences, yet almost immediately understand the benefit of living a life that is about acceptance and allowing difficult private experiences to loom rather than continue attempts to avoid, control, and escape.

In this artwork from a young girl suffering with fears and refusing to attend school, she depicted herself holding a rope where she is fighting with her monster in a tug-of-war. She drew soundwaves coming from her mouth illustrating herself shouting and arguing with her monster. The therapist skillfully asks, "What would happen if you used that rope to take your monster for a walk and took it to school with you?" The specifics of her answer, regardless of topography or what behaviors she might describe herself doing aren't what are most important. Rather, it is that she can describe doing more, broadening her repertoire in the presence of her fear. And with this new way of approaching fear and not withdrawing from it, the therapist can reinforce this young girl. A reinforcement from the therapist might be as simple as smiling and telling her "good job!" Although this new behavior is likely to be self-reinforcing for this young girl, remember that she has a history of attempting to escape, avoid, and control her fear, which has worked in the short-term. Therefore, multiple sources of reinforcement are helpful in the continuance of this new behavior. The therapist might encourage caregivers and school staff to also reinforce her for these new behaviors, shaping her behavior in the presence of fear to eventually go to school with her monster.

In the artwork at the bottom of page 139, from a young male client, he depicted himself holding a string that tethers him to his fears and sadness as if it were a balloon floating above him. He drew himself smiling as he goes outside to play with his friends, all the while bringing his fear and sadness with him.

TRAINING PARENTS

Throughout this chapter on assessment and adapting ACT with young people, we have encouraged you to engage primary caregivers in varying ways. This engagement may take a number of different forms early on in your ACT work with young people: information collection, uncovering caregivers' theories about what is happening with the young person you will be working with, educating caregivers about the function of their young person's behavior and encouraging caregivers' reinforcement of the skills you're using in session with their young person. There is some good empirical support for using ACT with parents to train them, and we'd like to encourage you to be flexible in how you deliver ACT with parents (Brown, Whittingham, Boyd, McKinlay, & Sofronoff, 2014; Whittingham, Sanders, McKinlay, & Boyd, 2014).

We have tried a number of different applications: parenting groups, working with parents for a single session before we see their young person in individual therapy and continuing to meet with caregivers for check-in sessions and debriefings after an individual session with their young person, and offering education and instructions that they can use at home. We've even tried putting together pamphlets and brief e-books for caregivers to read and implement at home. All of this is to say that being creative in engaging caregivers is an asset when requesting their buy-in. And buy-in is important. In our experience, caregivers want solutions in a hurry and they want them to work fast. In our practice, primary caregivers tell us that they consult the Internet as their number one source of information before anything else when it comes to issues with the young people in their lives. They want help and information, but don't necessarily know where to go to find accurate information. The behaviorally focused work you will be doing with ACT can have immediate positive gains but also requires long-term behavior change in caregivers, where they implement this program with effort. Without buy-in from caregivers, long-term gains become less likely.

Caregivers Giving Reinforcement

In our experience, primary caregivers often get frustrated with motivating behavior change in their children. Caregivers are largely doing the best that they can with what they have. They, like the young people in their lives, resort to what works and unfortunately what typically works for caregivers in the short-term is punishment, aversive control. We explain early on to caregivers that punishment tends to work in the short-term, but the problem is that behavior under aversive control isn't flexible and does not create a good environment to empower children and teach them to make the right choice. Instead, what we see in highly aversive environments are young people who become sneaky or better at hiding their behaviors that are frequently punished. We offer an alternative to parents: reinforcement, specifically, paying attention to the good behaviors the young person in their life does.

Assisting caregivers in understanding how to reinforce their young person in a way that leads to long-term, meaningful behavior change can be difficult. When we work individually with adults, the conversation is already hard enough as we seek to uncover their values as a source of reinforcement focused on who and what are most important to them. For young people, however, it isn't until later in life that they develop their values on a more abstract, hierarchical frame. Therefore, therapists need to be clever in exposing what reinforces a young person's behavior and pay attention to what else might be something a young person would find reinforcing to shape a new behavior. Early on, therapists and primary caregivers can draw on their own attention as a reinforcer for young people. Often the "who" that is important to young people is a person that they value, which is a source of reinforcement, especially when it comes to their attention. You read that right—a primary caregiver's attention is a source of reinforcement. Attention is generally an especially large reinforcer for children. As young people age into adolescence their primary attachment changes from primary caregivers to their peer group. In adolescence, primary caregivers may need to resort to monetary and other items or tokens as reinforcers.

Once a reinforcer is discovered or proved to be effective (e.g., a caregiver's attention is implemented and the child responds positively), they may even experiment in the effect of withdrawing attention to a child's acting-out behavior, minimizing it or decreasing its duration. Caregivers are instructed to find opportunities for the young people in their lives to be reinforced. You read that right, we tell caregivers to "try to catch your children doing the right thing." This might sound counterintuitive to you as a reader, and it will likely be interpreted that way by parents. However, with your newfound understanding that punishment and other forms of aversive control do not work to motivate long-term change, the agenda changes from getting better at punishing children and adolescents in an effort to limit their behavior and avert them from acting out to instead positively reinforcing and praising their good behavior so as to increase its frequency.

As we discussed in Chapter 2, crafting an ACT-consistent therapeutic contract is used to set the expectations of what therapy will be about, and working with parents is no different. Good stimulus control using behavioral principles involves an agreement that is not always obviously apparent to the caregiver, but it is evidence-based and it works. You are probably tired of reading it by now, but we are not concerned with what looks right or makes sense to a parent, we are focused on what works—the function of a behavior. Our hope is that this glimpse into using ACT with children and adolescents and their caregivers has created a sense of curiosity or excitement about the applications. It is our hope that you will do additional reading, seeking out more information on integrating behavioral plans into your work, that you'll begin to integrate ACT into your practice with young people and their caregivers, and advocate for interventions that are evidence-based focusing on the function rather than form of a behavior in your therapeutic work with schools, community agencies, and other stakeholders in the welfare of the young people you may work with in your pratice.

Chapter 9

The ACT Therapist

Within any type of theoretical orientation, the main focus is understandably on the person sitting across from us, typically referred to as a client. However, it would be remiss of us to not acknowledge that there is another person in the room as well, the therapist. One of the most helpful ways to learn this approach is to apply it to yourself. Being able to experience what it is like to do or to live this approach can give you insight into your clients' potential experience with the model as well as provide insight into your own fused self-as-content or experiential avoidance both as a person and as a professional.

LIVING THE ACT APPROACH

One of the most helpful ways to help your clients is to understand what you bring into the room: your own assumptions, biases, and history. To work from a functional contextualist model, you need to understand the context you are creating in the room and the function of your clients' and your behaviors, both observable and private experiences. If you only look at your client through this lens you are missing half of the equation: yourself. A good way to rid yourself of this habit of pretending you are a blank slate or completely unbiased, is to observe your own inner dialogue, mental verbiage, when you are in session. If you find yourself feeling frustrated with a client, for example, or feeling stuck, take some time to explore within that emotion and fill out a Life Map for yourself. Are you reacting to that experience in the room by acting in a way you otherwise wouldn't or that is inconsistent with your values as a therapist? Are you falling back on skills that feel safe rather than challenging yourself with this new approach and thereby developing your competence as a therapist? Are you sacrificing long-term development and progress for short-term relief? Our guess would be that the answer to that question is yes. Why? Because we've been there, in fact we still find ourselves there at times.

When we feel uncomfortable with trying something new or we try something and it does not turn out as we thought it would, our initial reaction might involve our mind throwing out thoughts such as, "See, you aren't as good of a therapist as you think you are" or "If you try this new thing your clients will realize how inadequate you are as a therapist and how you can't help them." We may have feelings of disappointment or anxiety pop up too, maybe even some fluttering in our chest, or Jessica's favorite: turning red. We might even remember embarrassing experiences of trying something before and being unsuccessful or feeling like a fraud when talking to a colleague who seems to only have successful experiences with clients. In reaction to these uncomfortable thoughts, feelings, and sensations we might have this urge to run away. *This is completely natural.* And it is exactly why we wanted to devote some time in this book to talking about your own experience as a therapist and as a person trying something new. If we do not pause to notice those experiences, if we choose not to look at them and understand their function, and if we cannot identify why those experiences are painful and what is important underneath, then we and our clients lose out on an opportunity to grow. This is not easy work. Leaning in when everything inside you is shouting to run away, go to your safe space, you aren't cut-out for this, *is hard.* And it is what we ask our clients to do every single day.

We have included a worksheet that we developed for your conceptualization of yourself as a therapist in the context of working with a specific client. This might sound like an odd place to put effort when so much of therapeutic training focuses on the people we work with, but the most useful clinical tool you have access to in your practice is yourself. There is value in understanding your own experiential avoidance, fusion, connection to the present-moment, self-content, values, and committed actions as a helping professional. We encourage you to use this worksheet on yourself for a client you're currently struggling with or find difficult to work with. Perhaps bring this worksheet to an ACT supervision or consultation session to see how you might be able to apply psychological flexibility to yourself and find new ways of connecting with yourself.

This worksheet can be a helpful jumping-off point for supervision or consultation sessions. Specifically, we can learn a lot about ourselves as therapists and make use of that learning in clinical situations when we can pay attention to the flow of our own experience in session and use that awareness effectively. We have included one of our own therapist conceptualization worksheets on page 145, with our own answers written in response to a challenging client.

Present Moment

What makes it difficult to stay present with this client? What distraction do you notice?

Values

What is important to you about working with this client? What stands out to you about them as special or significant?

Commitment

What behaviors do you want to do more of in session with this client? What can you plan and practice for yourself to do your best work?

Acceptance

What topics or clinical experiences do you find yourself avoiding or shying away from with this client?

Defusion

What stuck stories do you have about this client: assumptions, thoughts, feelings, and memories that you could be fused with?

Self-as-Context

What stuck stories do you have about yourself as a therapist?

Feelings of inadequacy, thinking about my next client

They have an amazing relationship with their spouse. Putting them first in a values-based way

Pause more: sitting with their pain engaging in more present moment in session work

Move on from uncomfortable topics → their medical decline & fact that they are dying

They don't want to try, they're so negative about everything

I can't help them, I'm wasting their time

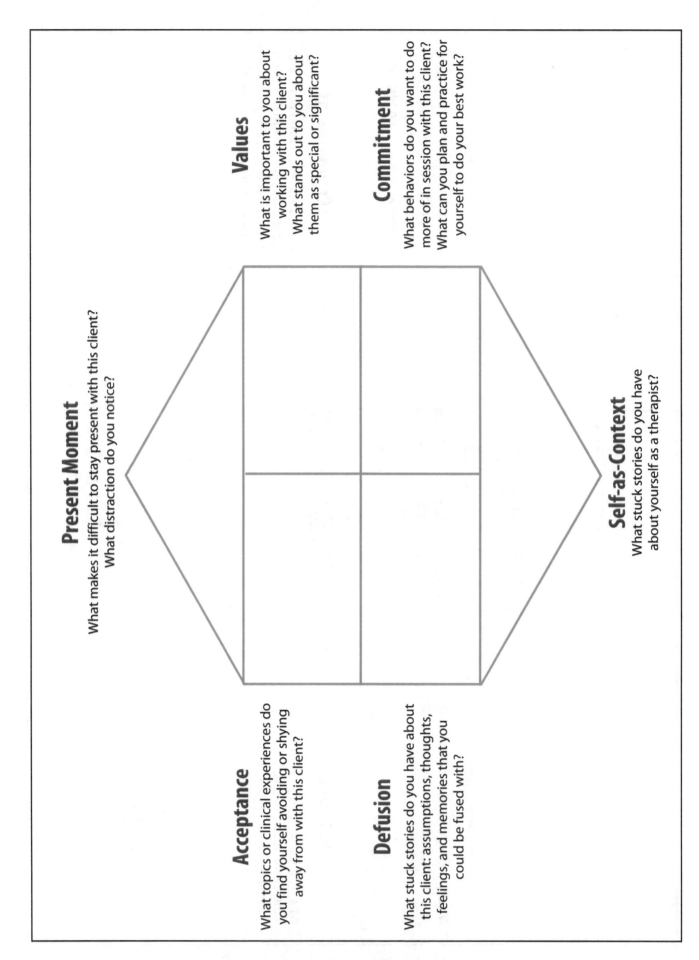

Present Moment

What makes it difficult to stay present with this client?
What distraction do you notice?

Values

What is important to you about working with this client?
What stands out to you about them as special or significant?

Commitment

What behaviors do you want to do more of in session with this client?
What can you plan and practice for yourself to do your best work?

Self-as-Context

What stuck stories do you have about yourself as a therapist?

Acceptance

What topics or clinical experiences do you find yourself avoiding or shying away from with this client?

Defusion

What stuck stories do you have about this client: assumptions, thoughts, feelings, and memories that you could be fused with?

We completed this worksheet by acknowledging our own experiential avoidance, fusion, values, and commitment in working with a client we find challenging. It's rare to find examples of clinicians publishing about cases that went wrong or therapy that was not done well, but the statistical reality of our work is that there will be difficult clients with whom we struggle, that we will have treatment failures, and that problems will arise. ACT fortunately has some empirical backing to support you with your own stress and burnout as a clinician (Brinkborg, Michanek, Hesser, & Berglund, 2011). We'd like to encourage you to print and use the worksheet on page 145 with your own clients to whom you're introducing ACT and especially with those clients with whom you struggle the most. We're hopeful that exploring your own experience and applying the model of psychological flexibility to yourself and your work will help inoculate you from burnout and breathe new life into your practice.

SELF-DISCLOSURE IN ACT

We wonder what it would mean to your clients to hear your own in vivo observation that you are feeling like a "bad therapist" and want to move on from this exercise or conversation, but instead you are pausing to acknowledge it and look at it and notice that it is showing up because you really want to help them and sometimes your mind tries to lead you astray. We bet it would feel pretty awesome, knowing they do not have to be perfect at all this ACT stuff, that it is an ongoing process, and that in the therapy room they are allowed to not be perfect, they are allowed to struggle. It would even be a cool way of demonstrating how you open yourself up to your experiences, become aware of every experience you are having, even the not-so-great-feeling ones, and engage in a behavior (talking to them about it) that is in line with your value of being an honest and effective therapist. Self-disclosure as a means of modelling the process, building therapeutic relationship, and transforming the function of that internal experience from something unpleasant to something that shows you how much you care about helping others.

Self-disclosing your own in vivo experiences with the client can also be an opportunity to explore interpersonal patterns of behaving that are not sensitive to feedback in their environment, which may be causing them difficulty in other domains in their life as well. Clients often respond in similar patterns in the therapy room as they do in their relationship with others in their lives (Kohlenberg & Tsai, 1991). These can be long-standing habits in reaction to private events. For example, have you ever felt frustrated with a client who often changes the subject, cracks a joke, or makes a provocative comment about the therapeutic relationship whenever the conversation veers toward a certain topic or level of emotional vulnerability?

In that context, those behaviors are all control strategies to attempt to remove or eliminate or escape from unpleasant internal stuff that is showing up. That client will often engage in these strategies even at the cost of damaging relationships or losing relationships entirely. It can be a profound conversation to pause and notice what is happening in the room, even so much as commenting on it, and working to ensure that you are not reinforcing the same patterns of behavior you are trying to extinguish in the client's life. Even saying, "I notice whenever we talk about your relationship with your wife you change the subject, what's happening there?" or pausing in the moment and asking, "What showed up for you just now?" can continue to model the process and enact meaningful change. It serves an important function.

MODELLING PSYCHOLOGICAL FLEXIBILITY

Throughout this book we have suggested that you can learn the six core processes of psychological flexibility and bring them to your clinical work, tracking those processes in your clients and encouraging their engagement with them in their most difficult moments to free clients from the tyranny of their minds. When we review our own therapy sessions and supervise others in ACT, we recognize a pattern in ACT-consistent interactions with clients, we've come to call good clinical work done with ACT as "ACT improvisation." It may sound strange, we know, but think back to Chapter 4 on case conceptualization where we described treatment planning itself as a flexible process in which ACT focuses not on the topography of a client's behavior but the function, a sort of ultimate transdiagnostic approach. In this way, you could use all six core processes in a single conversation with a client.

The following illustration includes examples of questions you might ask clients in a session, each focuses on a different process and seeks to put clients at the center of their experience.

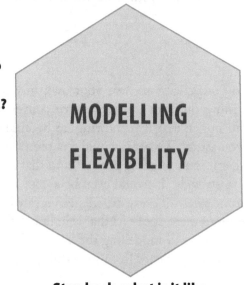

Where do you feel that in your body?

Would you being willing to hold that?
Could you make space for it?

MODELLING FLEXIBILITY

What's important about that?
Why does it matter?

What happens when that shows up?
What do you do next?

What could you do to move toward the life that is important to you?

Step back, what is it like to notice that? Is there a part of you that notices this? What is that like?

PRACTICAL CONSIDERATIONS

Now that you're using ACT and living it yourself in your practice, there are some practical considerations we use in our practice that can help set the context for flexibility and a focus on living a meaningful life. Clients often come in with a symptom reduction agenda. Unfortunately, I have yet to meet a therapist with a magic wand that removes symptoms; so, if clients continue on their symptom reduction mission, it's unlikely we will have much to offer. Therefore, the initial impressions and language we use to describe our practice and our approach need to be chosen with care. Without realizing it, we often prime our clients to come in and spill their guts: "What brings you in today?" We set the context for "tell me your problems" rather than working to shift the context and the goal of therapy to one of vitality and meaningful living.

Understanding the implications of practicing ACT with its new perspective on the world is an important distinction. Clients come to you from years of "talk" therapy, a few failed attempts at feeling heard, or with no basis other than movies that show a client lying on a couch and talking about their childhood. It is your responsibility to set the context, create stimulus control, for what therapy will look like with you. If you begin with a general open-ended question, you will often find clients will fall back on their default of "my problem is X, I need you to help me fix it." This tendency is even more prominent among clients with significant medical conditions or exposure to the medical health care system because they have been primed and shaped to come in and give a quick synopsis of their problem or pain and then have the doctor solve the problem. You can often tell who has chronic pain by using a 1–10 scale. They're the ones who laugh and finish the sentence for you because they have been conditioned to provide quantifiable data about their pain. So, what do we do when we are in a world that tends to be problem-focused and reductionist? We stack the cards in our favor.

Our initial language, even the way our informed consent is worded, can create a context in the therapy room for a different way of relating to what shows up for the client. We can begin in that first introduction to shift the perspective from one of symptom reduction to meaningful living. One way to do this is to frame the initial discussion within the context of who and what are most important to the client and what they are working toward. There are many ways to do this, and we encourage you to play around with language and different ways to set the tone of the session. One way to begin is to say, "Look, I spend the majority of the time talking with people about what is going wrong in their lives. I'd love to get to know you outside of that context and learn a little bit about who and what are most important to you in your life" or "I've found over the years that when clients first come in, their goal is to reduce or eliminate whatever they're currently struggling with, but I find that over time, the most meaningful gains in therapy come not from reducing or eliminating the unpleasant stuff but from adding and expanding their connection with who and what matter most to them. So, while I used to start with "what brings you in today?" if it's alright with you, I'd like to jump ahead and ask you who and what are most important to you."

Some clients may take some time to shift the way they approach their pain, but many feel extreme relief because we are confirming what their experience has already told them. Once they have identified who and what are important to them, it is a quick jump to talk about what has gotten in the way of living the life they want. Now many people will again respond with some type of symptom: "I can't be connected with my family until my depression goes away" or "Until my anxiety goes away, I am trapped in my house." Take time to explore what that symptom or pain looks like for them, asking them to describe what it feels like in their bodies, thoughts, feelings, memories; walk them through what they have tried in the past to escape, get rid of, or manage those experiences, focusing on the short-term and long-term costs and benefits, remembering that all behavior has a function and tying it back to whether those efforts have taken them closer to or farther from what matters to them. We have yet to meet a client who thinks staying inside their house all day is taking them closer to who and what matter most; generally those efforts are creating a cycle of experiential avoidance and suffering. You can use a Life Map to show them how they are spending a huge amount of time and effort in the top left quadrant avoiding or fighting the stuff that shows up in the bottom left quadrant, paying little attention to the right side of the model: valued living.

Now, some clients may think this is all a trick for you to show them another way, a better way, of controlling that yucky stuff that shows up. Be clear in this: the focus of therapy will be in connecting with all their experiences and helping them engage in behaviors that take them closer to who and what matter most to them regardless of what shows up along the way. And remember, if they're still not convinced, that's okay. There's no need to get into a battle of right and wrong, rather let them know they can always fall back on their old patterns of responding: "You have been trying all of these strategies to control, or avoid, or fight with all that painful stuff that shows up in an effort to get some relief from it, if only a moment.

From what you have said, it seems like you are extremely motivated to make the pain go away and have put a large amount of time and energy into these strategies, but from what you're telling me that's just not cutting it because the cost is just too high. It works for a little bit but the pain always comes back and now it's bringing more friends with it. It's taking you away from your life. Would you be willing to try something different with me, another approach to interacting with the pain that shows up, knowing you can always go back to your old strategies if you want?" Set it up like an experiment and ask them for their full effort during the trial period. This approach can also set a rationale for collecting process-based data—you are using science to see how well the experiment is working. Sounds kind of fun.

As a final note on your journey as an ACT therapist, we don't take this shift in worldview for granted and know ACT asks a lot of you: a strength of mind, a belief in the evidence for ACT, and your own courage to take on this radically different stance. You may feel like you're swimming upstream at times, which is why we encourage connecting with the larger ACT community in the Association for Contextual Behavioral Science. Do read on to the final chapter where we describe ways in which you can do your best to support yourself in growing into this work.

Chapter 10

Next Steps

By now you should have a good understanding of ACT as a model and the process of responding to whatever shows up in the therapy room. You might have even already started to incorporate this approach into your work, whether looking at your theoretical orientation through a functional contextualist lens or by jumping into ACT head first and trying to do all ACT all the time. We applaud any steps you have taken to move forward with this work in a meaningful way. And just like the steps our clients take, these first steps are the jumping-off point toward a lifelong journey of developing your approach. This means that after reading this book, you have vast and varied opportunities to continue your development as an ACT therapist. An exciting and often overwhelming idea—Help! Where do I start?

We recommend that you take some time after completing this book to begin practicing and applying the principles you have learned in the book into your practice. Use the worksheets, exercises, and case conceptualization model to guide how you take the approach into your setting, your context. Notice areas where you feel confident as well as areas you notice you still feel uncertain or even completely lost. As mentioned in the previous chapter, try to lean into those feelings. Developing your practice and competence in any approach is as much about your own self-reflection and honest appraisal of your abilities as it is your willingness to practice difficult or uncomfortable techniques. And remember as you begin this journey that you are working toward what matters to you, whether in service of your personal or professional development.

Although this book was written by two people, it was supported by a community. We would be remiss if we did not direct you to the vast network of professionals practicing and living the model who call the Association for Contextual Behavioral Science (ACBS) home. A self-disclosure note, although we do not receive any financial incentives for directing you to ACBS, we are actively involved in the community: Tim is a peer-reviewed ACT trainer and actively involved in his local chapter of ACBS and the ACBS Trainer Committee, while Jessica is a past board member of ACBS and actively involved in multiple committees within the organization. If you are looking for a community of diverse professionals passionately advocating and learning about ACT, functional contextualism, and everything within that realm, ACBS is the place for you.

As an ACBS member, you would have access to their website (contextualscience.org) and the *Journal of Contextual Behavioral Science*. The ACBS website also has a plethora of information that includes freely downloadable protocols, video, audio, and other written resources; ACT-consistent and process-based measures; journal articles; a directory of professionals and trainers; and an active professionals listserv as well as various special interest groups and local chapters to help you connect with others in your area or practice focus. Additionally, ACBS holds an annual world conference that alternates between North America and the rest of the world—it's always a good excuse to go on a vacation—that highlights the diverse and international representation of the organization.

Another excellent way to continue your learning and growth is to attend an in-person or online workshop. Given ACT's growing interest around the world, there is bound to be a workshop near you, whether you are looking for a brief two-hour webinar or a two-day immersion. Both of us give workshops and we'd love to have you join us for one [self-disclosure: we financially and professionally benefit from the workshops we give]. It is also important to note the importance of diversity of exposure. Every trainer has a different style, a different background, and comes at the model from a unique perspective. This variety creates an even greater flexibility in the approach, so we encourage you to seek out different opportunities to learn from various trainers in an effort not only to deepen your understanding of how to do and live ACT, but also to connect with different styles and perspectives. It is our hope that through diverse exposure you create a broader repertoire for your own practice and have the chance to try on different styles and find what works for you. There are many great trainers out there. A note on ACT: the organization that houses ACT (ACBS) does not certify people in ACT in an effort to not create rigidity nor punish innovation; however, it does offer a peer review process to become a trainer. On the website you can view the list of peer-reviewed ACT trainers (like Tim) who have completed this process. It is important to consider that many people who are giving trainings locally may not have completed the process, but are still excellent trainers, so even though the list is a good place to begin looking for trainers, it should not be the only place to look for trainers.

If you are looking for consultation or more direct feedback on an ongoing basis, we would recommend becoming involved in a local chapter of ACBS (they often have peer consultation groups) or reaching out to the ACT community to find a professional near you who provides consultation. Some of these options come with a financial obligation, although some peer support groups out there meet for the love of growth and development. Additionally, if you are simply looking for a way to get feedback on your implementation of this approach, why not engage in some scientific inquiry and measure yourself and your clients? Validated measures aren't only for research. They are important components of self-evaluation and feedback. It can be an intimidating endeavor to use process-based or outcome measures to track your clients' progress or ask them to fill out a feedback evaluation on you as a therapist or how satisfied or helpful they find therapy, but it is a worthwhile experience. We can't make progress if we do not know where we are right now. Another way to track your practice is to monitor your own competence through self-assessment and then create goals for yourself to, for example, practice a certain exercise or use a certain process in session without a structured exercise or begin an initial session with a new question or approach. The options are endless and can be tailored to your needs.

At the beginning of this book, we talked about the difficulty disseminating ACT because it is at times an abstract way of understanding the world. We hope this book has helped clarify some of your misconceptions. As you continue on with your training—and we really hope that you do—you will find a new voice or maybe an old friend who pops up and says, "you're doing this wrong," "You're going to mess up." When these thoughts occur and the related emotions that go with them, it's easy to fall back on a protocol or a skill rather than living the process. We ask that in those moments—just as you would ask of a client—you pause and ask yourself what is driving this behavior? Is this moving you toward what matters to you, or is it simply another control strategy to avoid discomfort or uncertainty? At the end of the day, we hope we have provided you with a jumping-off point and through our own passion for the model created a context that fosters excitement for flexibly embracing the ACT approach.

References

For your convenience, purchasers can download and
print worksheets and handouts from www.pesi.com/ACTapproach

Ainsworth, M., Bell, S., & Stayton, D. (1971). Individual differences in strange-situation behaviour of one-year-olds. In H. R. Schaffer (Ed.), *The Origins of Human Social Relations,* 17–58. New York: Academic Press.

Ainsworth, M., Bell, S., & Stayton, D. (1974). Infant-mother attachment and social development: "Socialization" as a product of reciprocal responsiveness to signals. In M. Richards (Ed.), *The Integration of a Child into a Social World,* 99–135. London: Cambridge University Press.

A-Tjak, J.G., Davis, M.L., Morina, N., Powers, M.B., Smits, J.A., & Emmelkamp, P.M. (2015). *Psychotherapy Psychosomatics,* 84(1), 30–36. DOI: 10.1159/000365764.

Bach, P. A. & Moran, D. J. (2008). *ACT in Practice: Case Conceptualization in Acceptance and Commitment Therapy.* Oakland, CA: New Harbinger.

Brinkborg, H., Michanek, J., Hesser, H., & Berglund, G. (2011). Acceptance and commitment therapy for the treatment of stress among social workers: A randomized controlled trial. *Behavior Research and Therapy,* 49, 389–398.

Brown, F. L., Whittingham, K., Boyd, R. N., McKinlay, L., & Sofronoff, K. (2014). Improving child and parenting outcomes following paediatric acquired brain injury: A randomized controlled trial of Stepping Stones Triple P plus Acceptance and Commitment Therapy. *The Journal of Child Psychology and Psychiatry,* 55(10), 1172–1183. DOI: 10.1111/jcpp.12227.

Catania, A. C. (1998). *Learning,* 4th ed. Upper Saddle River, NJ: Prentice Hall.

Coyne, L. W., McHugh, L., & Martinez, E. R. (2011). Acceptance and commitment therapy (ACT): advances and applications with children, adolescents, and families. *Child and Adolescent Psychiatric Clinics of North America,* 20, 379–399. DOI:10.1016/j.chc.2011.01.010.

Dixon, M. R. (2014). *ACT for Children with Autism and Emotional Challenges.* Carbondale, IL: Shawnee Scientific Press.

Dixon, M. R., Stanley, C. R., Belisle, J., & Rowsey, K. E. (2016). The test-retest and interrater reliability of the Promoting the Emergence of Advanced Knowledge-Direct Training assessment for use with individuals with autism and related disabilities. *Behavior Analysis: Research and Practice,* 16(1), 34–40. DOI:10.1037/bar0000027.

Dymond, S. & Roche, B. (Eds.) (2013). *Advances in Relational Frame Theory: Research and Application.* Oakland, CA: New Harbinger Publications.

Epkins, C. C. (2016). Experiential avoidance and anxiety sensitivity: Independent and specific associations with children's depression, anxiety, and social anxiety symptoms. *Journal of Psychopathology and Behavioral Assessment,* 38, 124–135.

Hayes, S. C., Barnes-Holmes, D., & Roche, B. (Eds.) (2001). *Relational Frame Theory: A Post-Skinnerian Account of Human Language and Cognition.* New York: Plenum.

Hayes, S. C., Strosahl, K. D., & Wilson, K. G. (2011). *Acceptance and commitment therapy: The process and practice of mindful change.* Guilford Press.

Hooper, N. & Larsson, A. (2015). *The Research Journey of Acceptance and Commitment Therapy (ACT).* London: Palgrave Macmillan.

Hughes, S. & Barnes-Holmes, D. (2015). Relational frame theory: Implications for the study of human language and cognition. In S. Hayes, D. Barnes-Holmes, R. Zettle, and T. Biglan (Eds.), *Handbook of Contextual Behavioral Science.* New York: Wiley-Blackwell.

Hayes, S. C., Strosahl, K. D., & Wilson, K. G. (1999). *Acceptance and Commitment Therapy: An Experiential Approach to Behavior Change.* New York: The Guilford Press.

Jablonka, E. & Lamb, M. J. (2014). *Evolution in Four Dimensions: Genetic, Epigenetic, Behavioral, and Symbolic Variation in the History of Life,* 2nd ed. Cambridge, MA: MIT Press.

Jacobson, N. S. & Christensen, A. (1996). *Acceptance and Change in Couple Therapy: A Therapist's Guide to Transforming Relationships.* New York: Norton.

Kabat-Zinn, J. (1994). *Wherever You Go, There You Are: Mindfulness Meditation in Everyday Life.* New York: Hachette Books.

Kohlenberg, R. J. & Tsai, M. (1991). *Functional Analytic Psychotherapy.* New York: Plenum.

McHugh, L., Barnes-Holmes, Y., & Barnes-Holmes, B. (2004). Perspective-taking as relational responding: A developmental profile. *The Psychological Record*, 54(1), 115–144.

McHugh, L., Bobarnac, A., & Reed, P. (2011). Brief report: Teaching situation-based emotions to children with autistic spectrum disorder. *Journal of Autism and Developmental Disorders*, 41(10), 1423–1428.

McHugh, L. & Stewart, I. (Eds.) (2012). *The Self and Perspective Taking: Contributions and Applications from Modern Behavioral Science.* Oakland, CA: New Harbinger.

Polk, K. L. (2014). The matrix, evolution, and improving work-group functioning with Ostrom's eight design principles. In K. L. Polk & B. Schoendorff (Eds.), *The ACT Matrix: A New Approach to Building Psychological Flexibility Across Settings and Populations.* Oakland, CA: New Harbinger.

Skinner, B. F. (1957). *Verbal Behavior.* New York: Appleton-Century-Crofts.

Skinner, B. F. (1971). *Beyond Freedom and Dignity.* New York: Knopf.

Skinner, B. F. (1984). The evolution of behavior. *Journal of the Experimental Analysis of Behavior*, 41(2), 217–221.

Slade, A. (2000). The development and organization of attachment: Implications for psychoanalysis. *Journal of the American Psychoanalytic Association*, 48(4), 1147.

Strosahl, K. D., Robinson, P. J., & Gustavsson, T. (2012). *Brief Interventions for Radical Change: Principles and Practice of Focused Acceptance and Commitment Therapy.* Oakland, CA: New Harbinger.

Villatte, M., Villatte, J. L., & Hayes, S. C. (2015). *Mastering the Clinical Conversation: Language as Intervention.* New York: Guilford Press.

Whittingham, K., Sanders, M., McKinlay, L., & Boyd, R. N. (2014). Interventions to reduce behavioral problems in children with cerebral palsy: An RCT. *Pediatrics*, 133, 1–9. DOI: 10.1542/peds.2013-3620.

Wilson, D. S. (2011). *The Neighborhood Project: Using Evolution to Improve My City, One Block at a Time.* New York: Little, Brown.

Zettle, R. D. (2007). *ACT for Depression: A Clinician's Guide to Using Acceptance and Commitment Therapy in Treating Depression.* Oakland, CA: New Harbinger.

Zettle, R. D. (2011). The evolution of a contextual approach to therapy: From comprehensive distancing to ACT. *International Journal of Behavioral Consultation and Therapy*, 7(1), 76–82.